Foundation Management

Foundation Management

Innovation and Responsibility at Home and Abroad

**Edited by
Frank L. Ellsworth
and Joe Lumarda**

JOHN WILEY & SONS, INC.

About the Editors

Frank L. Ellsworth joined The Capital Group Companies in January 1997 where he works primarily with Capital Research and Management Company (CRMC) and Capital Guardian Trust Company (CGTC). At CRMC he oversees and coordinates CRMC's various programs and services to endowments, foundations, and other nonprofit institutions. He is President and Chief Executive Officer of Endowments, a series of mutual funds managed by CRMC that are offered exclusively to nonprofits. The American Funds Group, managed by CRMC, is the third largest mutual fund complex in the United States. CRMC and its affiliates manage assets in excess of $350 billion.

Prior to joining the Capital Group, Dr. Ellsworth spent his entire career in higher education. Born and raised in the college town of Wooster, Ohio, he received his A.B. *cum laude* from Case Western Reserve University. He received Masters degrees from Pennsylvania State University and Columbia University in the City of New York. He was awarded his Ph.D. from the University of Chicago. He was awarded the honorary degree of Doctor of Laws from Pepperdine University.

For nearly 25 years he combined teaching and administration at Penn State, Columbia University, and Sarah Lawrence College. For nine years at the University of Chicago he served as a dean in its law school and taught the "Great Books" course in the College. In 1979 he was hired as President of Pitzer College, the youngest President in the history of the Claremont Colleges.

He is also active in many community affairs and serves on the Boards of Trustees of the Japanese American National Museum,

Southwestern University School of Law, Pitzer College, the Independent Colleges of Southern California, and the Japanese Foundation for International Education. He is Chairman of the Board of Trustees of The Center for the Preservation of Democracy and Global Partners in Canada.

His publications are numerous on topics ranging from classical philosophy, American history, Japanese prints, and Eastern philosophy. He has two books scheduled for publication in the fall of 2002, co-authored with Joe Lumarda, which will be published by John Wiley & Sons, Inc. as part of their nonprofit series: *From Grantmaker to Leader: Emerging Strategies for 21st Century Foundations* and *Foundation Management: Innovation and Responsibility at Home and Abroad.*

His daughter, Kirstin, is a graduate student at Indiana University. Dr. Ellsworth currently resides in Pasadena.

Joe Lumarda has held the position of Executive Vice President for External Affairs at the California Community Foundation for the past five years. He chairs the Foundation's management team and oversees its asset development program and donor-advised fund grant making. He started at the Foundation in 1990 as a program officer in the area of children and youth, was appointed Vice President for Development in 1991, and was named Executive Vice President for External Affairs in 1997.

Joe is a board member of the Saint Joseph Health System Foundation, Southern California Association for Philanthropy, Coro Southern California, the Peter F. Drucker Graduate School of Management, and the Council on Foundation's Community Foundation Leadership Team. He is also a board member of Endowments, a mutual fund trust serving nonprofit organizations nationwide.

Before coming to the Foundation, Joe served three years as an officer in the U.S. Navy, flying in the tactical navigator seat of the P-3 Orion aircraft. Prior to the Navy, he was Associate Director of Government Relations and Campaign Associate for the United Way of Orange County. He is a graduate of the Coro Foundation Orange County Public Affairs Leadership Program.

Joe received his bachelor's degree in philosophy at Saint John's Seminary College in Camarillo, California. In 1999 he attained an executive MBA at the Peter F. Drucker Graduate Management Center at the Claremont Graduate University. In 2000 Joe was named a German Marshall Fund Community Foundation Fellow. This fellowship sent him to Poland, where he studied and consulted with that country's growing community foundation movement.

Joe currently resides in Pasadena with his wife, Denise, and two sons, Malone and Elias.

Contents

Contents

Contents

Contents

Contents

Contents

Acknowledgments

First we want to acknowledge our authors. In glancing through the table of contents, the reader will see that we are fortunate to have the "best of the best" to present their ideas and strategies. Frank Ellsworth wishes to acknowledge the help of his assistant, Christine Imaoka Curry, and the support of Capital Research and Management Company, The Capital Group Companies. Joe Lumarda wishes to acknowledge the support of the California Community Foundation, in particular, its President Jack Shakely. Additionally, Joe wishes to convey his gratitude to fellow staff members at the community foundation who shared their wisdom, discriminating eye, forbearance, and good humor: in particular, Peter Dunn, Robin Kramer, Catherine Stringer, Judy Spiegel, Amy Fackelmann, and Sylvia Moraton. Finally, a very special thanks to Joe's wife, Denise, and two boys, Malone and Elias, for the patience, care, and smiles even when Dad was pounding on the computer or dragging in late.

Introduction

Innovation and responsibility in foundation management may strike the reader as paradoxical in nature, if not two concepts deserving separate consideration. We believe, however, that it is important for this book on perspectives on foundation management to address them together. Already in the course of events in this century fundamental issues of fiduciary responsibility loom large while projects and areas of innovation emerge quickly, many fresh and exciting, merging the new with the traditional. Thus issues of innovation and responsibility often intertwine in foundation management and are best viewed as co-related.

The purpose of this book, as for *From Grantmaker to Leader: Emerging Strategies for 21st Century Foundations*, is to move beyond information gathering and present strategies for management. Our audience is the practitioner: the trustee, the chief executive officer, the chief financial officer, members of the investment committee, the information and publication relations staff, the program officer and committee members, and indeed the wide range of people who work with foundations. Our distinguished authors in this book come to the task of writing with extraordinary experiences and keen analytical abilities. But their assignment was to move to the practical. They are writing for the individual who not only wants to understand an issue, but also wants and needs to gain insight on how to deal with the issues and create strategies whether they are of leadership or management in nature—or both. This book presents topics and issues that reflect the unspoken and spoken language of the world of foundations today with an eye toward helping the reader address them effectively.

Our intent is to be pragmatic and, at times, provocative as we attempt to provide a comprehensive and user-friendly guidebook on management innovation and responsibility.

Fiduciary issues and problems are everywhere today. Accounting scandals, executive and board accountability, ethical issues, the bear market, the economic recession in the United States and other parts of the world, terrorism, and other global events have had impact on foundations. Foundations cannot do business as usual. Several examples help demonstrate the point and illustrate the need for our audience to pay attention to fundamental needs: to address their responsibilities anew and when necessary the need for innovation within their foundations. Foundations with their assets invested solely in one company have seen their endowments dramatically decrease. The retreat to cash or certificates of despoit is not necessarily the answer. Newspaper and magazine articles have had story after story of foundations that have had to cut dramatically their giving programs because of steep decline in foundation assets. The raging bear market has pushed many consultants out of business. Foundations that had not paid attention to the costs of investments are now discovering that total costs of 2 percent to 2.5 percent, and sometimes more, are significant and are looking anew at the process of investment and the costs that go with it. Exotic investment vehicles, many of them created during the years when almost any equity fund could make money, but untried during down years in the market, have evaporated. The probability of bumpy times for some time ahead in the market poses a new challenge for many chief financial officers and trustees who are not old enough to have lived through a serious and long-drawn-out down market and are still waiting for the double-digit (plus) days of total return to return!

And what did happen to the "new economy?" Exotic and elaborate asset diversification models have devastated portfolios as many foundations whose assets soared with some of the exotic investment products have returned to the basics and fundamentals of investment. Some foundations have sued their advisors. Restrictions placed by the founders of some foundations on specific investments that had to be used have caused great pain and significant negative returns. The results have cut deeply into program expenditures and sometimes caused nasty lawsuits. Imprudent investments on occasion have been viewed by the courts as unlawful. Some lawsuits have been judged as self-dealing by trustees. Despite the attempts by the Internal Revenue Service to cause foundations to pay attention to potential situations of self-dealing, abuses continue to get headlines. Exposed conflicts of interest have torn apart boards and created deep wounds that will take years to heal.

The first section of the book looks to foundations abroad and the exporting of philanthropy. Twenty years ago this section would have been absent. Ten years ago it would have been short. Today it could be another book. The legal issues in international philanthropy are complex and in constant evolution. But the guide here is one that will serve anyone well who is entering this fascinating market place. Given our tendency for self-centeredness in America, we tend to see ourselves too often as the beginning—if not the end—of all discussions and understandings. Yet the foundation traditions in European are time honored and discussed along with some rapidly evolving new ones. Nongovernment organizations (NGOs) and foundations are exploding in Asia. Generalizations are meaningless yet some significant trends are merging. And looking south of the United States, we find philanthropy defined in different ways, often focusing exclusively on communities with governments playing a strong role in addressing a wide range of problems.

The next section of the book looks at a wide range of fiduciary issues. What is conflict of interest? How should a foundation define and monitor possible activities? Should trustees be compensated? If so, in what circumstances? Much attention is paid in articles, speeches, and conferences to concepts of *risk, diversification,* and *prudence.* What is the role of a consultant? A financial advisor? What is the role of an accountant? The lawyer? Who is responsible for their recommendations and their work? How does the board monitor their work?

Innovation and care is needed in the management of these issues. Foundation executives and trustees need to examine the way they are doing business to affirm that their house is in order.

But the challenge goes beyond that. Are the assets serving the mission of the foundation? And, in many cases, what is the mission of the foundation as it relates to the assets of the foundation? Does the management of the foundation serve that purpose? Are the shareholders of the foundation involved in the process of investment? What is the balance of prudence, growth, and mission? Moving beyond the rhetoric of these words, our authors look at specific strategies and alternative models. What model of investment best serves and allows for negotiations with all of the stakeholders? And if a foundation would want to start with a review of the process of investment, or, if a foundation were at the beginning stages of putting together the assets for a foundation, how could this be done? Here the role of the consultant and financial advisor is discussed and issues of accountability and monitoring of the process are detailed.

The final section turns to the role of the trusted counsel: the lawyer and accountant. The tax reform of 1969 was one benchmark that served to remind us that the IRS had issues with regard to foundations. But the issues have not gone away and the reader will find a current analysis of how the IRS eyes the foundation world today. What is the role of counsel? When should a foundation turn to a lawyer and what might the foundation expect from those consultations? With the recent corporate accounting scandals, foundations will be well served to pay special attention to the discussion on looking beyond the numbers. Here innovation may be in order to insure that the foundation has more than procedures in place for its audits. Have all of the trustees been educated about their responsibilities? What process is in place that allows for accountability? Is the process one that is user-friendly and in plain English? Traditionally few board members have understood the audit process or felt knowledgeable enough to know what questions to ask. Are board members comfortable that they are not involved in the shadows and mirrors of the audit jargon and process? Do they understand all of the fees involved in the cost of running the foundation?

Our readers will have differing views of the present and future roles for foundations in our country and throughout the world. Our readers will also have differing views of the roles of innovation as we move ahead in the twenty-first century. That is understandable and the way it should be. We hope, however, that these chapters will be useful for all of us playing our respective roles in innovation and responsibility in foundation management.

FRANK L. ELLSWORTH
Endowments, Capital Research and Management Company,
The Capital Groups Companies

JOE LUMARDA
The California Community Foundation

Los Angeles, California
October 1, 2002

Exporting Philanthropy: The Growing Presence of and Relationship with Foundations Abroad

CHAPTER 1

Emerging Legal Issues in International Philanthropy

By Jane Peebles

PERSPECTIVES

The immigrant roots of our nation are now emerging in philanthropy. Many of the large national foundations have established a grantmaking presence beyond our borders (such as Ford, Mott, and Soros), but what about smaller foundations without the resources to create an office or send staff abroad? Although tax laws and regulations governing public charities in the United States are standard, the rules of international grantmaking remain uncertain.

This chapter covers the major legal issues surrounding international philanthropy as it is practiced by foundations and individual donors. The author, Jane Peebles, is an expert in charitable giving across national borders; her contribution provides a practical and legal framework for international grantmaking. Peebles is a partner with the firm Freeman, Freeman & Smiley in Los Angeles. She is the author of *The Handbook of International Philanthropy* (Bonus Books, 1998).

THE RECENT EXPANSION OF INTERNATIONAL GRANTMAKING BY U.S. FOUNDATIONS

International giving by U.S. foundations has increased dramatically over the past decade. This growth is reflected not only in the total dollar amounts granted for use abroad, but also in the number of U.S. foundations active in the international arena and the number of grants made. A recent report by The Foundation Center in cooperation with the Council on Foundations indicates that, from 1990 to 1998, the amount of international giving by all U.S. foundations grew from an estimated $764.5 million annually to $1.6 billion annually.[1] The total amount granted increased 57 percent in actual dollars, or 43 percent adjusted for inflation, between 1994 and 1998.[2] In 1994, 50 percent of the foundations sampled by The Foundation Center reported making international grants.[3] From then until 1998, the number of U.S. foundations making international grants rose 20 percent.[4] International grantmaking averaged growth of more than 9 percent per year from 1994 to 1998, after adjustment for inflation, relative to the total number of grants made, with the number of international grants growing faster than the total number of grants made by U.S. foundations during the same period.[5]

Foundations grew in the late 1990s largely as a result of the booming U.S. economy and strong stock market. International giving grew as a result of the government's diminished role in overseas funding coupled with globalization and increased immigration to the United States, which have brought to the attention of U.S. grantmakers both urgent needs abroad and their impact on the United States itself. Drug-resistant infectious diseases are rampant and respect no borders; victims of ethnic conflicts and natural disasters require humanitarian assistance, global warming and other environmental problems can be effectively addressed only on a planet-wide scale; and the fall of the Soviet Union and end of the Cold War have given birth to fragile democracies in Central and Eastern Europe, which several U.S. grantmakers (including, notably, the Soros Foundation Network) are nurturing. The rapid expansion of international travel and trade, and global economic integration, have increased the interdependence of countries around the world and awareness that widespread and complex problems can only be effectively addressed globally. As new markets have opened up, corporate giving has increased. Local businesses have become first national and then international, and their corporate grantmaking programs have increased support for the communities abroad in which they have offices or conduct business. Impoverished populations do not produce strong consumer bases. Politically unstable nations do not provide the stability needed for continued viability of U.S. corporations operating abroad. Thus, enlightened self-interest has spread in the corporate sector.

Governments of postindustrialized countries have been and continue to be the primary donors supporting international development and relief; however, government support has decreased substantially since the end of the Cold War. Between 1992 and 1997, the gross national products (GNPs) of the leading industrialized countries jumped almost 30 percent, but their funds allocated to international development and relief decreased by 30 percent.[6] Many of the world's poorest countries pay far more for defense and for interest on their debts to foreign investors and governments of postindustrial countries than they pay for education, health care, and other basic human services.[7] A recent study released by the United Nations Children's Fund reported that the world's poorest nations slipped further behind developing and developed nations during the 1990s.[8] Statistics indicate that the majority of the world's population subsists on $2 per day, and 1.5 billion people live in abject poverty. The income gap between the richest fifth of the world's population and the poorest fifth is 74 to 1.[9] As governments of postindustrial nations have decreased their international development and relief efforts, corporations have increased their multinational aid.

Private foundations have also responded to the decrease in government funding. Currently, only 11 percent of all U.S. foundation grants, and less than 2 percent of all U.S. philanthropy, goes overseas;[10] however, recent statistics indicate that there has been enormous growth in international funding since the mid-1990s, and the percentage of foundation money dedicated to projects overseas is expected to continue to grow. The Foundation Center study sampled independent family foundations, corporate foundations, and community foundations. Among family foundations, five of the most active international funders ranked among the 100 largest U.S. foundations by grant amount. These included the Ford, W. Alton Jones, Rockefeller, Freeman, and John D. and Catherine T. MacArthur foundations.[11] Of the 1,020 foundations sampled, 85 gave at least one-fourth of their grant dollars internationally, and 27 gave at least one-tenth.[12] The most active international grantmakers ranged from some of this country's oldest modern foundations to some of its newest. The youngest foundations made more international grants as a proportion of their total giving. Twenty-two of the 36 foundations that gave at least 50 percent of their grants for international use were formed after 1970, and four of those since 1990. Almost half of the foundations that gave 25 percent or more of their grant funds internationally were younger foundations formed since 1970. Only 20 percent of the foundations that gave 25 percent or more of their grant funds internationally were created before 1950.[13] Newer foundations are expected to make more international grants as their endowments and staff grow over the coming years. The Foundation Center report indicates that these foundations will be a significant factor in the future growth of international giving. Family foundations already account for 90 percent of the total amount of U.S. foundation grants for overseas programs. New mega-foundations such as the Bill and Melinda Gates Foundation and the David and Lucille Packard Foundation have made substantial international grants, but older foundations, such as the Ford Foundation, have also contributed enough dollars to have a material impact on the regions and causes receiving the most U.S. support.[14]

Corporate foundations and community foundations have increased their international gifts at an even faster pace than family foundations. From 1994 to 1998, international grants by corporate foundations increased more than 120 percent, to $57 million, while giving by community foundations grew more than 150 percent, to $6 million.[15]

A strong U.S. economy and stock market, combined with the opening of new markets and increasing globalization of business, led to a huge jump in international grants by corporate foundations, which more than doubled from 1994 to 1998, outpacing by rate of growth all other corporate grants.[16] The Foundation Center study assessed corporate grants only through corporate foundations. The study also revealed that corporations make most of their overseas grants either through their foreign affiliates or through direct giving programs, rather than through their foundations.[17] Thus, international grants by corporate foundations included in the Foundation Center report represented only a small percentage of corporate giving overseas. If a U.S. corporation has subsidiary operations abroad, it is simplest for the foreign subsidiary to make a contribution to a charity established in the country in which the subsidiary operates. The overseas subsidiary will then claim whatever tax benefits are available under that country's laws. A charitable deduction or, commonly, a business expense deduction, is claimed against the subsidiary's foreign income tax owed to the country in which it is located, and U.S. tax laws are not involved.

The number and size of U.S. community foundations also grew rapidly in the 1990s. By their very nature, community foundations are formed primarily to support the geographic areas in which they are situated; however, they are playing an increasing role in international gifting. From 1994 to 1998, the number of community foundation grants for use abroad grew almost 200 percent, with the dollar value surging from $2.4 million to $6.3 million.[18] This trend is expected to increase as the number of community foundations increases in jurisdictions around the world and as partnerships among U.S. and foreign community foundations multiply and develop.

The numbers confirm the author's conclusion, based on her practice in international philanthropy, that a new awareness of global interconnectedness has developed in the post–Cold War era. A 1982 report on international grantmaking noted:

> . . . a fundamental obstacle to increased international philanthropy is a pervasive lack of knowledge or understanding among United States citizens of the interdependence of the United States' social, economic and political well-being with that of the rest of the world. Many of the grant-

makers interviewed consistently saw "domestic" and "international" issues as mutually exclusive spheres.[19]

Now grantmakers are increasingly recognizing that "the interplay between international and local events requires that foundations actively identify, monitor, and respond to international events and trends affecting their local interests."[20] The Foundation Center study reports that, although many foundations still distinguish between domestic and international grants, almost one-third of the foundations sampled in 1998 organized their grantmaking thematically, with no distinction between domestic and international grants.[21]

Some foundations are funding programs to educate Americans about the role of the United States in a globalized world.[22] As noted previously, several factors have led to this growing awareness among U.S. grantmakers and have facilitated international grantmaking:

- Partnerships between U.S. foundations and foreign non-governmental organizations (NGOs) are on the rise.
- Numerous conferences have been held around the world in recent years to focus attention on global issues and to facilitate dialogue among donors, business leaders, NGOs, and development specialists, leading to attempts to formulate and disseminate "best practices" in overseas giving as well as to educate attendees about policy and procedural matters.
- Several international philanthropic networks have been established, allowing grantmakers to share their knowledge and experience.
- The Internet has simplified research in connection with overseas grants; and the legal requirements for U.S. foundations making grants for use abroad are slowly but surely being clarified and somewhat simplified.[23]

Adding to these factors, wealthy immigrants to the United States have begun establishing foundations that provide funding for projects in their homelands, as well as donor-advised funds at local community foundations to support such projects.[24]

This increased awareness of globalization by U.S. donors has, for example, resulted in more grants for research on diseases that typically strike Third World populations and are therefore not profitable for U.S. pharmaceutical companies. A recent story reporting that research on cures for malaria and tuberculosis has received major funding from the Bill and Melinda Gates Foundation, the National Institutes of Health, and Britain's Wellcome Trust quotes Alfred Sommer, dean of the Bloomberg School of Public Health at Johns Hopkins University, as commenting: "What's not new is the severity of the diseases. What is new is the sudden urgency and interest on the part of donors."[25] Another example of this growing global awareness is that some community foundations near the Mexican border have started making grants for use in Mexico, in order to address such issues as disease brought in by immigrants, and pollution, which affects the quality of life in U.S. states adjacent to Mexico because it crosses the border. Janice Windle, Executive Director of the El Paso Community Foundation, which makes grants involving Mexico, has noted: "While it looks like we are acting very heavily in the international arena, in reality we're just dealing with our daily lives."[26]

These increases in international grantmaking are encouraging, but such grants remain only 11 percent of total grantmaking by U.S. foundations.[27] Factors inhibiting greater cross-border giving are that U.S. tax rules governing such grants are complex and intimidating; there is inadequate guidance for grantmakers regarding what constitutes compliance with those rules, and few lawyers, accountants, and other allied professional advisors are well-versed in the applicable requirements.

TECHNICAL REQUIREMENTS AND IMPEDIMENTS FOR FOUNDATIONS MAKING INTERNATIONAL GRANTS

International funding by U.S. family foundations can be effected by means of direct grants to overseas organizations or grants to U.S.–based groups that support projects abroad. This is largely a function of applicable U.S. tax laws. Private nonoperating foundations are generally required to make annual "qualifying distributions" equal to at least 5 percent of their net investment income after a brief startup period.[28] The rules governing when a direct grant to a foreign organization qualifies as part of the mandatory annual distributions are complex, unwieldy, and expensive to implement. The private foundation that wants to avoid dealing with the stringent requirements applicable to direct grants abroad may instead choose to make its grant to a U.S. public charity that will use the funds to support a charitable project overseas. This approach is common for smaller foundations, which lack the staff to process direct overseas grants and the funds for consultants to guide them in making such grants.

The Foundation Center study reports that, from 1990 to 1998, direct funding overseas experienced enormous growth. Grants to both overseas and U.S.–based programs for use abroad continued to grow rapidly, in terms of both total dollars granted and number of grants made. In the first half of the decade, foundations made more direct overseas grants than grants to U.S. charities operating and/or funding projects abroad; however, in the second half of the decade, funding of U.S.–based international programs outpaced direct overseas support. From 1994 to 1998, amounts granted to U.S.–based international programs grew 65 percent, while amounts granted directly overseas grew 47 percent.[29] The study found that new and newly international foundations tended to make such grants through domestic intermediaries, as did smaller and midsized funders. The older and larger grantmaking foundations tended to distribute substantially more of their international grants directly to overseas organizations.[30] Most grants for use abroad are still made through U.S. public charities, which act as intermediaries and regrant the funds overseas.[31]

Use of U.S. Intermediaries

U.S. public charity intermediaries are widely used because their use relieves the granting foundation of substantial responsibility for compliance with Internal Revenue Code (IRC)[32] rules aimed at ensuring that the granted funds are used for charitable purposes within the ambit of IRC Section 170(c). Grants to domestic public charities are generally qualifying distributions. Therefore, if a private foundation makes its grant to a U.S. public charity that is willing to regrant the funds for use abroad, the foundation does not have to comply with the stringent and often complex requirements applicable to direct overseas funding.

Several types of U.S. public charities may receive foundation grants for use abroad. Some U.S. public charities have a foreign branch office or subsidiary. Even if the grant is to be used by that foreign office or subsidiary, it is treated for tax purposes as made to the U.S. charity because the foreign branch or subsidiary is subject to complete administrative control by its U.S. parent.[33] Many U.S. charities, such as Oxfam, CARE, and the Red Cross, have broad-based direct programs abroad. It is possible for a foundation to specify that its grant is to be used for a particular overseas program of the grantee U.S. public charity as long as that program is subject to total control by the grantee.

In addition, a U.S. public charity may be formed exclusively to support one or more foreign organizations. Contributions to a U.S. public charity intermediary must be made for exclusively charitable purposes and must not be earmarked for distribution to a foreign grantee organization. Therefore, such U.S. organizations may not serve as conduits, merely funneling earmarked donations to non–U.S. charities. Revenue Ruling 63-252 addresses the deductibility of contributions by individuals to a U.S. charity that then transmits some or all of its funds to a foreign charity. No deduction is permitted unless the U.S. organization reviews and approves the charitable purpose of the grant as furthering its own charitable purposes.[34] The IRS has enumerated several additional procedures to be followed by U.S. public charities that make grants to foreign charities. These procedures are intended to ensure that the U.S. charity retains sufficient discretion and control over the use of such grants to ensure that the funds are used solely for charitable purposes.[35]

Community foundations can also facilitate overseas gifts if their governing instruments do not include geographic restrictions that preclude grants abroad. Overseas grants through U.S. community foundations are usually effected by means of contributions to donor-advised funds, with the private foundation's board acting as the donor advisor.[36]

IRS Recognition of Foreign Charities

A foreign charity may apply to the IRS for recognition as an organization exempt from taxation under IRC Section 501(c)(3); however, relatively few non–U.S. charities apply. One disincentive to such applications is that, even if the foreign charity has obtained IRS recognition, direct contributions from U.S. individual donors still cannot be deducted against income tax liability because the organization is not formed in the United States. Legal costs and complicated ongoing reporting requirements (including U.S. information returns for each year in which the foreign charity has more than $25,000 of U.S.–source income) are also disincentives.

Although IRS recognition of a foreign charity does not qualify donations to it for U.S. income tax deductions, it does offer important benefits to the foreign charity. U.S.–based private foundations can make grants to such a foreign charity without worrying about the requirements of an equivalency determination or expenditure responsibility (both discussed as follows). Grants from U.S. public charities to foreign charities with IRS determination letters also do not require ongoing monitoring by the grantor. Therefore, foreign charities that want to receive funds from U.S. charities should consider going through the application process; however, most foreign charities do not obtain IRS recognition, and a complex set of rules governs the process of making grants to those organizations in order to ensure that grant funds are expended for solely charitable purposes.

Rules Governing Grants Abroad by Private Foundations

Private nonoperating foundations making grants abroad will want to determine whether the foreign grant counts as a "qualifying distribution" for purposes of the IRC Section 4942 minimum distribution rules and to avoid running afoul of the IRC Section 4945 prohibition against grants to organizations other than public charities unless the grantor exercises "expenditure responsibility."

If a private foundation fails to make sufficient qualifying distributions annually of amounts equal to 5 percent of the aggregate fair market value of all of its assets held for investment, it will be subject to an excise tax in that year.[37] The taxable expenditure provisions of IRC Section 4945 also have a substantial impact on grants abroad by private foundations. A private foundation makes a taxable expenditure subject to excise tax if it makes a grant (1) for any purpose other than one specified in IRC Section 170(c)(2)(B) or (2) to an organization that is not a public charity (or foreign equivalent of a U.S. public charity) unless the private foundation exercises "expenditure responsibility" with respect to the grant.

Good Faith Determination

A grant by a U.S. private foundation to a foreign organization that has received an IRS determination letter that it is a public charity is always a qualifying distribution for purposes of the 5 percent minimum distribution rule. If the foreign donee does not have such a determination letter, the private foundation will generally first try to make a good-faith determination that the donee is the equivalent of a U.S. public charity. If this determination can be made, the foreign grant will be a qualifying distribution even if the U.S. grantor does not exercise the ongoing monitoring of the funded project known as "expenditure responsibility."

In making a good faith determination, the private foundation may rely on an opinion from its counsel or the grantee's counsel or an affidavit of the grantee.[38] If this method is used, however, each potential U.S. grantor private foundation must obtain its own lawyer equivalency letter or grantee affidavit, and the cost may be prohibitive for smaller foundations. In Revenue Procedure 92-94,[39] the IRS approved a form of equivalency affidavit of the foreign grantee that may be relied on by multiple U.S. grantors as long as it contains current information. This helps small foundations make their good-faith determinations at a reasonable cost.

Expenditure Responsibility

If the private foundation cannot determine that the proposed foreign donee organization is the equivalent of a U.S. public charity, then the grantor private foundation must exercise "expenditure responsibility" over the grant. Exercising expenditure responsibility entails making a pregrant inquiry to allow the grantor to make a reasonable determination that the proposed grantee can fulfill the charitable purpose of the grant. An officer or director of the foreign grantee must also sign a written grant agreement specifying the charitable purpose of the grant and committing the grantee to:

- Repay any funds not used for the grant's purpose.
- Submit annual reports detailing how the funds have been used, compliance with the grant agreement, and the grantee's progress in achieving the purpose for which the grant was made (these grantee reports must usually be made until all of the grant funds have been expended).
- Maintain books and records that are made reasonably available to the grantor.
- Refrain from using any of the funds for lobbying, direct or indirect influence on any public election or voter registration drive, or any activity for a noncharitable purpose, to the extent that such use of the funds would be taxable to a private foundation.

The agreement will typically also prohibit the grantee from regranting the funds to other organizations or individuals because that triggers additional complicated rules. If the foreign grantee is not the equivalent of a U.S. private foundation, the agreement must also require the donee to maintain the grant money in a separate fund dedicated to charitable purposes so that the grantee may properly account for the funds.[40]

Special rules also address the situation where a director, trustee, or employee of the U.S. grantor foundation becomes aware of or suspects diversion of grant funds by a foreign grantee to any use not furthering any charitable purpose specified in the grant agreement. If that occurs, immediate follow-up may be required, and any future installments of grant funds may need to be suspended or cancelled. The grantor foundation may even have to take reasonable steps to recover funds already granted if it has evidence that the grantee has misused the funds.[41]

The Treasury Regulations on expenditure responsibility recognize that "[a] private foundation is not an insurer of the activity of the organization to which it makes a grant."[42] The Regulations provide that the grantor foundation will not be found to have violated the taxable expenditure rules if it has followed the prescribed expenditure responsibility procedures, even if funds are in fact diverted by the grantee or something else goes wrong.[43]

The U.S. grantor private foundation must take all reasonable efforts to establish adequate procedures to see that the grant is spent solely for the purposes for which made and must obtain detailed annual reports from the grantee on how the funds are spent. It must also provide the IRS with annual reports on all expenditure responsibility grants.[44] In order to satisfy its IRS reporting requirement, the grantor private foundation is required to provide information about each expenditure responsibility grant on its annual Form 990-PF information return.

Grants to Governmental Units

Grants to foreign governmental units do not require either an equivalency determination or expenditure responsibility. The Treasury Regulations provide that a foreign organization will be treated as a public charity if it is a "foreign government, or any agency or instrumentality thereof . . . even if it is not described in IRC Section 501(c)(3)";[45] however, any grant to such a governmental unit must be for charitable, not public purposes. Therefore, the U.S. grantor foundation should obtain documentation establishing that the grantee is a foreign government or governmental unit, and it should enter into a grant agreement obligating the grantee to use the grant for charitable purposes.

The Out of Corpus Requirement

IRS rules specify that one private foundation cannot make grants to endow another. A grant from one private foundation to another (whether overseas or domestic) will not meet the definition of a qualifying distribution for purposes of application of the 5 percent minimum payout rules to the grantor unless the grantee satisfies the so-called out of corpus rule.[46] Therefore, if the foreign charity grantee is the equivalent of a U.S. private foundation, the U.S. foundation's grant to it must also meet the out of corpus requirement. The out of corpus rule requires that any grant from one private foundation to another must be spent by the grantee within 12 months after the close of the taxable year in which it received the funds. The grantee must take the grant funds "out of corpus" and spend them within the required amount of time. This policy is designed to ensure that such private foundation grants will be used for the public benefit and not to build the recipient organization's investment portfolio.

Furthermore, the grantee foundation must provide records to the grantor foundation showing that the grantee met its minimum payout requirement before it received the grant, and the grantee satisfied its minimum payout requirement for the year in which the grant was received in addition to spending the grant. Because most foreign charities are unfamiliar with the minimum payout rules and do not maintain the records necessary to compute it, satisfying the out of corpus requirement is often not possible.[47]

The procedure approved by the IRS in Revenue Procedure 92-94 has helped simplify the process of collecting the data necessary to attempt to make a good-faith determination that a proposed foreign grantee is the equivalent of a U.S. public charity, and it has also potentially decreased the cost of that process because several U.S. grantors may rely on a single currently qualified Revenue Procedure 92-94 affidavit; however, the process is still generally expensive and often impossible. The affidavit requires the grantee to provide its governing documents and local law translated into English. Moreover, the grantor must obtain and review several years' financial data of the grantee in order to try to determine whether it meets the public support test applicable to U.S. public charities. As a practical matter, grantees in underdeveloped nations do not readily or easily provide such data. Even when they do, differences between U.S. law and the law of the grantee's jurisdiction may make it very time-consuming for the grantor, or more often its counsel, to tell whether, for example, the grantee's assets are required to be distributed to other charities upon dissolution of the grantee,[48] or whether private inurement, private benefit, and substantial lobbying and political activities are prohibited. Even if the grantor is able to clear all of these hurdles, it will still need sufficient staff capacity to exercise the required ongoing oversight, and grantors can become quite frustrated chasing financial reports and other follow-up data needed for expenditure responsibility grants.

In addition to the complex maze of IRC requirements, other laws may impede a foundation's ability to make cost-effective grants abroad. Grants to organizations in embargoed countries are a good example of situations requiring substantial legal advice, which is cost prohibitive for most small to midsized foundations. Counsel to such grantors must have working knowledge of rules imposed by the embargo, exceptions to the embargo, and how to obtain necessary government permission or licenses to make such grants.[49]

RECENT DEVELOPMENTS IN TECHNICAL REQUIREMENTS FOR OVERSEAS GRANTS

Some foundations avoid making grants to overseas organizations because they are concerned about possible failure to comply with all of the requirements for expenditure responsibility.[50] Sometimes, the U.S. foundation lacks adequate staff to comply, and sometimes it lacks funds for professional counsel in connection with such grants. The author has also helped arrange for community foundations to facilitate international grants by acting as intermediary, where the size of the grant or the frequency with which the foundation anticipates making international grants does not warrant the grantor's developing the forms, policies, and procedures needed to administer expenditure responsibility grants. Particularly during the 1990s, several efforts were made to simplify the applicable procedures. This section describes the outcomes of those of such efforts that have succeeded to one degree or another.

"Good-Faith Determinations"

A U.S. foundation wishing to make a grant to a foreign organization has traditionally first attempted to make a good-faith determination that the grantee is the equivalent of a U.S. public charity and has then resorted to expenditure responsibility only if that determination could not be made. This has been an expensive and time-consuming process in many cases, particularly when laws governing NGOs in the country of the proposed grantee are not similar to U.S. laws governing nonprofits. As noted earlier, in order to attempt a good-faith equivalency determination, the grantor must review the grantee's governing documents, analyze local governing law, and review several years' financial data of the grantee. The governing documents often must be translated and the financial data, if available at all, converted to U.S. currency. If the proposed foreign grantee is a hospital or school, the grantor must also obtain and review patient admission and student racial discrimination policies and standards. In collecting the necessary data, each U.S. grantor to the same foreign grantee has typically had its own counsel collect and analyze this data and then, where possible, issue a letter opining that the grantee is the equivalent of either a U.S. public charity (in which case no expenditure responsibility is required) or a U.S. private foundation (in which case the grantor must exercise expenditure responsibility, and the grant must satisfy the out of corpus rule). The process of obtaining this legal opinion has been prohibitively expensive for some grantors.

Revenue Procedure 92-94

In 1992, the IRS issued Revenue Procedure 92-94,[51] which provided a form of equivalency affidavit that may be relied on by multiple U.S. grantors to the same foreign organization as long as it is current or has been updated by the foreign grantee to include current data. Although the Revenue Procedure's approach is an admirable attempt to simplify the process of international grantmaking by U.S. foundations, the author has found it to be of little utility. There is no central repository for Revenue Procedure 92-94 affidavits (although the International Center for Not-for-Profit Law is building one on its Web site), so use by multiple grantors most often depends on fortuitous communications among them. Occasionally, a grant application from a foreign grantee is referred by a larger U.S. foundation to a smaller one, and the latter is given access to an affidavit obtained by the referring foundation, along with supporting materials. Even then, the smaller foundation will be hesitant to rely on its own data analysis, or even on the analysis performed by or for the larger foundation, and will therefore still incur the expense of having its counsel analyze the data and issue an opinion regarding equivalency. Thus, while the process approved by the Revenue Procedure has promise and may save substantial time and costs once such a central database is available, it has limited utility as a cost and time saver at this point. Its primary benefit, in the author's experience, has been to provide foundations with IRS-approved forms of an equivalency affidavit and financial schedules designed to elicit the necessary information from the foreign grantee.

IRS General Information Letter on Equivalency Determination

Following a two-year effort by the Council on Foundations, on April 18, 2001, the Department of the Treasury issued a general information letter that will streamline overseas grantmaking.[52] The letter, which may be relied on by all U.S. private foundations, indicates that foundations do not need to attempt to make a good-faith determination that a proposed foreign grantee is the equivalent of a U.S.

public charity before deciding to make the grant subject to expenditure responsibility. This development is welcome because the equivalency determination process is so complex, costly, and time-consuming. This change will be particularly helpful when the foreign organization is unable to provide the financial data needed to determine whether it meets the U.S. charity public support test. The letter was needed because the IRC and applicable Treasury Regulations seemed to indicate that an equivalency determination had to be attempted before the U.S. grantor foundation could make an overseas grant subject to expenditure responsibility. Treasury has now provided this guidance and confirmed that the Regulations do not, in fact, require this determination.

The letter makes clear that a U.S. private foundation may treat an overseas grantee as a noncharity from the outset. It also notes that a private foundation is not bound by another private foundation's determination regarding whether the same grantee is the equivalent of a U.S. public charity. Moreover, unless the foreign grantee has applied for and received an IRS determination letter, the IRS will respect the grantor foundation's conclusion that the grantee is either the equivalent of a U.S. private foundation or a noncharity. The letter does not affect specific treaty rules, such as those under our treaties with Mexico and Canada. The April 18, 2001 letter should encourage international grantmaking by U.S. foundations by meaningfully streamlining the due diligence process.

Regranting of Expenditure Responsibility Grant Funds

When a U.S. private foundation makes an overseas grant, stringent requirements often apply if the foreign grantee will regrant the funds to other organizations or to individuals. Regranting can be attractive because foreign grantmaking organizations have better access than U.S. grantors to information regarding which local projects are the best and most effective. Therefore, a U.S. donor foundation may make a grant to a foreign entity (the initial grantee); which in turn regrants the funds to other local entities or individuals (secondary grantees).

If the initial grantee is a U.S. public charity equivalent, the U.S. grantor is not required to monitor the regranting. If it is not, however, the secondary grant must comply with all of the normal requirements for grants by U.S. private foundations.[53] A secondary grant to an individual must be made on an objective and nondiscriminatory basis, and according to procedures preapproved by the IRS. If the secondary grant is to a foreign organization that is not the equivalent of a U.S. public charity, the initial grantee must exercise expenditure responsibility regarding the grant. These requirements have raised concerns that the U.S. grantor must somehow guarantee the initial grantee's compliance with these rules.[54]

In 1997, the IRS issued a private letter ruling that answered a lot of questions about a U.S. donor's responsibility with respect to such secondary grants.[55] The ruling takes a pragmatic approach, which does not hold the U.S. grantor responsible if the initial grantee fails to meet all requirements of exercising expenditure responsibility over the secondary grant. Specifically, the ruling held that:

- The U.S. grantor's expenditure responsibility requirements regarding the secondary grants are satisfied if the initial grantees are bound by written grant agreements to meet the applicable requirements in connection with the secondary grants, as long as the initial grantees also provide the grantor with satisfactory reports, the grantor has no reason to doubt the accuracy of those reports, and the grantor properly reports the initial grants on its Forms 990-PF.
- If the initial grantee makes a secondary grant to an individual, it may use procedures for which the U.S. grantor has received pre-approval from the IRS.
- The initial grantee need not make reports to the IRS regarding the regrants even though, technically, a pledge to exercise expenditure responsibility entails proper reporting to the IRS.

The pragmatic approach taken by this ruling is a comfort to U.S. grantmakers. Although U.S. grantors must still take care to comply with many technical requirements, the IRS has indicated that the grantor is not an insurer with respect to the proper exercise of expenditure responsibility by overseas initial grantees who make secondary grants of the funds.

New Tax Withholding Requirements for Certain Foreign Grants

On a less positive note, new Treasury Regulations under IRC Section 1441 may require U.S. foundations to withhold taxes on grants to foreign individuals or organizations.[56] The new Regulations, which became effective on January 1, 2001, require U.S. foundations to withhold U.S. income taxes on grants they make to foreign individuals or organizations that perform all or a portion of the activities funded by the grant within the United States. The new rules do not affect grants that do not involve activity taking place within the United States, so they will not affect most international grants; however, if grant funds will be used to allow a foreign individual to attend a conference in the United States, teach here, intern with a company here, or perform other activities here, or will allow a foreign entity to perform activities within the United States, withholding on the portion of the grant funds to be used for the U.S. activity will be required unless:

- The recipient qualifies under a treaty exception.
- The recipient is an entity, and it can be proven that the recipient could qualify as a U.S. tax-exempt organization.
- The grant is intended to be used solely to acquire property.[57]

Trends in Technical Requirements

A cooperative effort to streamline and simplify procedures for international grantmaking has existed for several years. The Council on Foundations' U.S. Giving Abroad Initiative grew out of its Strategic Plan for International Programs. The goal of the initiative is to facilitate communication and reporting procedures for overseas grantmaking by U.S. foundations.[58] Initial planning for the initiative occurred at an October 1, 1996 meeting in New York called "Facilitating U.S. Giving Abroad: Current Solutions, Current Problems." Representatives of 17 foundations attended the meeting, which was co-hosted by the Council on Foundations, the American Express Corporation, and the International Center for Not-for-Profit Law.

The scope of the U.S. Giving Abroad Initiative is to share best practices among foundations that make overseas grants; explore much-needed revisions to IRS guidelines for cross-border grants; and collect in a central, readily accessible place, forms (such as Revenue Procedure 92-94 affidavits) and information about nonprofit law in various countries. The work of the Initiative's Administrative/ Legislative Task Force on simplifying and clarifying procedural requirements is critical as international philanthropy grows. Many of the current rules were developed when such grants were rare, and in the same atmosphere of suspicion, and perhaps xenophobia, that gave rise to the U.S. law denying U.S. donors income tax deductions for direct gifts to foreign charities.[59] The Task Force has identified as areas of concern the duration and level of reporting requirements for certain types of grants,[60] the out of corpus rules, restrictions on re-granting, and the rules governing equivalency determinations.

A task force of the Exempt Organizations Committee of the Section of Taxation of The American Bar Association is also focusing on suggesting revisions to the rules governing international grantmaking by U.S. foundations. Although the project encompasses work on rules governing both domestic and overseas grantmaking, the Task Force will be working to clarify and simplify the rules governing expenditure responsibility, with a focus on reporting requirements and program-related investments.[61] Program-related investments (PRIs) are private foundation investments in ventures that help achieve the foundation's charitable purposes.[62] The Treasury Regulations on PRIs are limited and offer examples that are often difficult to apply in a foreign context. The goal of the Task Force will be to flesh out guidance on the permissible terms of PRIs and the examples offered.

The projects discussed previously are just a couple of the many current projects whose goals are to facilitate communication among

NGOs around the world and to help governments, the private sector, and NGOs to work together to solve communities' needs by opening lines of communication, analyzing interaction among these sectors, and developing uniform best practices for international giving. For example, the Active Learning Network for Accountability and Performance in Humanitarian Assistance is working with other NGOs to establish universal codes of conduct in humanitarian assistance.[63]

Community foundations around the world are also joining forces to promote and support the development of community foundations. For example, WINGS-CF, an informal network of community foundations around the world, helps its member organizations work with their peers to share information and experiences.[64] Another current project of interest is the Community Foundation Transatlantic Fellowship program sponsored by the King Baudouin Foundation of Belgium and the United States (KBF) and the German Marshall Fund of the United States (GMF), with the support of the Charles Stewart Mott Foundation. During each year of the program, American and European senior staff representatives of community foundations are participating in the new peer exchange program for community foundation professionals. Participants spend three weeks at a host community foundation on the other side of the Atlantic to learn about the social, cultural, and other circumstances affecting the development of community foundations in a country other than their own. While at the host foundation, the community foundation senior staff members participate in day-to-day office operations; explore issues of governance, strategic planning, grantmaking, and investment; and learn about public/private partnerships. They are expected to hold informal briefings for their hosts on the needs and foundation practices in their own communities.[65]

One of the reasons that equivalency determinations are so difficult and cumbersome is that laws governing NGOs vary widely among jurisdictions. Another complication for international grantmakers is that existing legal systems around the world are inadequate to support the development of solid, independent, transparent, and responsible NGOs.[66] Insufficient local regulation permits lack of accountability, which often results in fraud and diversion of funds.

Several cooperative efforts are afoot to educate various jurisdictions about each others' not-for-profit laws, develop such legal structures where there are none or where they are in their infancy, and provide technical assistance in writing laws and regulations, while developing global standards and guidelines for best practices for incorporation into the laws governing NGOs in countries all over the globe. The International Center for Not-for-Profit Law (ICNL), in cooperation with the Council on Foundations, is developing a database of NGO laws of various jurisdictions that, when available on ICNL's Web site, will be an invaluable resource for counsel performing equivalency determinations. The Web site already has these data available for some jurisdictions. Data on some other jurisdictions that are not yet available online can be obtained at no charge from the ICNL.

The process of standardizing NGO laws globally is a fascinating one for counsel who participate. The author was fortunate to have the opportunity, in April 1998, to meet for a day with a delegation from mainland China that was touring the world to discuss best practices and legal frameworks governing philanthropy.[67] The delegation's mission was to craft a statutory structure for philanthropy in China, including oversight of NGOs. Detailed discussions of U.S. practices regarding enforceability of pledges, U.S. laws forbidding private inurement and private benefit, and tax benefits for charitable contributions not only highlighted some vast cultural differences but also confirmed that many concerns about best practices were shared by the Chinese and U.S. representatives at the meeting.

Progress is being made toward normalizing laws and regulations governing the NGO sector, with a focus on communication, development of training and educational materials and programs to facilitate learning about not-for-profit laws, and administrative and judicial systems. Many organizations around the world are conducting and supporting legal, sociological, and other research needed to strengthen and improve laws and legal systems for NGOs. Ultimately, these efforts should lead to substantial simplification of U.S. laws governing international grantmaking. The legal and nonprofit communities will continue to work with and educate the IRS and the legislature as not-for-profit laws around the world adopt similar standards and regulatory systems, and concerns about lack of oversight of NGOs by local governments decrease. This is an era of enthusiasm and optimism in the not-for-profit sector, but much work remains to be done.

THE EVOLVING ROLE OF COUNSEL

The role of counsel in working with foundations that are active in the international arena is not unique. Counseling such foundations—like counseling foundations whose grants are solely domestic—requires thorough knowledge of the arcane rules governing such grants as well as knowledge of current developments in this evolving field of law. We must educate the donors with whom we work; assist them in developing forms, policies, and procedures appropriate to international grantmaking; and help them work through the frustrations that often accompany operating subject to a maze of technical requirements. At the end of 2000, the author worked on several equivalency determinations and grant agreements for a midsized foundation that funds only projects connected with the incidence of AIDS in sub-Sarahan Africa and its impact on local youth. The young founder, visionary and impassioned, was impatient with the process and applied pressure to release funds as soon as possible. Her focus was the severity and urgency of the need for assistance. As counsel, we not only have to be sure our clients observe IRS requirements, but we must also act as trusted advisors/counselors who can reassure the foundation directors or trustees that the funds will indeed be released. Just as in the domestic arena, it can be hard to tell a client that you need more time for due diligence when the client is thinking primarily of the deaths occurring during the pregrant compliance period and how many fatalities might be averted by prompt funding of the project. This particular foundation funds primarily grassroots projects. Because the grantees lacked sophistication and often had little experience, the process of ensuring that they had the wherewithal to carry out the project, and of obtaining adequate data from them, was slower than it is when the grantee has been operating for many years and has experience with U.S. legal requirements for grants abroad. In Third World countries, however, grassroots organizations are often best positioned to deliver services because of their intimate familiarity with the culture and potential local impediments to success. Their input in refining the scope and purpose of the grants was invaluable, and counsel, the founder, and the foundation's Programs Director all knew this to be true.

The emphasis on accountability in the U.S. philanthropic sector is generally increasing.[68] One result of this is that so-called venture philanthropists in particular seem comfortable with the idea of post-grant ongoing due diligence. This attitude tends, in the author's experience, to make all of the ongoing procedural requirements for expenditure responsibility grants more palatable to them. Impatient as these clients may be, they realize that ongoing monitoring of the project should increase the odds of its success.

It is an exciting time for counsel to international grantmakers. As overseas funding grows, many challenges face us. It is perhaps easiest to pinpoint how changes in U.S. laws governing such grants can be simplified while still protecting our government's interests—certainly far easier than dealing with issues such as how best to deliver services abroad and how to measure the success of overseas projects. The IRS has signaled its willingness to revise and simplify outdated and complicated rules, and much progress in the effort can be expected to occur over the next decade as grantmakers and allied professionals throughout the country join forces to facilitate this process.

ADDITIONAL RESOURCES

ALNAP: *www.odi.org.uk/alnap*
Council on Foundations: *www.cof.org*
eldis: *http://ntl.ids.ac.uk*
The Foundation Center: *www.fdncenter.org*
German Marshall Fund of the United States: *www.gmfs.org*
Grantmakers Without Borders: *www.internationaldonors.org*
The Grantsmanship Center: *www.tgci.com*

International Center for Not-for-Profit Law: *www.icnl.org*
Nonprofit Sector Research Fund: *www.nonprofitresearch.org*
Oxfam: *www.oxfam.org*
U.S. Agency for International Development: *www.usaid.gov*
United States International Grantmaking (COF): *www.usig.org*
Worldwide Initiatives for Grantmaker Support (WINGS) (COF):
    www.wingsweb.org

NOTES

1. *International Grantmaking II: An Update on U.S. Foundation Trends* (New York: Foundation Center, in cooperation with the Council on Foundations, 2000), p. 16, hereinafter sometimes referred to as "the Foundation Center Report." The term *international grantmaking* as used herein includes both direct grants overseas and grants to U.S. charities which then regrant the funds overseas.
2. *Id.*, p. xiv.
3. *Id.* To collect the data reported in *International Grantmaking: U.S. Foundation Trends* (New York: Foundation Center, in cooperation with the Council on Foundations, 1997), the predecessor to *International Grantmaking II*, the study analyzed grants of $10,000 or more authorized or paid by 821 family, corporate, and community foundations in 1990 and 1,020 such foundations in 1994. Grants of $10,000 or more authorized by 1,009 foundations in 1998 were analyzed for the update report, *International Grantmaking II*.
4. *Id.*
5. *Id.*, p. 18.
6. "Five Reasons to Give Internationally," Grantmakers Without Borders Web site: *www.internationaldonors.org*.
7. *Id.*
8. "World's Poorest Countries Falling Further Behind Developing World: UNICEF." United Nations Children's Fund press release dated May 16, 2001, regarding a study entitled "Poverty and Children: Lessons of the 90s for Least Developed Countries" prepared for the Third UN Conference on Least Developed Countries.
9. See note 6.
10. See note 1, p. 12. Also see, for example, S. Bruce Shearer, "The Role of Philanthropy in International Development," paper prepared for the October 1995 Rockefeller Foundation Bellagio Conference on Human-Centered Development: The Role of Foundations, FLOs and NGOs. Available at the Web site of the International Center for Not-for-Profit Law: *www.icnl.org*.
11. See note 1, p. 30.
12. *Id.*, p. 24.
13. *Id.*, p. 30.

14. *Id.*, pp. 2 and 30.
15. *Id.*, p. 17, Table 2-2 and p. 19, Table 2-3.
16. *Id.*, p. 19.
17. *Id.*, p. 3.
18. *Id.*, p. 17, Table 2-2, and p. 19, Table 2-3.
19. Sheila Avrin McLean, *U.S. Philanthropy: Grantmaking for International Purposes* (Washington, D.C.: Council on Foundations, 1982), p. 18.
20. Emmett Carson, *Grantmaking for the Global Village* (Washington, D.C.: Council on Foundations, 1997), p. 1.
21. See note 1, p. 8.
22. *Id.*, p. 7.
23. See note 1, pp. 8-11.
24. Id., p. 12; See note 20, p. 18. As Carson notes, these donor-advised funds have led to increased community foundation involvement in international philanthropy.
25. Anthony Shadid, "Fighting Scourges with Funds," *Boston Globe*, May 30, 2001.
26. See note 20, p. 4.
27. See note 1, p. 12.
28. IRC Section 4942.
29. See note 1, p. 44.
30. *Id.*, pp. 45–47.
31. *Id.*, p. 52.
32. All references to the IRC are to the Internal Revenue Code of 1986, as amended.
33. See Rev. Rul. 63-252, 1963-2 C.B. 101, Ex. 5; *Bilingual Montessori School of Paris, Inc.*, 75 T.C. 480 (1981).
34. See Rev. Rul. 63-252, Ex. 4. Also see Victoria B. Bjorklund and Jennifer I. Goldberg, "How a Private Foundation Can Use 'Friends Of' Organizations," *International Dateline*, August 1998, Issue 48 (Council on Foundations). U.S. public charities specifically formed to support foreign organizations are sometimes referred to as "friends of" organizations because they often bear names such as American Friends of Oxford University.
35. For more details on these procedures, see, e.g., John A. Edie, *Beyond Our Borders: A Guide to Making Grants Outside the U.S.* (Washington, D.C.: Council on Foundations, 1994); Jane Peebles, *The Handbook of International Philanthropy: Policies and Procedures for Planned Giving Beyond Our Borders* (Chicago: Bonus Books, 1998).
36. For a fuller discussion of the use of U.S. intermediaries, see Timothy R. Lyman, "Simpler Approaches to Cross-Border Giving Through Domestic Collaborations," *International Dateline*, Winter 1998, Issue 47 (Council on Foundations).
37. I.R.C. §4942.
38. Treas. Reg. §53.4945-5(a)(5).
39. Rev. Proc. 92-94, 1992-2 C.B. 507.
40. See Treas. Regs. §53.4945-5(c)(3)(ii), §53.4945-5(b)(8) and §53.4945-6(c).
41. Treas. Reg. §53.4945-5(e)(1).
42. Treas. Reg. §53.4945-5(b)(i).
43. Treas. Reg. §53.4945-5(e).

44. I.R.C. §4945(h).
45. Treas. Reg. §53.4945-5(a)(4)(iii).
46. Treas. Reg. §53.4942(a)-3(c).
47. For a detailed discussion of the out of corpus rule, see Milton Cerney and Doug Varley, "The Out of Corpus Rule Reviewed," *International Dateline*, April 1999, Issue 51 (Council on Foundations).
48. For a discussion of differences in the laws governing NGOs in various jurisdictions, see Karla W. Simon, "Dissolution Dos and Don'ts." Also see Simon's "Legal and Regulatory Frameworks for the Not-for-Profit Sector: A Comparative Analysis." Both are available at the International Center for Not-for-Profit Law Web site: *www.icnl.org*.
49. Timothy S. Bugett and Timothy R. Lyman, "Grantmaking and Embargoed Countries: An Overview Using Kosovo as a Case Study," *International Dateline*, October 1999, Issue 53 (Council on Foundations).
50. See, e.g., Thomas Chomicz, "Grantmaking by Private Foundations in the International Arena," *International Dateline*, November 1998, Issue 49 (Council on Foundations).
51. See note 39.
52. "IRS Endorses Streamlining of International Grantmaking Procedures," Council on Foundations press release (May 15, 2001); Department of the Treasury letter to John A. Edie, Senior Vice President and General Counsel to the Council on Foundations (April 18, 2001).
53. See Treas. Reg. §§53.4945-5(a)(6) and 53.4945-5 (b)(1).
54. See Milton Cerney and Beth Sellers, "Private Ruling Takes Pragmatic Approach to International Regranting," *International Dateline*, Fall 1997 (Council on Foundations).
55. Private Ltr. Rul. 9717024 (January 23, 1997).
56. Treas. Reg. § 1.1441-1(b).
57. A memorandum on these requirements can be accessed at the Council on Foundations' Web site at: *www.cof.org/legal/index.htm*. The full text of the new regulations is also available at that Web site.
58. See "U.S. Giving Abroad Initiative" on the Council on Foundations' Web site at: *www.cof.org/whatis/types/international/intgiving/intgiving.htm*.
59. IRC §170(c) allows a U.S. individual donor an income tax deduction only for contributions to charities organized in the United States. Congress has justified this rule because, in its view, the U.S. derives no benefits from such gifts. In 1939, it expressed its reason for disallowing an income deduction for direct gifts abroad saying: "[When a contribution is made to a U.S. charity, the] government is compensated for the loss of revenue by its relief from financial burden which would otherwise have to be met by appropriations from public funds, and by the benefits resulting from the promotion of the general welfare. The United States derives no such benefit from gifts to foreign institutions." H. Rep't. No. 1860, 75th Cong., 3rd Sess., pp. 19-20, 1939-1 C.B. (Part 2) 728, at 742.
60. For example, cross-border grants for the purchase of capital equipment or to build an endowment raise reporting issues because capital equipment and en-

dowments typically have a useful life longer than the terms of the grant. Grantees must usually report annually to the U.S. grantor until all of the grant funds have been expended. The Treasury Regulations do not specify how long a foreign grantee must continue to make written reports to the U.S. grantor foundation when the grant is for the purchase of capital equipment or for endowment. See Treas. Regs. §§ 53.4945-5(b)(3) and 53.4945-6(c)(2). Moreover, no cases or IRS rulings to date have addressed this issue. A logical approach as to purchases of capital equipment is to require reports over the useful life of the equipment, based on IRC depreciation rules and generally accepted accounting principles. Grants for endowment are problematic because the life of an endowment is potentially permanent. Therefore, the grantee might have to report indefinitely, and the grantor would also have to continue reporting on the grant to the IRS. Clearly, guidance and safe harbors in these areas are much needed.

61. Richard S. Gallagher, "Bar Association Task Force Revisits Private Foundation Rules: Implications for Foreign Grantmaking," *International Dateline*, Winter 2001 (Council on Foundations).

62. See Treas. Reg. § 53.4945-(b)(4).

63. See Raymond Apthorpe and Philippa Atkinson, "Towards Shared Social Learning for Humanitarian Programmes," a study prepared for the Active Learning Network for Accountability and Performance in Humanitarian Assistance (July 1999), available at ALNAP's Web site: *www.odi.org.uk/alnap*.

64. Dagne Forrest and Monica Patten, "Philanthropy Support Organizations Worldwide," *Alliance*, Vol. 6, No. 1 (March 2001); Eleanor W. Sacks, "The Growth of Community Foundations Around the World: An Examination of the Vitality of the Community Foundation Movement," prepared for the Council on Foundations and the Worldwide Institute for Grantmaker Support—Community Foundations (WINGS-CF) (2000).

65. Interview with Joseph Lumarda, Executive Vice President, External Affairs, California Community Foundation (June 8, 2001). In the 1999–2000 inaugural year of the project, Mr. Lumarda visited with two Polish community foundations as a part of this project, and the California Community Foundation has hosted representatives of foreign community foundations who are visiting the United States as a part of this project. For more information on the project, go to *www.gmfs.org*.

66. See note 48.

67. The delegation included Mao Qi Xiong, Vice-Director of the Research Office Overseas Chinese Committee of the National People's Congress of the P.R.C.; Wang Shihu, Director, State Organs Law and Administrative Law Commission, Standing Committee of the National People's Congress; Xu Anbiao, Division Director, State Organ Law and Administrative Law Department Legislative Affairs Commission, Standing Committee of the National People's Congress; and Yang Tuan, Vice-Chairman Research of Interchange Committee, China Charity Federation. The U.S. representatives were Dr. Frank Ellsworth of Capital Research and Management Co., Joseph Lumarda of the California

Community Foundation, the author, and Michael Rea, the Asia Foundation's Program Officer for its Asian-American Exchange.

68. There are several projects in process that are working to establish uniform standards for accountability. So-called Participating Monitoring and Evaluation (PM&E) focuses on the tools and methods for promoting participation by beneficiaries and other stakeholders in decision making as well as monitoring and evaluation of projects. See "Background to PM&E" at the eldis Web site: *http://ntl.ids.ac.uk/eldis/hot/pm3.htm*. Practical and effective delivery of services is also a focus, with much attention paid to rhetoric without effective action. See, e.g., "Millennium Summit: Closing the Credibility Gap?", Oxfam International Policy Paper (August 2000), available at Oxfam-UK's Web site at: *www.oxfam.org.uk./policy/papers/millsum/millsum.htm*. Another excellent resource on accountability is Peter Raynard, "Mapping Accountability in Humanitarian Assistance," a study performed for the Active Learning Network for Accountability and Performance in Humanitarian Assistance (ALNAP, May 2000). Also see M. Edwards, "International Development NGOs: Legitimacy, Accountability, Regulation and Roles," a Discussion Paper for the Commission on the Future of the Voluntary Sector (CFVS) and the British Overseas Aid Group (BOAG) (1996). CFVS is a U.K. organization set up by the National Council for Voluntary Organizations. BOAG is a coalition of five U.K. development agencies: ActionAid, CAFOD, Christian Aid, Oxfam—U.K., and Save the Children—U.K.

CHAPTER 2

The Old and New Traditions of European Foundations

By John Richardson, Peter Walkenhorst,
and Jakub Wygnanski

PERSPECTIVES

Foundations and charitable trusts are a time-honored tradition throughout Europe as vehicles for the largesse of individual land-holders and members of the ruling class. The emergence of European foundations as instruments of civil society mirrors a shift among foundations in the United States toward the broader social visions embraced by corporations, entrepreneurs, and families. With this growth in European foundations, do opportunities exist for transatlantic communication and the exchange of knowledge regarding foundation development?

This chapter consists of four parts. The first, a position paper produced by the European Foundation Centre's European Union Committee, outlines the specific characteristics of foundations and emphasizes the role they can play in fostering democracy and promoting socioeconomic development to improve the quality of citizens' lives in Europe and worldwide. The second, from the executive director of the European Foundation Centre, John Richardson, surveys the services provided by European foundations and the support they receive from the Centre. The European Foundation Centre promotes and underpins the work of foundations and corporate funders active in Europe.

The third part is by Peter Walkenhorst, director of philanthropy and foundations for the Bertelsmann Foundation in Gütersloh, Germany. In it, Walkenhorst describes the German foundation tradition and emerging trends in foundations' structure and activities. He recently edited the book *Building Philanthropic and Social Capital: The Work of Community Foundations* (Bertelsmann Foundation Publishers, 2001).

The final part is an interview with Jakub Wygnanski (known as Kuba) of the Stefan Batory Foundation. Kuba describes the history and recent rapid growth of foundations in Poland. He touches on philanthropy's role in civil society and the emergence of the community foundation model in his country. The Stefan Batory Foundation supports the development of a democratic and open society in Poland.

Working with Foundations in Europe: Why and How?

From the European Foundation Centre

Across Europe, foundations are receiving increased attention and are taking up a more central role in discussions about the future of economic, social, environmental, and other policies. Their characteristics and the role that foundations can play remain, however, largely unfamiliar to the public in general and to decision makers and political leaders in particular. This chapter part outlines what they are, and how they work and reach out to other actors in our society.

Foundations represent a small but important part of the nonprofit sector. They are active in such fields as education, research, and culture, and are involved in programs aimed at fostering democracy and socioeconomic development in many world regions. At a time when governments are reviewing their spending for new social programs and cooperation with the nonprofit sector, one may look at how public needs could be addressed through initiatives launched and funded with and within the sector.

A DIVERSE COMMUNITY WITH A COMMON AIM: ASSOCIATING PRIVATE WEALTH TO BENEFIT THE PUBLIC

The role and activities of foundations are driven by a public benefit purpose and a general philanthropic impulse that aims at an improving the living conditions and quality of life of the general public and specific disadvantaged groups and individuals as well as promoting civic initiatives and active citizenship.

The foundation landscape in Europe is richly varied, partly because of the many cultures and the different legal environments from one country to the next. The estimated 200,000 European foundations, although diverse, share common essential features:

> Foundations are *independent, separately-constituted non-profit bodies* with *their own established and reliable source of income,* usually but not exclusively from an endowment, and *their own governing board.* They have been attributed goods, rights and resources for the performance of work and support for *public benefit purposes,* either by supporting associations, institutions or individuals etc., or by operating their own programs.

Grants for postgraduate studies, support to school reform, research against muscoviscidose, prizes for television programs, cross-border parliamentary exchanges, employment and business creation programs, research into risk prevention, and improving management in health services are only a few examples of foundations' activity in Europe. Their action ranges from environmental protection to early childhood development, violence prevention to health care services, work with senior citizens to assistance for fostering participatory democracies, and civil dialogues across Europe and beyond.

Foundations constitute an expression of civic awareness of responsibility toward the community and are an indispensable element of an active civil society expressly protected by the rule of law.

Empowering Individuals and Creating Social Linkage

Foundations place the individual at the center of their work and concerns. Organized philanthropy is very much about increasing the efficiency of citizen participation by strengthening civil society.

Promoting Equal Access and Quality of Access

Foundations work toward a better distribution of wealth. In an economic context, foundations are about a more equitable and sustainable environment where all members of society can find a useful role whatever their talents, possibilities, or disabilities.

Building Social Capital: Civil Society's Development Arm

Foundations are too often only considered as financial retailers and venture capital banks for civil society. They are primarily bodies of knowledge and expertise whose primary purpose is to *create added value* in society in their respective fields of operation. Foundations can convert this body of expertise into long-term development policies. Their financial position, their *independence* and *continuity* give them the appropriate means to do so. They often play a valuable role as leaders daring to step onto contentious territory, where government could not venture, to help achieve the following goals:

- Bring about far-reaching change, including the search for innovative solutions to problems through the promotion of academic, scientific, and new technology programs.
- Introduce new variables into society's discourse.
- Bring new players to the decision-making table, and develop a more community-based process of change making. This trend is increasing with the development of foundations set up to help local communities address social, economic, and environmental challenges.

Today, foundations are one of the driving forces behind social change as well as benefactory institutions for the public at large.

Sustaining Research to Act Upstream

Foundations work to help tackle the root causes of problems, rather than just reacting downstream to their consequences in order to alleviate negative impact and effects. Foundations may support relief actions to assist other nonprofit organizations and public authorities in tackling emergency humanitarian, environmental, social, and other needs; however, the bulk of their action is to help address causes and try to anticipate changes in particular by supporting research, building expertise, and testing new approaches, thereby acting as catalysts for innovation.

Advancing European Cooperation

Over the last decade, the foundation community has witnessed a distinct change in Europe. Supporting the development of emerging democracies and market economies in Central and Eastern Europe, and the development of the single market, foundations are increasingly operating cross-frontier in Europe, awarding grants or operating programs, and developing cooperation schemes at a European level. Building on their respective cultures, traditions, and structures, foundations perceive the importance of working together, the concrete added value of partnership, sharing expertise, pooling resources, and promoting European solidarity and integration.

In 1989 a group of seven leading European foundations set up the European Foundation Centre (EFC) to underpin their work and collaboration at a European level and in other world regions. The EFC serves as a platform for exchange of expertise and the development of joint projects, as well as a key information resource center on the work of foundations in Europe. The Centre today serves a core membership of more than 200 funders, as well as 250 community philanthropy initiatives, and serves a further 48,000 organizations linked through networking centers in 37 countries.

A Commitment to Openness and Transparency

The greater involvement of foundations in the public policy arena goes hand in hand with increased responsibility. Members of the EFC have been in the forefront of foundations' efforts to promote openness, integrity, accountability, good stewardship, and optimal use of resources and evaluation of their work. This was the thrust of the *Prague Declaration* issued by the membership of the Centre in 1993. These considerations also motivated the 1996 *EFC Code of Practice*. The code sets out principles and procedures that independent funders are enjoined to respect to foster effective grantmaking and optimize accountability, toward the public at large, their grantees, regulatory authorities, and toward each foundation's own mission and objective.

WORKING IN PARTNERSHIP: LINKING RESOURCES AND NEEDS

In their respective fields of operation, foundations have engaged in a range of leadership and partnership activities with charities, businesses, and public authorities at the local, national, European, and global levels. They help *build partnerships across sectors* by bringing together different actors of our society, from multinational agencies, central governments, local authorities, the private and charity sectors to jointly address and devise effective responses to social, environmental, educational, scientific, and economic challenges facing European citizens. Their independence and flexibility allow foundations to play this catalyst role and pool resources, expertise, and know-how to tackle critical needs. Partnership is at the core of the work of many foundations, including those foundations working at a local level.

Partnering with foundations can represent a most attractive option for the following four principal reasons:

1. Foundations give a *human dimension* to public actions—in other words, they focus on the rule of law and civil society, respect for minority rights, freedom of the media, tolerance and pluralism, and can reach parts of society that government cannot reach.
2. They have the ability to work in a long-term perspective unlike elected governments, for-profit companies, and fundraising associations faced by shorter-term considerations and needs. Thus foundations are able to *experiment and take risks*. In doing so they are in a position to provide flexible

social venture capital for citizens supporting and acting through charities and other forms of nonprofit entities to develop useful models for long-term public action.

3. They can enter into *joint funding partnerships* where every euro of partners' funds goes to the recipient. An essential aspect of the uniqueness of foundations is their financial independence that is in stark contrast with other nonprofit bodies that do not have their own resources to cover their own administrative costs.

4. They can *complement public authorities and the private sector* or add resources where the latter are unable to operate because of legal or other restrictions.

EFC members have put into practice these partnership approaches with the public and private sectors by supporting initiatives where other sectors cannot intervene, and partnering in other projects with public and corporate funders leveraging and matching their resources.

Services Provided by European Foundations

By John Richardson

The institutions of organized philanthropy have centuries-old traditions and deep roots in the European consciousness. Organized philanthropy aims to increase the efficiency of citizen participation by strengthening civil society, the bedrock of democracy. In an economic context, foundations and corporate funders aim for a more equitable and sustainable environment in which all members of society can find a useful role whatever their talents, possibilities, or disabilities. In a global society that relies less and less on the mechanism of the state, which is gradually passing its power to mega-institutions, the respect for and protection of the needs and rights of individuals must be nurtured.

While the power of national governments is eroding in some areas, private wealth in Europe has reached unprecedented levels. This prosperity is largely the result of the new power, influence, and wealth of corporations both large and small. To secure continuous growth and development of organized giving for public benefit, the philanthropic instincts of increasingly wealthier Europeans must be harnessed.

Across Europe, foundations and corporate funders are receiving increased attention from policymakers and are taking up a more central role in discussions on the future of economic, social, and other policies. For governments, independent funders represent a most attractive option for four principal reasons: (1) they give the government a human dimension; (2) they can enter into funding partnerships with governments where every euro of government money goes to the recipient; (3) they complement governments or add resources where the latter are unable to operate because of legal or other restrictions; and (4) they are free of short-term considerations faced by elected governments.

Today, foundations and corporate funders are prominently involved in debates on the future of a plethora of issues, including the social welfare system, education, research, arts and culture, and the fostering of democracy. European Union (EU) institutions see foundations as an integral and key component of the social economy. United Nations agencies are entering a new era of private–public partnerships. The EFC aims to be a vehicle for independent funders to engage EU and global institutions.

As the nations of Europe come together, with national boundaries becoming ever-more transparent, so must civil society actors in Europe reach out across borders to act together. The European Foundation Centre (EFC) promotes and facilitates this cooperation, giving a unified voice to independent funders in Europe.

ABOUT THE EFC

The EFC was established November 9, 1989, by seven of Europe's leading foundations. It serves a core membership of more than 200 members, associates, subscribers, and 250 community philanthropy initiatives, as well as a further 48,000 organizations linked through a network of information and support centers in 37 countries worldwide. The EFC Secretariat is based in Brussels, Belgium. The EFC's stated vision and mission are as follows:

- *Vision.* A community of informed, inspired, committed, independent funders engaged in seeking solutions to challenges facing humanity in Europe and internationally.
- *Mission.* The EFC is a knowledge-based membership association dedicated to strengthening organized philanthropy, which is embedded in and supports civil society, in Europe and internationally. The EFC helps nurture efforts aimed at supporting independent, accountable, and sustainable funders throughout the New Europe, particularly when this fundamental human right to associate private capital for public benefit needs fostering.

EFC Membership

EFC membership comprises foundations and corporate funders from across all regions of Europe. Membership is also open to funders worldwide with interests in Europe, thus the EFC counts in its membership funders from Japan and the United States. In addition to the two main categories of membership—EFC Member and EFC Funding Member—provision is made for EFC Guests. This category for Central and Eastern European foundations is underwritten by a Charles Stewart Mott Foundation grant. Fundação Oriente sponsors a Guest program for Portuguese foundations.

EFC Policy Committees

The strength and effectiveness of the EFC lies in its structure as a member-led organization. Members use their seats on two major policy committees to guide the work of the Centre, taking it in directions that matter to them as independent funders. The European Union Committee and the International Committee empower members by broadening their participation in EFC affairs and increase the Centre's impact by widening its outreach. The EFC Enlargement Task Force links the two committees and focuses on EU enlargement issues. The committees report to a Governing Council that is also made up of EFC members. The Governing Council is supported by a Management Committee. Technical assistance for committee activities is provided by the EFC Secretariat.

European Union Committee

One of the core functions of the EFC is the representation of members' interests at the EU level, and the monitoring of developments within EU institutions. This work is guided by the member-led European Union Committee, which advises the Centre's Governing Council on developments with regard to EU internal issues, interfaces with EU institutions, and focuses on promoting an enabling operating environment for independent funders in the EU, and encouraging research on organized philanthropy.

International Committee

The member-led International Committee advises the EFC Governing Council on developments in organized philanthropy in the wider Europe and in the Americas, Africa, the Mediterranean, and Asia. The committee works in close contact with associations of funders in other world regions with which the Centre has concluded cooperation agreements, in particular the Foundation Center and the Council on Foundations (COF) in the United States. (Staff of the EFC and COF assist at each other's annual conferences.)

The International Committee maintains a representation and monitoring role in relation to governmental bodies, such as the EU institutions concerned with external relations, the United Nations organizations, the World Bank, and the North Atlantic Treaty Organization (NATO).

Enlargement Task Force

The EFC's new Enlargement Task Force complements the roles of the European Union Committee and the International Committee by representing the needs and interests of EFC members from accession countries. The Task Force reports directly to the Management Committee.

EFC CORE FUNCTIONS

To carry out its aims, the EFC focuses on three core functions: representation and monitoring, networking and convening, and information and communication.

Representation and Monitoring

The EFC fulfills its representation and monitoring role primarily through its two policy committees.

EU Representation and Monitoring

The EFC European Union Committee works to ensure that EFC members have a voice in the development of policy at EU level. EFC representation runs throughout the relevant EU institutions, up to the Office of the President of the European Commission. At a meeting with EFC delegates in April 2001, President Romano Prodi proposed that the European Commission join with foundations in a project aimed at promoting European cultures. The proposed project will take place during the Belgian presidency of the EU in the second half of 2001.

In addition to the activities of the European Commission, the EFC closely follows the activities of the European Parliament, the Council of Ministers, the Economic and Social Committee, and the Committee of the Regions.

The Centre builds its capacity to serve and represent members' interests at the level of the EU and its institutions through the following activities:

- Cementing relations with commission services, including the commission's service for social economy organizations
- Reinforcing contacts with other commission departments, notably in the fields of education and training, social affairs and employment, and culture
- Further developing relations with the Commission's external relation services dealing with Central and Eastern Europe, Asia, North America, and the Mediterranean
- Responding to EU position papers concerning civil society and foundations in particular

The EFC maintains contacts with other European and international organizations, such as the World Bank, the Council of Europe, the United Nations, and the United Nations Educational, Scientific, and Cultural Organization (UNESCO).

A bid to improve and refine relations between foundations and EU institutions prompted the European Union Committee to prepare a document on the role and characteristics of foundations in Europe with the aim of promoting better knowledge, understanding, and recognition of foundations in EU circles. The EFC position paper "Working with Foundations in Europe: Why and How?" outlines the unique characteristics of foundations and emphasizes the potential role they can play in fostering democracy and promoting socioeconomic development. The paper is used as a basis for dialogue with the European Commission.

As part of its monitoring function, the EFC publishes approximately 60 information releases per year, covering EU initiatives and partnership opportunities in the fields of culture, education, youth and training, the environment, health, employment and social affairs, minorities and multiculturalism, and global funding. This information is delivered to EFC members through *EFC Alerts, Briefings*, and *Communiqués* and made available on the EFC Web site. The items on EU developments also appear in the quarterly *efc newsline*, which is distributed to independent funders in Europe and worldwide, as well as to EU institutions.

European Union Committee Legal and Tax Task Forces

The Legal and Tax Task Forces of the committee work toward improving the regulatory and fiscal frameworks for independent funders in the EU by benchmarking best practices and regulations in the field.

The Legal Task Force is developing a European legal template for foundations, which will serve as a model for new foundation laws and law revisions at a national level as well as an alternative to potential EU proposals and regulations on the European Association Statute and a possible statute for foundations. The task force is comparing best practices, developing a toolkit of legal models, and further investigating the possibility of developing an additional comprehensive legal model at the European level.

After 30 years of negotiations, an agreement by the EU Member States to go forward with the European Company Statute has paved the way for the adoption of a European Association Statute. The statute is aimed at creating an optional EU-wide legal personality for nonprofit organizations, enabling them to operate across boundaries within the EU. The agreement on the Company Statute was reached at the European Council in December 2000.

The EFC Legal Task Force is reviewing the legal and practical implications for foundations regarding the proposed statute. The Legal Task Force also examines the self-regulation mechanisms and practices of foundations, including a review of the EFC Code of Practice.

The European Union Committee Tax Task Force closely monitors fiscal and taxation issues involving the funding sector and serves as an information exchange and alert network that reports on fiscal developments affecting foundations both at EU and national levels. The Tax Task Force is researching national fiscal provisions that can be used as benchmarks for other EU countries.

CEP-CMAF

In November 2000, the EFC—together with a group of European-level nonprofit networks—set up an independent platform for consultation and advocacy at the EU level in the form of a Standing European Conference of Cooperatives, Mutuals, Associations and Foundations (CEP-CMAF). The Standing European Conference of CMAF will work on EU competition and taxation issues, among other things.

Representation and Monitoring at International Level

The International Committee monitors and advises on developments in organized philanthropy in the wider Europe and in the Americas, Africa, the Mediterranean and Asia. The committee works in close contact with EU institutions and the Council of Europe, as well as umbrella associations of funders in other world regions with which the Centre has concluded cooperation agreements.

Achievements of the committee include the Disaster Response Initiative, which is a joint effort of the International Committee and the Council on Foundations (COF). The initiative aims to provide funders with a useful tool in responding to global emergencies. The Disaster Response Initiative Working Group comprises six EFC members and six COF members.

The International Committee's work on Southeast Europe involves maintaining a dialogue with the European Commission to raise awareness of the challenges within the Balkan region and promote cooperation with foundations. The International Committee has also formed an EFC Interest Group for funders interested in sub-Saharan Africa.

In addition to the aforementioned activities, the International Committee contributes to the Worldwide Initiatives for Grantmaker Support (WINGS), a collaborative platform for organizations engaged in building a support infrastructure for philanthropy, including community foundation support bodies. The International Committee also acts in an advisory role for the Trans-Atlantic Donors Dialogue, the Trans-Mediterranean Dialogue, the Europe-Asia Civil Society Dialogue, and the Grantmakers East Group, and produces a quarterly e-mail bulletin for international funders.

Networking and Convening

Annual General Assembly and Conference

The EFC Annual General Assembly (AGA) and Conference typifies the work of the EFC. It has become the premier event on the European independent funding community's calendar, convening independent funders from Europe and the globe, allowing EFC members, public authorities, and grantees to exchange ideas and best practice, to form partnerships, and to learn about the latest developments in the independent funding sector in Europe and the world.

During the course of the conference, the EFC convenes its Annual General Assembly of Members. This assembly gives EFC members an opportunity to discuss their views and determine EFC policy. The work of the main EFC committees and the CFO's and CEO's reports are also available for discussion by EFC members.

Each year, the EFC holds its AGA and Conference in a different European city at the end of May or beginning of June, with Brussels serving as the host city every third year. Members in the country where the conference is to take place form a Host Committee, which plays an important role at the conference.

At the 2002 AGA and Conference, "Foundations for Europe: Science and the Citizen," participants tackled crucial science and health issues. The event focused on the ethical and social policy questions raised by the incredible pace of scientific advancement in recent decades as well as the serious challenge of global health issues faced by civil society. The implications of living in a nuclear society, long-term impacts of genetically modified food, the ethical issues surrounding genetic engineering and cloning, the global problem of HIV/AIDS, and the division between digital haves and have-nots are among some of the critical issues that were examined.

The AGA and Conference is key to the work of the Centre because it launches and facilitates other EFC networking and convening initiatives, including International Dialogues, the Community Philanthropy Initiative, the EFC Corporate Citizenship Europe program, and EFC Interest Groups.

International Dialogues

The EFC's International Dialogues are aimed at promoting cooperation and exchange of best practice among funders, governments, and civil society leaders across geographic boundaries, with the goal of strengthening civil society worldwide.

The Trans-Atlantic Donors Dialogue (TADD) helps build bridges between European and U.S. private and public donors who actively support and promote the development of people-to-people links and the strengthening of civil society on both sides of the Atlantic. The

Trans-Mediterranean Civil Society Dialogue (TMCD) aims to initiate, reinforce, and expand cooperation among foundations, corporate funders, public authorities, and civil society organizations across the Mediterranean Region to help develop and sustain civil society mechanisms and structures. The Europe-Asia Civil Society Dialogue sets out to map, network, convene, and promote civil society exchanges between Europe and Asia.

Community Philanthropy Initiative

The EFC's Community Philanthropy Initiative (CPI) focuses on strengthening and increasing organized philanthropy at the local level in Europe by promoting and sustaining the development of community philanthropy organizations.

Community philanthropy organizations collect, manage, and redistribute donations from a range of local donors to meet critical needs and improve the quality of life in a specific geographic area. They can be found in a variety of organizational forms.

The CPI aims to (1) strengthen existing community philanthropy organizations and facilitate the establishment of new ones; (2) build the capacity of emerging and established national community philanthropy support organizations and informal networks; and (3) increase awareness, knowledge, and understanding about issues, trends, needs, and opportunities affecting community philanthropy organizations.

Interest Groups

As part of realizing its convening function, the EFC hosts several interest groups led by members. These include the Intermediaries Interest Group, the Education and Youth Interest Group, the Minorities and Multiculturalism Interest Group, the Grantmakers East Group, and the sub-Saharan Africa Interest Group.

The EFC's Corporate Citizenship Europe group convenes senior executives from EFC corporate and corporate foundation members who are committed to the development and promotion of corporate citizenship. To achieve greater impact internationally and locally, the group members actively encourage business partnerships with private foundations, public authorities, and civil society organizations.

These groups promote partnerships and cooperation by bringing together foundations with common interests to develop projects and influence policy.

WINGS and CIVICUS

The EFC occupies a seat on the board of WINGS, the Worldwide Initiative for Grantmaker Support, which supports associations of grantmaking foundations and other organizations assisting grantmakers in their work to promote philanthropy. More than 85 associations and organizations make up the WINGS network. From January 1, 2003, WINGS will be headquartered at the EFC offices in Brussels.

The EFC was instrumental in setting up the World Alliance for Citizen Participation (CIVICUS) and has acted as a hub for CIVICUS-Europe. Today, the relationship with the EFC is mutually reinforcing, as reflected in joint activities, meetings, and exchange of publications. Both CIVICUS and the EFC are committed to developing a strong, independent, and active civil society in Europe and internationally.

Information and Communication

The Orpheus Programme, the public record of private funding, is the EFC's information and communication wing. It specializes in collecting, analyzing, and disseminating funding information and facilitates a network of national-level resource centers that serve independent funders throughout Europe. These national or regional-level information and support centers or associations of foundations are responsible for developing and maintaining national dossiers, which hold foundation and corporate funding information for their specific country or region.

Drawing on its extensive contacts and information gathering expertise, the Orpheus Programme maintains a database of detailed profiles of hundreds of funders across Europe and worldwide. The

Orpheus database serves as a model for national-level databases throughout Europe. The EFC Secretariat also houses the Social Economy Library and Documentation Centre, a public resource of information on funders from Europe and worldwide.

The Orpheus Civil Society Project, launched in 1994, facilitates the exchange of knowledge and expertise among information and resource centers in Central and Eastern Europe and the newly independent states that serve foundations, associations, and other nonprofit organizations. It is owned and driven entirely by the needs and participation of the centers.

The project also supports the Orpheus Civil Society Network, which exists to promote civil society development in these regions. Most of the members are part of national networks of support organizations, which serve more than 30,000 nonprofit organizations and other institutions in Central and Eastern Europe and the newly independent states. They provide services in the following five key areas:

1. Information and communication, including information about funding from foundations, corporates, and other sources
2. Training and other educational programs
3. Advocacy of a positive legal and fiscal environment for the sector
4. Mediation within the nonprofit sector
5. Partnership building

The network is open to all support organizations that work in these five areas.

Publications

Through its Orpheus Programme, the EFC produces numerous publications, including *Independent Funding: A Directory of Foundation and Corporate Members of the EFC*. The directory outlines EFC members' funding interests, areas of expertise, and grantmaking guidelines. Inclusion in the directory implies subscribing to the EFC brand.

The EFC publishes topic-based directories of funders active in Europe in the areas of Mediterranean funding, culture, the environment, youth, education, and minorities and multiculturalism. *The Social Economy and Law Journal* (SEAL), which is published three times per year, covers the law of foundations, associations, and other nonprofit organizations. The journal focuses on all regions of Europe, including Central and Eastern Europe, the newly independent states, and EU countries. The journal is part of a wider initiative that promotes an informed dialogue on developing a favorable legal and fiscal operating environment for the European nonprofit sector.

To fulfill its monitoring role, the EFC publishes information releases in the form of *EFC Alerts*, *Briefings*, and *Communiqués* on EU funding opportunities, as well as on fiscal and legislative initiatives concerning the independent funding community. These releases are disseminated to all EFC members and partner organizations. The International Committee produces a monthly electronic bulletin, updating EFC members, public authorities, and other civil society stakeholders on international developments. The Community Philanthropy Initiative also produces a monthly electronic bulletin.

The EFC Social Economy Library produces bibliographic information on its most recent acquisitions through the *efc bookshelf*. The quarterly *efc newsline* details current projects and updates on EFC Secretariat activities and is sent to organization executives in Europe and worldwide.

Funders Online (**www.fundersonline.org**)

Funders Online is the online information resource for information on hundreds of funders as well as references to the Web sites of more than 400 independent funders who are based or active in Europe. Information on the site is automatically updated through the Orpheus database. The service offers free model templates for foundations wishing to develop a Web presence. Funders Online has been featured in several of the most widely read journals for philanthropy and nonprofits, such as the *Chronicle of Philanthropy* and the *Philanthropy Journal Online*.

Efforts are underway to enhance the existing Funders Online, making it more interactive and dynamic. This enhanced version of Funders Online is intended to be the collective voice for independent funders in Europe. This proposed Internet-based knowledge management program for the funding community is designed to integrate online information and convening elements into a powerful resource that will allow funders to turn information into shared knowledge. The project will aim to make this knowledge available to staff members at all levels of a funding organization to help them make sound decisions in their work, thus strengthening European philanthropy as a whole.

FINAL THOUGHTS

Europe stands at a crossroads. After some 50 years of uneasy peace in much of the continent, the nations of Europe now face the biggest-ever intergenerational transfer of wealth, creating a new generation of donors. Successful young entrepreneurs are giving at a much earlier age than did their predecessors, creating new foundations and helping established foundations grow their endowments. This unprecedented growth in philanthropy comes at a time when short-term political pressures on democratically elected governments are leading to withdrawal of state support in some crucial social areas.

The continuity and independence essential to the work of foundations are increasingly called on to provide strategic vision in the new Europe. The EFC continues to underpin the independent funding community in this endeavor.

Foundations in Germany: Growth, Professionalization, and the Search for a New Balance between the State and the Nonprofit Sector

By Peter Walkenhorst

The German foundation sector has experienced a period of sustained growth during the last two decades, and it is quite likely that this trend will continue in the future. This growth is the result of the long period of political stability and economic prosperity since 1945 that allowed for an accumulation of private wealth that was unprecedented in German history. The ongoing intergenerational transfer of this wealth has already left its mark on philanthropy, but there is still untapped potential for more giving. In addition, the growth of the German foundation sector has been encouraged by the shift from traditional social welfare policies to new forms of public–private partnerships. Increasingly, the responsibility of national, state, and local government agencies for the funding and delivery of social services is devolving to either private for-profit institutions or nonprofit organizations that operate outside the public and private sector. The increase in both the number and size of foundations implies at the same time that issues of strategic focus, key competencies, and organizational effectiveness are becoming ever-more important. Against this background, this chapter part tries to provide a brief overview of the history, size, and structure of the German foundation sector and to identify key challenges German foundations are facing at the beginning of the twenty-first century.

HISTORICAL BACKGROUND

In Germany, foundations have contributed to the public good for more than a millennium. Historically, charitable foundations are among the oldest existing social institutions. Some existing foundations can trace their history as far back as the Middle Ages. Although the motives, practices, and legal framework for philanthropic activities have changed over the centuries, this long tradition of institutionalized charity needs to be remembered when talking about contemporary developments.

Throughout the Middle Ages, foundations in Germany evolved much as they did in other Continental European countries. Medieval charity was devoted to "pious causes"(*piae causae*), describing all philanthropic purposes that were motivated by striving for personal salvation through good works. Medieval foundations, therefore, primarily developed in the form of hospitals and orphanages. The church as well as some monastic orders collected bequests and donations to create such foundations. Beginning with the High Middle Ages, however, the emerging urban middle class gradually replaced the gentry and the clergy as the dominant donor group, while municipal governments were assuming greater supervisory authority over charitable institutions. As a consequence, from the twelfth and thirteenth centuries onward, new and more diverse types of foundations were established, which were often linked and dedicated to particular trades or crafts guilds. Throughout that period, the purposes of foundation work also widened in scope to include arts, social services, and other activities. These processes of secularization and growing regulation by the municipal authorities accelerated in the sixteenth century, as many cities began to centralize assistance to the poor and to exercise stricter control over charitable institutions.[1]

The end of the Holy Roman Empire in 1803 marked a new stage in the development of German foundations. In the aftermath of the Napoleonic Wars, foundation property formerly in the hands of ecclesiastical establishments was transferred to the surviving German states as compensation for territories lost to French occupation. The secularization of church property corresponded with the process of state building that resulted in the expansion and consolidation of state powers. Within the newly emerging states, foundations enjoyed only a very limited autonomy. Between 1815 and 1848, Friedrich Carl von Savigny and other legal theorists devised a theoretical justification for private foundations that is still relevant for German foundations today. Savigny introduced a theory of legal personality that stressed the importance of the consent of state authorities for the creation of a legal person, thus providing a justification for the existence of private foundations, albeit under tight control and regulation of the state. His theory became the dominant outlook on foundations in the nineteenth century.[2]

After the founding of the German Empire in 1871, the number of foundations increased considerably. The new wealth and increasing economic prosperity generated by the industrialization period provided the basis for a foundation boom that reached its height during the late nineteenth century. Foundations blossomed as successful industrialists discovered philanthropy both as an arena for experimenting with social welfare initiatives and as an instrument for influencing public policy. Around the turn of the twentieth century, many prominent foundations, research centers, cultural organizations, and institutions of higher education were created by private donors. In addition, for many members of the urban middle classes, philanthropic giving, especially for the fine arts, became a symbolic expression of their wealth and social status.

The outbreak of World War I abruptly ended this golden age of philanthropy. After 1918, hyperinflation and the Great Depression destroyed thousands of foundations, a loss from which the foundation sector has still not recovered completely. Although the Nazi regime left many foundations untouched, Jewish foundations were dissolved and their assets confiscated. A sharp decline in the number of foundations was the obvious result of this policy as well as of the devastation caused by World War II. The postwar division of Germany further accelerated this decline. In East Germany, foundations were dispossessed, and basically barred until 1989. Only in recent years have their numbers and wealth recovered to some degree.

DIFFERENT TYPES AND LEGAL FORMS OF FOUNDATIONS

In Germany the term *foundation (Stiftung)* is not defined by law. The German foundation sector, therefore, is characterized by a variety of different legal forms. A foundation can be granted legal personality under either civil or public law. Most foundations are civil law foundations established under the Civil Code (*Bürgerliches Gesetzbuch*). They are independent legal persons with assets designed to serve specific statutory purposes in perpetuity as laid down by the founder(s). In contrast, public law foundations are established by an act of parliament or government. Church foundations constitute another significant segment of the German foundation sector. They are established under canon law, which is constitutionally equivalent to public law. Church foundations are regulated not by public authorities but by internal church structures. In addition to these different types of foundations, there are other legal forms, such as the limited liability company or the registered association, that can serve the functions of a foundation. Despite its name, the *Robert Bosch Stiftung GmbH*, for example, is actually not a foundation but a nonprofit limited liability company. The German political foundations like the *Friedrich-Ebert-Stiftung, Konrad-Adenauer Stiftung*, or *Heinrich Böll Stiftung* are, in legal terms, registered associations with no significant assets of their own. Their operating budgets are primarily covered by annual subventions from the government. Because of their paradigmatic role for the sector at large, the following discussion concentrates on private law foundations.

A PROFILE OF THE GERMAN FOUNDATION SECTOR

Any profile of the German foundation sector has to start with a word of caution: an accurate assessment of the number, size, and activities of foundations in Germany is hampered by a lack of basic statistics. Only little is known about the exact size of the German foundation sector in solid empirical terms. This lack of empirical data exists because there is no legal obligation for foundations to provide information to the general public. German law requires a foundation only to report to the tax authorities and the state supervisory bodies (*Stiftungsaufsicht*). This information, however, is classified. All available statistics, therefore, rely on information provided voluntarily by individual foundations.

Despite this lack of solid empirical data, the knowledge about the foundation sector has improved in recent years. In its latest survey, the *Federal Association of German Foundations* counted 9,663 foundations, ranging in size from very small organizations without any professional staff to large foundations like the *Volkswagen* or *Bertelsmann Foundation*. Some 94.3 percent of these foundations are recognized as charitable organizations, which means they are granted exemptions from income, gift, and inheritance tax. The data on total assets and annual expenditures are also incomplete and can only be estimated. According to the mentioned survey, the assets of those 4,538 foundations that have disclosed their financial data amount to about €30 billion, but even these figures have to be interpreted with great caution because no generally accepted principles of validation exist. The same holds true for the estimated total expenditure of approximately €18 billion per year. In addition, it must be noted that this expenditure is not derived solely from assets, but also from revenues, services, donations, government grants, and other sources.[3]

Probably the most significant characteristic of the German foundation sector is its expansion during the second half of the twentieth century. According to the data available, two out of three of all existing foundations were established after 1945. Although the number of newly established foundations was rising slowly in the first three postwar decades, the 1980s and 1990s have brought a foundation boom. In less than two decades, between 1982 and 1999, close to 50 percent of all existing foundations were established. In 1998 the number of new foundations reached a record high of 416, followed by 402 in 1999, and for 2000 similar figures were expected.[4] These figures demonstrate that, notwithstanding its century-long history, the German foundation sector represents essentially a late-twentieth-century phenomenon, and that in Germany "the key to understanding foundations lies not in the past, but in the present."[5]

The foundation boom of the last two decades can be attributed primarily to the unprecedented accumulation of private wealth in the post–World War II period. The ongoing transfer of this wealth to the next generation must be seen as the main reason for the recent expansion of the foundation sector. It is also providing a unique opportunity for further growth and new resources to flow into philanthropic activities. The sheer size of this intergenerational transfer of wealth, as well as the emergence of a new generation of donors with new interests, values, and approaches to philanthropic giving, are likely to change the face of organized philanthropy in Germany in the not-so-distant future.

CURRENT TRENDS AND CHALLENGES

German foundations often assert to have the primary responsibility for encouraging, promoting, and supporting civic engagement and the nonprofit sector. Yet contrary to most current expectations, the German nonprofit sector receives only a limited portion of its total revenue from private philanthropy. As recent findings of the *Johns Hopkins Comparative Nonprofit Sector Project* indicate, philanthropy contributes only 3.4 percent of the sector's total revenues. The overwhelmingly dominant portion of income of nonprofit organizations comes from public-sector sources, which account for 64.3 percent of all nonprofit revenues, while fees and charges account for 32.3 percent. This pattern of nonprofit sector financing reflects the tradition of subsidiarity built into the German welfare state system, a tradition that is characterized by extensive partnership arrangements between nonprofit organizations and the state, especially in fields such as health and social services.[6] Notwithstanding the structural particularities of the German nonprofit sector, however, these figures make clear that private foundations can and probably should play a more important role in the development of the nonprofit sector. Although they constitute only a small share of the overall number of nonprofit organizations, they are strategically positioned to strengthen the capacity and work of nonprofit organizations. As philanthropic entrepreneurs, they can facilitate new trends and developments or they can support constituencies and interests that are ignored or neglected by the market or the public sector. In other words, foundations have a unique opportunity to expand and nurture the diversity of nonprofit activities, and thus, make a lasting contribution to the development of a viable civil society.

This challenge is reinforced by the changing relationship between the state and the nonprofit sector. Similar to other industrialized countries, the traditional roles of the state, the private sector, and the nonprofit sector are currently renegotiated in Germany. Increasingly, new forms of public–private partnership, which emphasize enabling rather than service provision or state regulation, are being discussed and tested. This shift in the political culture presents a historically unprecedented opportunity for increasing the space of the nonprofit sector, and, thereby, opportunities to expand the scope of foundation work. Consequently, foundations are at the core of the search for a new balance between the state and the nonprofit sector.

The growing importance of foundations has been recognized by policymakers and the general public alike, and a political debate on reforming the legal framework governing foundation activities is gaining momentum. As a first step toward a new legal framework, the German parliament passed a law reforming the fiscal treatment of charitable foundations in July 2000, improving the tax deductibility for donations to existing foundations, as well as for establishing a new foundation.[7] The growing public awareness of their role and importance presents both challenges and opportunities for German foundations. They are called on new roles that were previously the domain of the state and government agencies. At the same time, they are asked to perform them in better and more efficient ways. Organizational effectiveness, therefore, constitutes a major challenge for German foundations that has led to an increasing interest in evaluation methods and instruments.[8] This quest for effectiveness and efficiency is all the more important given the slowly growing professionalism of organized philanthropy in Germany. Lagging behind developments in the United States, German foundations are just beginning to realize the need to invest in management capacity building and professional training to ensure that their resources are being used effectively and creatively.

Similarly, more and more foundations are realizing the need to legitimize their activities against the background of increased demands for openness and accountability. In the absence of any legal requirements to provide information to the general public, most German foundations, however, are still showing only little concern with public accountability. According to a recent survey, less than 10 percent of foundations publish annual reports, and no more than 8 percent have printed information available, while only 6 percent ever issue press releases.[9] Thus, while foundations are widely perceived as doing good in some way, the general public and the media do not have much opportunity to appreciate or critically discuss the activities of individual foundations or the role of foundations in general. This lack of transparency and accountability poses a permanent danger to the public acceptance of foundations because it can foster misperceptions, misunderstandings, and mistrust.

In addition to these challenges, the European integration process requires German foundations to expand their strategies and programs beyond national borders. They cannot ignore the tremendous changes that are likely to result from applying a European-wide economic and political framework to activities supporting the public good. Currently, the different legal and fiscal frameworks within the European Union applying to foundations are still based on the rationale of giving back to national societies. In the future, however, cross-border philanthropy will become increasingly important as a result of an integrated economy with a common market and currency. These developments are already reflected in the growth of cross-border giving on the global level. In the long run, they will lead foundations throughout Europe to a continued redefinition and repositioning of their strategies and programs, and the future of German foundations will be ultimately decided in this wider economic and political context in the twenty-first century.[10]

An Interview with
Kuba Wygnanski

Kuba Wygnanski: It's quite late here, but that's what I was asking for. It's 11:00 p.m. here, but everything's okay.

Frank Ellsworth: By 11:00 o'clock, you should either be home in bed or at the local pub.

KW: No. I'm at home. I had the last meeting, which has just finished here at home, and I'm ready, at least, to try to answer your questions.

FE: Well, I know when Joe returned from his trip as a German Marshall Fund Community Foundation Fellow—it certainly was an extraordinary experience for him.

Joe Lumarda: Kuba? It's Joe Lumarda. Hello. How are you?

KW: I'm doing well.

JL: In looking at general strategic and operational issues for foundations in the United States, we found that various philanthropists and foundation executives are increasingly interested in the international aspect of philanthropy and foundation operations. Before we begin, please introduce yourself.

KW: I shall try. I'm a sociologist by profession. I'm 36. I spent much of my life more as a political animal working with the Solidarity Trade Union. This was until the Round Table Talks on creating a new democracy in 1989, where I was the chief of the youth delegation of solidarity. I mention that because one of the outcomes of the Round Table Talks was not only free election, but also the freedom of association. At that time, we were working with the companies to introduce the precedence of the registration of the Independent Students' Union. And from that time, I broke away from politics and began my study on the role, opportunities, and responsibilities of nongovernmental organizations in a new Polish civil society. I've not only studied the subject for over 10 years, I have, along with associates from the University of Warsaw, compiled an extensive database on nonprofits in Poland. This is known as the Database Klon, *K-l-o-n*, which means like a legal copy, but in Polish it also means the name of a tree.

I'm also the vice president of Batory Foundation, one of the few grant-giving foundations in Poland. It's the part of the Open Society Network in Europe.

Last, but not least, I am the founder and president of the Forum of Nongovernmental Initiatives, which is a nonprofit umbrella organization. As you know, both are quite anarchic, so it's rather kind of a movement. It's not a formal organization. In terms of the functions, its closest parallel in the U.S. is the Independent Sector. I'm also a member of the Council on Foundations in the U.S. and part of its International Committee. That's my schizophrenic existence: activist, researcher, and donor.

FE: *I think it would be—and I hope at some point—possible for the three of us to enjoy a glass of vodka or good wine together because it seems that our minds, careers, and many of our own dreams, if you will, are quite similar.*

For clarification, since we're taping this, would you give me, please, the name again of the information system? I wrote down K-l-o-n.

KW: K-l-o-n.

FE: *Very interesting. And is that, perchance, on the Internet?*

KW: Yes. This database is more or less equal to what GuideStar is doing in the U.S. You have the publicly available data on all NGOs in Poland. The address—Web address for that is *www.ngo.pl.*

FE: *That may be the first thing I do after we finish this interview is check that out. I've been on GuideStar most of the morning doing some research on another project, and it'll be interesting to see what you've set* *up there. Also you mentioned the Batory Foundation. Could you tell us a little bit about that?*

KW: This foundation is a part of the Open Society Network created by George Soros. I believe Batory was established in 1988 as part of the Soros philanthropic family in this country. We are not huge by American standards and not endowed. We distribute approximately 8 million zloty ($1.9 million) in grants for NGOs across Poland.

FE: *Interesting. Let me ask the first question: Give us a short history—that is to say, when did the foundation movement start; what motivated it; and what are any other issues that you think are relevant to its beginning.*

KW: First, may I establish that Polish foundations are part of a long history of philanthropy. The first foundation in Poland was founded in the twelfth century. It operated until Poland lost its independence in 1795 for 123 years.

Then after regaining the independence in 1918, the whole sector (and I use the term loosely) was connected to the rebuilding of an independent Poland. After the Second World War, the communists, while trying to seize as much as possible, banned all foundations. They nationalized the capital of foundations, and between 1952 and 1984, there were no foundations in Poland. Remnants of exiled foundations still survive in different European countries, especially in England.

The most significant action happened in 1984. The 1984 Act of the Foundations was the first legislative act in the former Soviet Bloc that recognized and ratified the NGO and foundation community.

Therefore, in 1984 the Act on Foundations was introduced in Poland. This development was very exciting since it connected the efforts of Polish nonprofits to support from U.S. (both private and governmental). This new sector supported economic growth, the agricultural infrastructure, the water system, and the like. Until 1989, there was like—I don't know—20, 30 foundations.

Since 1989, the number of foundation growth has been very rapid. It was kind of a foundation baby boom after 1989—with exponential growth until 1995, when we reached a social saturation point and created a regulatory process that scrutinized foundation applications.

JL: Just for clarification, foundations that could exist, were those foundations as program service NGOs or foundations that grant funds?

KW: That's probably the most crucial clarification. Anyway, right now, we have about 5,000 registered foundations, but we don't have the kind of a capital limit for that. So basically, you can register a foundation with a meager symbolic sum of money—for about $2,000. I would say that 95 percent of all foundations in Poland are the grant-seeking or operating foundations.

FE: Two questions: You said that the first foundation dates back to the seventeenth century.

KW: The first Polish foundations are dated back to the twelfth century.

FE: Twelfth century?!

KW: Not 1-7 but 1-2. I remember one of the oldest ones, which is dated 1392, was a foundation supporting an orphanage for the Catholic Church in Krakow. I have a picture in my house that shows a monument of the foundation. Most of these were connected to the charitable activities of the church, and mostly to support the poor or orphans.

FE: And the best of the tradition is called Caritas, I guess. Let me ask another question regarding the 1984 legislation: Are there tax incentives, tax breaks involved in—for people, organizations, or companies that create foundations?

KW: First, let me say that NGO activists in Poland will often state that we don't have tax breaks—knowing that in modern democracies, including the U.S., you have much more incentives for philanthropy. It is not true. Donors may deduct up to 10 percent or 15 percent from their income before tax to be tax-deductible from the tax base. That's very important. Compared with many other countries in Europe and around the world, it is a generous incentive.

We have been conducting much research on giving. About 60 percent of people give in an informal way to different charitable purposes. This includes giving directly to a poor or otherwise needy person. About 25 percent of people give in an intentional, organizationally based way (NGOs). Only 2, maximum 3 percent—because it's in the range of the statistical error—give money with a tax deduction in mind. The wealthy and the corporations are just discovering the tax advantages of giving.

FE: One other question regarding brief history: You said that in 1995 after that six-year period of pretty dramatic growth, things slowed down. Was there something—was there an event, was it the economy? Why did things slow down in 1995?

KW: There is a very practical answer to that. There was only one court that approved the registration of foundations—the court in Warsaw. In 1995 they became strict on the registration of foundations. Until 1995, it was very flexible. Any given purpose imaginable was acceptable and eligible for establishing foundations. And, in fact, we don't have, as you have, the different internal differentiation of foundations—for example, public charities versus private foundations. "Foundation" is one word for everything. So since 1995, the registration court cracked down on applicants. After 1995, courts will ask you what you specifically mean by the stated charitable purpose. They have much leeway for judgment. For example, they may not register a foundation because too many organizations exist for that cause or the applying organization has no funds for operation.

JL: So there's now more quality control with the creation of these organizations or foundations?

KW: Yes, but you should also know that since 1999, the registration process was decentralized to 16 courts. So, in a way, if you are not happy with the Warsaw court, you can go to another and they will register your foundation.

JL: To change the subject a bit, in Poland right now, other than Batory, what are the top three or four grant-making foundations?

KW: In specific terms of grant-giving, I need to distinguish three types of foundations. First (and I understand that it's not the subject of our discussion) are those operating from outside Poland, like Ford, Mott, Rockefeller, etc. They are active in Poland and they are very important. We still are trying to persuade them not to decrease their activity, not only from Poland, but also from this region. They are a significant presence and model for philanthropy in Eastern Europe.

In terms of the pure private foundations, Batory is one of them, but it's not the biggest foundation. Right now, the first of the two biggest foundations is the Polish-American Freedom Foundation. But again, in the formal sense, it's not a Polish foundation. It operates purely for Poland, but it's registered in the U.S.

The other big one supports Polish science. This is an interesting case since it was created from privatized state funds—special funds dedicated to scientific activities before 1989. Now it acts like a private foundation. They have the biggest endowment in Poland of, I think, 300 million zloty ($70 million). They are the biggest grant givers in Poland.

FE: Kuba, let me ask a question with regard to endowment assets. Are endowment assets regulated? Are they carefully invested? Are they invested in assets in Poland? Talk a little bit about how the endowments are treated.

KW: Interesting you should ask that. It was, I believe, in 1994 that legislation changed the whole system. Before that, there was the legal push to spend all funds that were given to a foundation within a period of two years. So there was no talk about endowments because you had to spend everything. Then, through the lobbying efforts of foundations, limits on payout were lifted. Unfortunately, we have a saying: "Foundations are a great refrigerator of your money." You can donate money to a foundation tax-free and then can keep that money warehoused for even a hundred years.

But the government is concerned with this activity (or lack of charitable activity). This, along with the budget problems of the state, causes increased criticism of foundations. Some lawmakers are clamoring for tax on the income of foundation endowments. Currently, this is a big debate.

FE: Okay. You were—you stopped at number two. What was the third other type of foundation that is part of the sector? You said outside foundations and then the private foundations and then . . .

KW: Okay. The third type, not in terms of the volume of money, but in terms of the number of foundations, would be the so-called operating foundations. They don't base their activity on the endowment or capital. These foundations are not very different from associations or the plain vanilla service NGO. The difference is that you don't have the legal regulations or regulatory agencies to oversee their democratic management.

I intentionally used the word *democratic*. Now, one person can create a foundation and be its board of the member. It does not have internal control mechanisms, which might be enforced by law. The concept behind that was that the foundation should, because they don't have the internal control mechanism, report to the state.

JL: Where do your community foundations fit?

KW: Ah, community foundations—there are 16 community foundations right now. These are also called local funds.

JL: Where do they fit in the landscape? How do you feel that they're serving the philanthropic needs of Polish people?

KW: I'm probably not the best person to ask. I'm a big fan of the community foundations in Poland. The only problem is, even having in mind that there's a big, big, big success of the community foundation, which is mainly due to the very hard work of the Academy of Philanthropy in Poland, which is supporting that movement. But it's very important to have in mind that there are only 16 communities in Poland, and there are two and a half thousand deserving communities in Poland. These 16 lucky ones were able to fundraise money for the local endowment with matching funds from Batory, Mott, and others. My main problem is, and I have no problem with the fact that they have perfect DNA for the local works—my question is how do we replicate this DNA. That's the main challenge for the Academy of Philanthropy and for Poland. How do we put this car into second gear because the first gear is perfect.

JL: When you look at the philanthropic history of the United States—Ford, Mott, Carnegie—you see individuals who, out of the success of their industry or company, have created these large philanthropic institutions. If you're looking into your crystal ball, with Poland's entry into the European Union and the forecasted economic success, do you find such individuals like the company I met in Bilgoraj?

KW: Yeah.

FE: Very philanthropic. The name escapes me. I'll think of it . . .

KW: It's Mr. Palico.

JL: Yes. Do you see them creating foundations? Do you see anything getting in the way? What's the opportunity there?

KW: In terms of individual wealth, we need to make a distinction. Most people of such means are not giving from personal wealth but from their corporation.

One example of prominent individual philanthropy is Wislawa Szymborska, who is a Nobel Prize winner in literature from maybe four years ago. She decided to put a big part of her prize, Nobel Prize, to endow one of the foundations in Poland to give—actually, the annual award for poetry.

But the potential lies first with the corporate sector. There is a need to colonize the corporate sector with the good philanthropic behaviors of other countries. I don't know whether it's good or bad, but 18 percent of small to medium size companies are giving money for charitable purposes (less than 500 employees). The average amount of money is 5 percent of their profits. Again, it's like talking about the glass is half empty or half full.

JL: I think Frank has one last question.

FE: Final question: You've been describing today and you've also made some comments about tomorrow as you look into your crystal ball. My question requires you to look further into your crystal ball. What do you think the role of foundations will be in Poland 25 years from now?

KW: Twenty-five? It's really—I mean, remember that the whole history of this sector is only 10 years old right now. I can name some major challenges for foundations.

FE: That would be quite appropriate and, I think, very interesting that even though this is a relatively new sector, it does have a tradition going back many, many years.

KW: I would say that the big challenge is the internal communication between and among donors and foundations. I think that what we need in this part of Europe is what's already happening in many countries: communication and cooperation among donors.

The second challenge is the whole question of the self-reflection and having in the mind, with very limited resources that you can imagine are valuable to the private foundation in Poland, is the understanding what are the crucial moments, what are the key opportunities where your money can make a difference. I think a lot of foundations don't even think this way. There should be more emphasis on outcome-based giving. Basically, what is the best value for the money you can give.

Also, you asked what will be my dreams? I would give nonprofits the instruments of self-regulation as opposed to state regulation of ranking or a system so people can understand to whom it's worthwhile to give money. We need to address the challenge of ethics—creating a code of conduct for the nonprofits. You call it the Better Business Bureau. People and foundations need to know where their money is going before they give it.

Externally, I would say my dream would be that the whole culture of philanthropy will somehow grow. This means that it is not just for the rich or for corporations. This means that people will treat it not as a kind of exceptional unique moment that you are able to dedicate some of your money to the purposes closest to your heart. It means that it would be a natural instinct.

NOTES

1. James Allen Smith and Karsten Borgmann, "Foundations in Europe: The Historical Context," in Andreas Schlüter, Volker Then, and Peter Walkenhorst (Eds.), *Foundations in Europe: Society—Management—Law* (London: Directory of Social Change, 2001), pp. 2–34; Rupert Graf Strachwitz, "Germany," in Schlüter, Then, Walkenhorst (Eds.), *Foundations in Europe*, pp. 133–144.
2. See note 1, Strachwitz, "Germany," p. 134; Andreas Richter, "German and American Law of Charity in the Early 19th Century," in Richard Helmholz and Reinhard Zimmermann (Eds.), *Itinera Fiduciae: Trust and Treuhand in Historical Perspective* (Berlin: Dunker & Humboldt, 1998), pp. 427–467.
3. Bundesverband Deutscher Stiftungen e.V. (Ed.), *Verzeichnis Deutscher Stiftungen* (Darmstadt: Verlag Hoppenstedt GmbH, 4th edition, 2000), pp. ix–xiii.
4. See note 3, Bundesverband Deutscher Stiftungen (Ed.), *Verzeichnis Deutscher Stiftungen*, p. A18. For a detailed analysis of the German foundation sector, see Helmut K. Anheier and Frank P. Romo, "Foundations in Germany and the United States. A Comparative Analysis," in Helmut K. Anheier and Stefan Toepler (Eds.), *Private Funds, Public Purpose: Philanthropic Foundations in International Perspective* (New York: Kluwer Academic/Plenum Publishers, 1999), pp. 79–118.
5. Helmut K. Anheier and Stefan Toepler, "Why Study Foundations?" in Anheier and Toepler (Eds.), *Private Funds, Public Purpose*, pp. 255–259 (quotation: p. 258).
6. Eckhard Priller, Annette Zimmer, Helmut K. Anheier, Stefan Toepler, and Lester M. Salamon, "Germany: Unification and Change," in L.M. Salamon, H.K. Anheier, R. List, S. Toepler, S.W. Sokolowski, and Associates, *Global Civil Society: Dimensions of the Nonprofit Sector* (Baltimore, MD: The Johns Hopkins Center for the Civil Society Studies, 1999), pp. 99–1118 (especially p. 109).
7. For details see note 1, Strachwitz, "Germany," p. 143.
8. Bertelsmann Foundation (Ed.), *Striving for Philanthropic Success: Effectiveness and Evaluation in Foundations* (Gütersloh: Bertelsmann Foundation Publishers, 2001).
9. See note 1, Strachwitz, "Germany," p. 141.

Notes

10. Cathy Pharoah, Michael Brophy, and Paddy Ross, "Promoting International Philanthropy through Foundations," in Schlüter, Then, Walkenhorst (Eds.), *Foundations in Europe*, pp. 587–601; Helmut K. Anheier, "Foundations in Europe: A Comparative Perspective," in Schlüter, Then, Walkenhorst (Eds.), *Foundations in Europe*, pp. 35–81.

CHAPTER 3

Philanthropic Foundations in East Asia

By Barnett Baron

PERSPECTIVES

Even within the context of considerable political turmoil, rapid economic development over the past two decades has helped spur the growth of foundations across Asia. The centralized governments of many Asian countries would like to foster foundation growth in an effort to shift burdens from governmental agencies, but have had mixed results.

Several years ago, the editors of this book met with representatives of China's People's Party to discuss the institutionalization of the nonprofit/nongovernmental organization system in mainland China. We discovered then the difficulties and challenges a highly centralized government would face in creating independent organizations to do what was traditionally the work of the state.

That meeting was organized by the Asia Foundation, which collaborates with partners from the public and private sectors to build leadership, improve policy and regulation, and strengthen institutions to foster greater openness and shared prosperity in the Asia Pacific region. The author of this chapter, Barnett Baron, is executive vice president of the Asia Foundation.

International interest in Asian philanthropy and Asian foundations blossomed in the late 1980s and early 1990s, fueled by Asia's continuing economic boom; the growing presence of Asian multinational corporations in the United States, Europe, and Southeast Asia, and the publicity surrounding several blockbuster grants to prestigious American universities and museums from Japanese foundations and corporations. At the same time, as official development assistance from the United States and European donors began to shift from Asia to other, more economically destitute parts of the developing world, Asian and international nongovernmental organizations (NGOs) began to explore whether local sources of funding could be developed to replace declining levels of international development aid. Facilitated by the pioneering work of the Japan Center for International Exchange (JCIE), and beginning in 1989 with a series of academic research conferences in Bangkok, Seoul, and Osaka that led to the creation of the Asia Pacific Philanthropy Consortium late in 1994, the study of Asian philanthropy began in earnest.[1] Unfortunately, Asian philanthropy's very promising growth during the 1980s and 1990s, spearheaded by the rapid growth of primarily corporate foundations, suffered a setback with the onset of the economic crisis that swept across Asia beginning in July 1997. The region appears to be en route to economic recovery, but it is too early to know how quickly renewed economic vigor may be followed by renewed local philanthropy.

Economic growth, political reform, and the globalization of business practice were the catalysts for the growth of Asian foundations during the 1980s. A very small number of modern charitable foundations in Asia can be traced back as far as the first decades of the twentieth century, but Asian philanthropic foundations are generally of much more recent vintage. The decade of 1987–1997 was the period of most rapid growth in the number, size, and scope of East Asian foundations, for three reasons.

Capital formation is the first requirement for philanthropy. The stage was set for the emergence of modern Asian philanthropy during what has come to be called the East Asian "economic miracle," the longest, most sustained, and probably most equitably shared period of economic growth in recorded history. Between 1965 and 1990, the

23 countries of East Asia grew at historically unprecedented rates, averaging 5.5 percent annual growth in real terms. All countries in the region benefited from growth, but eight were at the core of the "miracle": Japan, followed by the "Four Tigers" of Hong Kong, Korea, Singapore, and Taiwan; followed in turn by the newly industrialized economies of Indonesia, Malaysia, and Thailand.[2] In comparative terms, these eight countries grew more than twice as fast as the rest of East Asia, roughly three times as fast as Latin America and South Asia, and five times faster than sub-Saharan Africa. They also significantly outperformed the industrial economies of North America and Europe and the oil-rich Middle East–North Africa region. Between 1960 and 1985, real income per capita increased more than four times in Japan and the Four Tigers and more than doubled in the newly industrialized countries of Southeast Asia.

In addition to creating the economic preconditions for the growth of philanthropy, the decade 1987–1997 saw the replacement of authoritarian regimes by elected governments in Korea, Taiwan, and Philippines, and the acceleration of Deng Xiaoping's policy of "opening and reform" in China. Several other Asian countries also experienced a decline in bureaucratic control over their economies and increasing political participation during this period.

Beginning earlier in the 1980s, formidable domestic and global forces began to place heavy strains on centralized systems of governance in Asia, including the rise of increasingly prosperous and demanding middle classes, extraordinary advances in low-cost communications technologies, the globalization of trade and investment, and an exponential increase in the flow of ideas and information on a global scale. Privatization, deregulation, marketization, and related economic trends (sloganized in China as the move toward "small government, big society") have all contributed to a rethinking of the historically dominant role of central governments in economic and social life. Key allocation and policymaking functions began to move *down* to local levels of government, *up* to regional and international economic institutions, and, in many cases, *out* to the voluntary and nonprofit organizations of civil society. In the process, national governments began to face tremendous pressures to restructure themselves, moving away from the historical model of the East Asian Development State with its command-and-control mode of operating, toward hybrid forms of governance that facilitate and support at least quasi-independent initiatives by individuals, organizations, businesses, and communities lying outside the formal apparatus of the state.[3]

As political space opened and economies boomed, traditionally tight government control over the marketplace loosened throughout the region, even in the realm of corporate philanthropy. Whereas government-initiated philanthropy, sometime referred to as "quasi-taxes," had once been the norm in countries such as Indonesia, Japan, Korea, and Taiwan, corporations were no longer required to devote most of their discretionary funds to officially determined charitable purposes. They began to see the value of corporate contributions as an integral part of their corporate strategies directed at market-opening and improved community relations.

In addition, the failure of governments to respond quickly, efficiently, and adequately to major natural disasters in Japan (the Great Hanshin Earthquake, 1995), China (the floods of 1996), and Taiwan (the September 1999 earthquake) provided eye-opening contrast to the rapid and relatively more efficient response of local, nongovernmental, voluntary relief efforts, thereby contributing to increased public awareness and appreciation of the potential role of charitable and nonprofit organizations, including philanthropic foundations.

Thus the decade beginning in 1987 saw a fundamental transformation in the way that increasingly educated and economically secure populations throughout East Asia began to view the proper relationship among governments, corporations, and civil society—the vast and amorphous collection of nongovernmental, nonprofit, charitable, voluntary organizations that exploded across East Asia during this period.

The third, related factor contributing to the growth of foundations in East Asia, particularly the dominant form of corporate foundations, was the globalization of business practice beginning in the late 1970s and 1980s. As Japanese, Korean, and other Asian multinationals began to expand their operations to other countries, they faced unanticipated pressures from local communities to contribute funds to local causes and community needs. Yamamoto describes the impact that the expansion of Japanese corporate investment in Southeast Asia and the United States had on Japanese corporate philanthropy in response to local community demands and expectations—demands and expectations that had not featured prominently in corporate governance within Japan itself.[4] In addition, a growing number of Asian corporations began to share the view that philanthropic contributions to community and other nonprofit organizations may constitute a prudent investment in a company's long-term success. Among the potential direct benefits to the corporation of successful partnership with local communities and NGOs are enhanced reputation, positive brand identity, and a license to operate in local communities; enhanced management, motivation, training, and retention of top-quality employees; improved market positioning; improved operational efficiency by lowering nonproduction costs; improved capacity to anticipate and manage risk and conflict; enhanced capacity to reach otherwise inaccessible groups, shape public perceptions, and increase public understanding of business-centered approaches; and an improved operating environment resulting from a more stable local society and a healthier local economy.[5] For many corporations in Asia, under pressure to demonstrate heightened social awareness and good corporate citizenship, projecting a philanthropic dimension became an increasingly accepted part of corporate business strategy.

GENERAL CHARACTERISTICS OF FOUNDATIONS IN EAST ASIA

A review of the available descriptive research suggests several salient characteristics of contemporary East Asian philanthropy. First, very few empirical data are currently available on foundation assets, levels and purposes of grant-making, organizational structure, or their management and decision-making practices. The Japan Foundation Center (Tokyo) and the Himalaya Foundation (Taipei) are the two most developed sources of data in East Asia, but both are still evolving and provide only partial coverage of their respective foundation communities. Corporate contributions are regularly monitored in Japan and

Korea by the Federation of Economic Organizations and the Federation of Korean Industry, respectively. The Johns Hopkins University Comparative Nonprofit Sector Project is making important progress toward providing aggregate-level data in a few Asian countries. Overall, however, reliable and comprehensive data at either the country level or the level of individual foundations are still not available.

Second, there is great diversity in the types of philanthropic institutions and foundation-like entities. Formally organized philanthropic entities include endowed private foundations, publicly funded grantmaking foundations established by national legislatures, community trusts, a vast number of operating foundations (particularly in the form of schools, research institutes, hospitals, cultural and religious institutions), and a growing number of corporate foundations and giving programs. There are also many successful rural credit and loan programs that are philanthropic in intent but operate as not-for-profit businesses. Many Asian foundations are both fundraisers and grantmakers, and several large Asian NGOs are also grantmakers. Developing classification systems that will allow international comparisons among Asian philanthropic institutions, and between Asian institutions and those found elsewhere, continues to be a serious challenge.[6]

Third, unlike the United States, there are still very few endowed private foundations based on individual or family wealth. The limited number of private foundations in East Asia reflects, in part, cultural traditions in which the ostentatious display of personal (or family) wealth is considered unacceptable. Political, social, and business leaders are expected to be personally generous to those in need, and demonstrations of personal charity at critical times are an important part of demonstrating and legitimizing high social position. In general, displays of personal wealth are contrary to traditional norms in many Asian cultures. That pattern appeared to be changing to some extent in the years just before the economic crisis of 1997. The Japan Foundation Center's 1990 survey of grantmaking foundations in Japan, for example, found that 112 of the 394 large foundations covered in the survey (28%) were established by wealthy individuals, compared to 229 corporate foundations (58%). In Korea, many corporate-sponsored foundations were initially endowed by wealthy business families acting in their personal capacity, followed by corporate donations only later when corporate wealth increased. Anecdotal evidence from Hong Kong also suggests an increase in the number of family foundations, many of them making donations in Mainland China, especially since 1997. Even in Thailand, a very small number of then wealthy individuals had established grantmaking foundations, such as the Chaiyong Limthongkul Foundation, which supported activities related to public policy, international relations, the arts, and culture. With increased pressure for improved corporate governance throughout the region, including calls for greater financial transparency and more responsiveness to stakeholder concerns, some corporations are giving increased authority to professional managers outside the founding family and to making sharper distinctions between family wealth and corporate assets. In Korea, at least, this change is beginning to result in increasing individual philanthropy on the part of some industrialists and may eventually lead in time to the creation of more private foundations.[7]

At present, though, most philanthropic entities in the region are corporate foundations or, even more commonly, corporate giving programs funded on an annual basis rather than endowed.

Fourth, there are numerous examples of innovative fundraising for philanthropy. Community foundations are just beginning to emerge in Japan (e.g., the Osaka Community Foundation and the Asian Community Trust, a community foundation-like entity staffed on behalf of eight trust banks by the Japan Center for International Exchange). Several recently established foundations in Korea depart from the traditional corporate model and seek to raise funds from the general public for diverse causes, such as the Beautiful Foundation (which seeks to raise funds for political and social justice advocacy organizations), the Women's Fund, and the Korea Human Rights Foundation.[8] Community chests are increasingly popular, thanks to the assistance of United Way International in several countries, including Hong Kong, India, Indonesia, the Philippines, Singapore, and Taiwan. Many Chinese cities have also established community chest-like charitable organizations, often to provide support for laid-off workers, orphans, the elderly, and poor students. With the exception of Hong Kong, the amounts collected are still small, but payroll deductions and annual charity drives are increasingly common and growing in public acceptance throughout the region.

Philanthropy based on horse racing, motor boat racing, or other forms of gambling is big business in the region. The Jockey Club in Hong Kong is the major philanthropic force in the territory, providing more than US$143 million in charitable contributions in 2000–2001 and accounting for roughly 12 percent of total annual tax revenue in Hong Kong.[9] The Royal Bangkok Sports Club and the Turf Club are major sources of charitable contributions in Thailand. Three of the largest Japanese foundations (by grant spending) in 1998 derived their funds from horse racing (National Horse Racing Welfare Foundation), automobile racing (Vehicle Racing Commemorative Foundation), and motor boat racing (Sasakawa Peace Foundation), respectively.

JAPAN

The Japanese foundation sector is the most developed in East Asia. It has been regularly surveyed since 1987 by the Japan Foundation Center, which publishes a biannual *Directory of Grant-Making Foundations in Japan*. The 1988 directory covered 419 grantmaking foundations and reported the results of a more detailed survey of a subset of 171 foundations. The 2000 edition analyzes data from 849 foundations that have participated in annual surveys since 1987 and on a subset of 615 foundations which responded to a detailed questionnaire in July 1999 covering the Japanese fiscal year 1998 (April 1, 1997 to March 30, 1998).[10]

As indicated in Exhibit 3.1, the number of newly established grantmaking foundations has been declining since 1991. The last years of the 1980s witnessed the beginning of a period of rapid growth in new foundations, with more than half of the 847 respondents having been established between 1980 and 1989. The number of newly established foundations then dropped sharply from 1991, reflecting Japan's deepening economic recession.

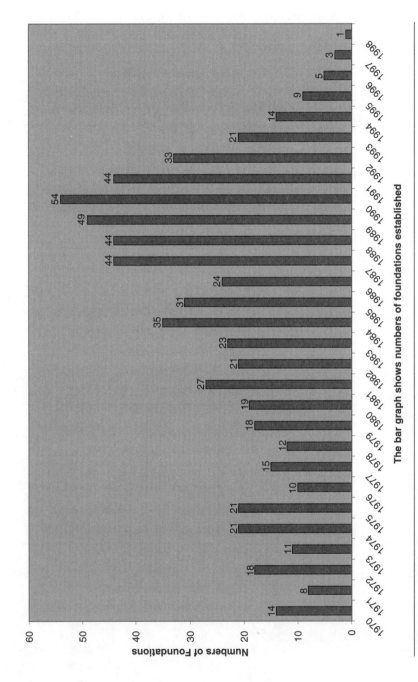

Exhibit 3.1 1970–1998 Trends in Foundation Establishment (Japan)

Exhibit 3.2 shows the distribution of assets of the 615 foundations for which data are currently available.

In each edition, the *Directory* has noted that the endowments of Japanese foundations are very small compared to the asset base of American foundations. In 1998, for example, the 20 largest Japanese foundations had combined endowments of only 4,105.63 billion yen, compared to 98,624 billion yen for the 20 largest American foundations. To put it another way, the combined endowments of the 20 largest U.S. foundations was more than 24 times as large as the combined endowments of the 20 largest Japanese foundations. The comparison is somewhat misleading, however, in that almost all of the Japanese foundations listed operate on the basis of annual budgets provided by their parent or sponsoring corporation (or government agency) rather than from income earned on their endowments. Reporting on 464 foundations, the *Directory* reports than in 1998, an average of only 19 percent of their income derived from endowment earnings, while 28 percent came from current donations received in that year, 7 percent from income earned by affiliated units operated by the foundation, and 46 percent from other sources ("operating income, subsidies/grants, or gains on the sale of property/fixed assets"). See Exhibit 3.3.

In terms of grant spending, the 615 foundations surveyed reported total grant expenditures in 1998 of slightly less than half a billion yen, or about U.S.$456 million (see Exhibit 3.4).

Asset Range	Number of Foundations	Percentage	Total Assets
Less than Yen 500 Million	169	27	504
Yen 500mm–1 Billion	160	26	1,164
Yen 1 Billion–3 Billion	193	31	3,141
Yen 3 Billion–10 Billion	74	12	3,863
More than Yen 10 Billion	19	3	4,006
Totals	615	100	12,678

Exhibit 3.2 Size of Japanese Foundation Assets, 1998 (in hundred-million yen)

Foundation Name	Total Assets	Grant Spending	Established	Government Agencies
The Sasakawa Peace Foundation	730.65	4.20	1986	Ministry of Posts and Telecommunications
Peace Nakajima Foundation*	518.32	3.09	1992	Ministry of Education
The Inamori Foundation	435.83	2.00	1984	Science and Technology Agency
Foundation of River & Watershed Environment Management	279.85	4.33	1975	Ministry of International Trade and Industry Agency of Cultural Affairs
The Toyota Foundation	270.16	4.38	1974	Ministry of International Trade and Industry Ministry of Construction
The Ishibashi Foundation*	163.28	1.14	1956	The Prime Minister's Office Ministry of Education
The Sumitomo Foundation*	160.73	3.56	1991	The Prime Minister's Office
The Vehicle Racing Commemorative Foundation	157.95	10.46	1975	Ministry of International Trade and Industry Ministry of Education
The Mitsubishi Foundation	149.67	4.43	1969	Ministry of Health and Welfare
Hoso Bunka Foundation, Inc. (HBF)	133.77	1.71	1974	Ministry of Posts and Telecommunications
Nagao Natural Environment Foundation	131.93	0.11	1989	Environment Agency
Research Institute of Innovative Technology for the Earth	123.13	8.46	1990	Ministry of International Trade and Industry
Nippon Life Insurance Foundation	119.98	4.58	1979	The Prime Minister's Office
The Asahi Glass Foundation	117.16	4.31	1934	Ministry of International Trade and Industry
The Saison Foundation	104.78	1.11	1987	Agency of Cultural Affairs
Expo '90 Foundation	104.03	0.40	1991	Ministry of Agriculture, Forestry and Fisheries Ministry of Construction
Yoshida Scholarship Foundation	103.66	2.71	1967	Ministry of Education
The Telecommunications Advancement Foundation	100.85	3.52	1984	Ministry of Posts and Telecommunications
Iijima Memorial Foundation for the Promotion of Food Science and Technology	100.59	1.31	1984	Ministry of Agriculture, Forestry and Fisheries
East Japan Railway Culture Foundation	99.33	0.24	1992	Ministry of Posts and Telecommunications
	4105.65	66.05		

*Originally translated by TAF staff. Note US$1 = Yen 105

Exhibit 3.3 Assets of the Twenty Largest Japanese Foundations (1998) (yen 100 million)

Size of Grants	Number of Foundations	Percentage	Total Grants
Less than Yen 25 Million	308	50	39
Yen 25–50 Million	144	23	51
Yen 50–150 Million	107	17	82
Yen 150–500 Million	45	7	116
More than Yen 500 Million	11	2	191
Totals	**615**	**100**	**479**

Exhibit 3.4 Japanese Foundation Grants, 1998 (hundred-million yen)

As in the case of endowments, the *Directory* consistently notes that Japanese grantmaking pales in comparison with the grant-making of American foundations. In 1998, the 20 largest Japanese foundations made a total of approximately $247.7 *million* in grants, compared with $3.2 *billion* in grants from the 20 largest U.S. foundations (see Exhibit 3.5).[11] Moreover, the trend in grantmaking in recent years is down. The 153 foundations that have responded to this question in the annual survey every year since 1988 reported that their total grant spending declined from its peak of 239 billion yen in 1992 and 1993 to 18.0 billion yen in 1998. Such a decline clearly reflects generally stagnant economic conditions since the early 1990s and the sharp decline of interest rates to almost zero today.

By subject matter, science and technology projects continue to receive the largest number of grants, followed by education and medical research, as indicated in Exhibit 3.6. Unfortunately, data on actual expenditures are not available.

In terms of types of grants made in 1998, the largest number of grants supported research (425), scholarships for foreigners to study in Japan (159), projects directly related to business development (152), study visits abroad (149), scholarships for Japanese to study in Japan (148) or abroad (28), competitive prizes (144), and conferences (114).[12]

Foundation Name	Total Assets	Grant Spending	Established	Government Agencies
The National Horse Racing Welfare Foundation	56.49	91.85	1969	Ministry of Agriculture, Forestry and Fisheries Ministry of Health and Welfare
Osaka Scholarship Foundation	46.63	45.72	1952	Osaka Prefectural Educational Committee
Rotary Yoneyama Memorial Foundation, Inc.	18.63	93.34	1967	Ministry of Education
The Society of Nephrology*	12.85	10.92	1972	Ministry of Health and Welfare
Japanese Foundation for International Cooperation*	12.40	96.32	1997	Ministry of Foreign Affairs
The Vehicle Racing Commemorative Foundation	10.46	157.95	1975	Ministry of International Trade and Industry
Research Institute for Environmental Industry and Technology	8.46	123.13	1990	Ministry of International Trade and Industry
Uehara Memorial Foundation	7.13	64.22	1985	Ministry of Health and Welfare
Kagoshima Scholarship Foundation*	6.73	4.66	1968	Kagoshima Prefectural Educational Committee
Exchange Association*	6.21	1.82	1972	Ministry of Foreign Affairs
Nagasaki Scholarship Foundation*	5.03	46.48	1960	Ministry of Trade and Industry Nagasaki Prefecture
Nippon Life Insurance Foundation	4.58	119.98	1979	The Prime Minister's Office
Japan Brain Foundation	4.52	10.35	1981	Ministry of Health and Welfare
The Mitsubishi Foundation	4.43	149.67	1969	Ministry of Education
The Toyota Foundation	4.38	270.16	1974	Ministry of Health and Welfare The Prime Minister's Office
Foundation of River & Watershed Environment Management	4.33	279.85	1975	Ministry of International Trade and Industry
The Asahi Glass Foundation	4.31	117.16	1934	Ministry of Construction Ministry of International Trade and Industry
The Sasakawa Peace Foundation	4.20	730.65	1986	Ministry of Posts and Telecommunications
Okinawa Prefectural Government Human Resources Development Foundation	3.79	55.60	1972	Okinawa Prefectural Educational Committee
Kyoto Promotion Society for Medical Science*	3.64	7.30	1986	Kyoto Prefectural Educational Committee
	229.20	2477.13		

*Originally translated by TAF staff. Note US$1 = Yen 105

Exhibit 3.5 Grants of the Twenty Largest Japanese Foundations (1998) (units: yen 100 million)

Field	Number of Grants
Science and Technology	397
Education	390
Medical Research, Public Health	229
Social Welfare	136
Humanity, Society	133
Culture and the Arts	120
International Cooperation	82
Environment	58
Public Affairs	28
Other	82
	1,655

* Some grants covered more than one field of interest.

Exhibit 3.6   Japanese Grants by Field of Interest, 1998 (615 foundations reporting 1391 grants*)

Japanese Corporate Philanthropy

Japan's corporate philanthropy became active in the late 1980s with the growing corporate appreciation of the need to participate in socially responsible activities. Although several major corporations established foundations, more emphasis was placed on direct giving because of the cumbersome process of incorporating a foundation under Japanese law as well as limited endowment revenues generated by low interest rates. More and more corporations have established departments or sections that specialize in socially responsible programs. The Japan Federation of Economic Organizations (Keidanren) established its "Committee for Promotion of Social Contributions" and the "One Percent Club" in 1990 to enhance this trend further. The Japan Association of Corporate Executives (Keizai Doyukai) has also promoted corporate social responsibility, sometimes in the context of corporate governance. Despite the economic stagnation that has lasted for almost a decade, and the absence of tax incentives, the level of corporate giving has remained remarkably stable.

Based on a July 1999 survey of 378 member companies, Keidan-ren (Federation of Economic Organizations), the major association of large Japanese companies, reported on patterns of corporate philanthropy for fiscal year 1998.[13] Exhibit 3.7 shows total expenditures in millions of yen for the period 1992–1998.

The data indicate a decline of 7.7 percent in average contributions per company between 1997 and 1998. Keidanren's 1999 survey (published in 2000) reported a 5.5 percent *increase* in average corporate contributions from 382 million yen to 430 million yen. Among the respondents in the 1999 survey, 80 corporations, or 32.4 percent of total respondents, registered more than a 10 percent increase in financial contributions over the previous year. On the other hand, 98 corporations, or 39.7 percent, registered more than a 10 percent decline in giving over the same period.[14]

Exhibit 3.8 shows Japanese corporate donations by field of interest. Japanese foundations (and other nonprofit organizations) are governed by an extraordinarily complex set of overlapping regulations and laws administered with a high degree of bureaucratic discretion.[15] Although the Law to Promote Specified Nonprofit Activities enacted in March 1998 made it somewhat easier for Japanese nonprofit organizations to register and receive formal legal status, the Diet postponed for two years any consideration of favorable tax status for most nonprofits. In March 2001, the Diet enacted the Law Amending in Part the Special Tax Measures Law, which provided some modest tax benefits, under very restrictive conditions, to selected nonprofits. The passage of these two laws had the unintended effect of creating a de facto two-tier system consisting of a very small number of tax-privileged nonprofits established under Article 34 of the Civil

	1992	1993	1994	1995	1996	1997	1998
Total Amount	167,000	149,400	154,200	145,400	162,000	155,700	137,600
Number of Companies	381	398	404	367	405	376	360
Average per Company	438	450	382	396	400	414	382

Exhibit 3.7   Corporate Expenditures on Philanthropic Activities, 1992–1998 (in million yen)

Field Type	Percentage
Academic Research	19.8
Community Activities	14.4
Education	12.3
Arts and Culture	9.5
Social Welfare	7.1
Health/Medicine	6.1
Sports	6.1
International Exchange	5.8
Environmental Protection	4.8
Historical Preservation	2.3
Disaster Relief	1.2
Other	11.0

Exhibit 3.8 Japanese Corporate Donations by Field, 1998 (329 companies)

Code and the many more tax-privileged nonprofits registered under the March 1998 NPO law.[16]

In addition to the difficulties encountered in registering any nonprofit organization in Japan, foundations operate under the close scrutiny and administrative guidance of their supervising ministry. In many cases, this requires advance approval from the supervising ministry before grants can be made. An issue of paramount importance for Japanese foundations is tight government control over their ability to invest foundation endowment assets.

According to Japanese legal experts, the scope of administrative guidance exercised by supervising ministries frequently extends beyond existing law. For example:

> In many instances, administrative guidance is given to incorporated foundations advising them to maximize their principal assets so that they can conduct public interest activities on a stable basis, using the revenues from their principal assets. Furthermore, the supervisory agencies prefer cash to real estate or similar assets for the principal assets of an incorporated foundation. . . . In addition, the [foundation]

will be instructed under administrative guidance to set aside a "principal fund" consisting of several tens of millions of yen. However, there is no basis in law for either of these requirements.

In addition, according to the 1996 Accounting Standards for Public Interest Corporations, "with the exception of assets necessary for the sound operation of the corporation (notably cash and buildings), the corporation must invest and manage its investment assets in a manner by which there is a high probability that the principal can be recovered, and which yields as much investment income as possible." In practice, this results in most foundations placing their endowments in secure term deposits, either in a postal savings account or with a bank.[17] With interest rates at or near zero for the past several years, many Japanese foundations are realizing significant declines in income.

KOREA

Most of the largest foundations in Korea were created or sponsored by corporations, often with an initial endowment provided by the CEO in his personal capacity, and later with donations contributed through the corporation itself as the economy boomed. These corporate foundations are surveyed annually by the Federation of Korean Industries (FKI), the counterpart to Keidanren in Japan. The most recent survey of corporate foundations is based on research conducted in December 1999 and January 2000.[18] Ninety-seven foundations were polled through mailed questionnaires, to which 70 replied. Taken together, the respondents represent the bulk of foundation activities in Korea in terms of asset size and grants made.

As in Japan and Taiwan, most Korean foundations were established during the boom years of the late 1970s through early 1990s, as shown in Exhibit 3.9.

The total assets of the 70 foundations included in the survey amounted to 1,704,279 million won at the end of 1999 (approximately

Year Established	Number	Percent
Before 1960	3	4.3
1960s	4	5.7
1970s	19	27.1
1980s	20	28.6
1990s	24	34.3
TOTAL	70	100.0

Exhibit 3.9 Establishment of Korean Foundations

$1.43 million at the then exchange rate of $1 = won 1190). Approximately 29 percent of total assets were in the form of real estate, 26 percent in stock, and 19 percent in cash and certificates of deposit. Exhibit 3.10 shows trends in asset size among the corporate foundations included in the FKI survey.

Endowment building continues to be a shared investment of the corporate owner in his personal capacity and the corporation itself. In 1999, 11 of the 70 foundations received contributions to their endowments from the corporate owner alone, 16 from the corporation alone, and 43 from both sources.

As in Japan, Korean foundations face strict government control over their ability to invest endowment assets, although there is no law or regulation that bars Korean foundations from specific types of in-

Asset Size	1991		1996		1998		1999	
	N	%	N	%	N	%	N	%
Less than 100 million	0		1	1.2	0		0	
100M–1 Billion	26	32.1	13	15.5	9	12.9	9	12.9
1–5 Billion	34	12.0	32	38.1	25	35.7	25	35.7
5–10 Billion	8	8.9	5	6.0	7	10.0	7	10.0
10–50 Billion	11	13.6	23	32.9	23	32.9	23	32.9
Over 50 Billion	2	2.5	5	7.1	5	7.1	6	8.6
TOTALS	81		86		70		70	

Exhibit 3.10 Assets of Korean Corporate Foundations

vestments. Indeed, Article 11(4) of the Nonprofit Act, which imposes a prudent management standard, implies that foundations may invest just as other fund managers do; however, foundations must report any changes in their basic assets to their supervising ministry, thereby inviting ministerial intervention. "Thus the pertinent ministry can easily notice changes of property, including investments in stock. Government ministries very often do not permit or accept the transfer of basic assets to stocks because if the stocks fall in value, the foundation will lose its permanent property."[19]

Exhibit 3.11 shows the impact of the Korean economic crisis of 1997–1998 on foundation expenditures. During this period, the won fell dramatically against the dollar, unemployment reached unprecedented highs, and more than one-third of Korea's midsize and large *chaebol* (corporate conglomerates) fell into bankruptcy or had to sell off significant assets. Total foundation grant expenditures declined by 33 percent between 1996 and 1997 and fell a further 27 percent in 1998, but then rose by almost 80 percent in 1999. These trends are skewed, however, by the disproportionate impact of increased spending by a few large foundations in 1999, particularly increased spending for hospitals and medical facilities by the Asan Foundation and the construction of an expanded cultural complex by the LG Yonam Culture Foundation.

Korean corporate foundations have traditionally provided most of their support for health and medicine, arts and culture, provision of educational scholarships and research, and social welfare activities, in that descending order. In recent years, there appears to have been a relative increase in expenditures for health (albeit skewed by increased spending by one major foundation) and a decline in funding for scholarships and academic research. Support for environmental

	1995 N = 84	1996 N = 84	1997 N = 67	1998 N = 68	1999 N = 65
Total Expend	230,800	273,100	146,750	108,326	186,147
Average Expend	2,747	3,251	2,190	1,593	2,846

Exhibit 3.11 Trends in Annual Expenditures, 1995–1999 (million won)

issues appears to be on the rise, but still represents a small fraction of overall foundation spending. Exhibit 3.12 shows trends in foundation expenditures by field of interest.

One of the unanticipated findings of this series of surveys is the increased professionalization of Korean foundations, as measured by the number of staff and the percentage that are assigned to full-time foundation work. The 70 foundations included in the KFI survey in 1999 had a total of 418 employees, of whom 369 (88%) were on full-time assignment to the foundation, while 49 (12%) had dual roles within the corporation (see Exhibit 3.13). Larger foundations tended to have a higher ratio of full-time staff than smaller foundations, which rely more heavily on part-time staff and outside consultants. The trend compares favorably to the situation in 1991, when very few foundations had any full-time staff.[20]

With the rise of civic activism among Korean advocacy organizations in recent years, unable to raise funds from government or existing corporate foundations, several new advocacy-oriented foundations have been created during the past two years. The Beautiful Foundation was established in 2000 to raise funds from the general public to support the activities of Korean environmental, economic

Field of Interest	1997 (N = 68)		1998 (N = 69)		1999 (N = 66)	
Health and Medicine	22,911	15.6	14,587	13.5	70,956	38.1
Arts and Culture	27,492	18.8	20,692	19.1	61,044	32.8
Scholarships/Research	29,365	20.0	24,097	22.2	18,260	9.9
Disaster Relief and Restoration	35,490	24.2	19,824	18.3	12,482	6.7
Social Welfare	13,356	9.1	10,261	9.5	11,651	6.3
Education	2,563	1.7	2,483	2.3	2,128	1.1
International Exchange	499	0.3	446	0.4	529	0.3
Community Social Development	443	0.3	173	0.2	359	0.2
Environmental Preservation	—		176	0.2	608	0.3
Other	14,627	10.0	15,581	14.4	8,120	4.4
TOTALS	146,746		108,320		186,137	

Exhibit 3.12   Trends in Foundation Expenditures, 1997–1999 (million won)

Rank	Name	Donor Corporation	Year of Establishment	Assets in Year of Establishment	Total Assets	Annual Expenditure
1	Asan Foundation	Hyundae	1977	5,000	483,756	72,404
2	Samsung Foundation of Culture	Samsung	1965	11,549	267,951	14,722
3	LG Yonam Foundation	LG	1969	1,549	146,219	52,290
4	The Daewoo Foundation	Daewoo	1978	5,000	88,818	4,789
5	Yonkang Foundation	Doosan	1978	63	63,893	566
6	Kumho Cultural Foundation	Kumho	1977	200	59,559	7,106
7	Ilju Scholarship and Culture Foundation	Taekwang Industry, etc.	1990	100	46,050	2,358
8	Lotte Welfare	Lotte	1983	500	37,307	1,288
9	Ko-chon Foundation	Chonggundang	1973	20	30,334	865
10	LG Welfare Foundation	LG	1991	1,000	30,023	3,419
11	Samsung Welfare Foundation	Samsung	1989	10,200	29,300	2,675
12	Owoon Foundation	Kolon	1981	269	27,781	408
13	Daesang Culture Foundation	Daesang	1971	10	27,340	967
14	Seoam Scholarship Foundation	Taeyoung	1989	100	23,104	1,137
15	Sungkok Art & Culture Foundation	Ssangyong	1995	13,236	22,812	614
16	The Korea Foundation for Advanced Studies	S.K.	1974	55	21,798	3,406
17	The Yangbaek	Daenong	1988	500	21,283	68
18	Yuhan Foundation	Yuhanyangheng	1970	42	16,979	656
19	Silla Cultural Scholarship Foundation	Shilla trade	1978	100	14,875	825
20	Daesan Culture Foundation	Kyobo Life Insurance	1992	2,630	13,819	1,309

Exhibit 3.13 Twenty Largest Korean Corporation Foundations (1999) (one million won = $840,000)

justice, and social advocacy organizations. Based broadly on the community foundation model in the United States, the Beautiful Foundation offers donors a choice of activities and organizations to support. The Women's Fund, established in January 2000, supports various types of women's organizations. It is seeking to encourage firms to allow employees to make contributions through payroll deductions. The Korea Human Rights Foundation, established in November 1999, is another of these new publicly funded foundations intended to raise funds for Korean NGOs. The Community Chest of Korea, originally established in 1975 by the Ministry of Health and Welfare as a quasigovernmental construct, was reorganized in 1998 as an autonomous and privately governed body similar to community chests in other countries. Approximately $2 million was transferred from the ministry to the new community chest in 1998, and an autonomous board of directors began making fundraising and allocation decisions. Whether these new initiatives will be successful in raising significant amounts of funds and become an established part of Korean philanthropy remains to be seen.

TAIWAN

The Himalaya Foundation in Taipei has served as an informal information center on foundations in Taiwan since 1997, when it published its first *Directory of Foundations in Taiwan* (in Chinese). In the same year it published a bilingual (English-Chinese) *Directory of 200 Major Foundations in Taiwan*, and in 1999 a *Directory of 300 Major Foundations in Taiwan*. The two latter reports are based on questionnaire surveys and interviews with major foundations selected from a comprehensive database of 1649 registered foundations.

In October 1999, the foundation opened to the public its Taiwan Philanthropy Information Center, with a reading room, a library of more than 500 books on nonprofit management, and access to an online database containing information on more than 2000 Taiwan foundations and 900 other nonprofits that provide social services and resources.[21]

In the year 2000, 3,014 foundations of all types were formally registered and operating in Taiwan. Newly established foundations financed by individual donations or corporate entities dominate Taiwan's foundation landscape. More and more corporate foundations have been established since the 1980s, and their increasing importance in Taiwan's nonprofit world reflects the growing concern and involvement of the business community in matters of public interest. Charitable and welfare foundations are the most numerous types of foundations, followed by public interest research, education, culture and arts, international cultural exchanges, and social activism. The vast majority of foundations in Taiwan are operating foundations rather than grantmaking foundations.[22]

Two-thirds of the foundations in Taiwan were formed after 1987—the year Taiwan's democratization process formally began. These foundations vary greatly in terms of the size of their governing boards (six to 65), number of staff (one to 873), and size of endowments. More than 85 percent of these foundations have endowments of less than NT$10 million (about U.S.$240,000 at current exchange rates) and 49 percent have endowments below NT$5 million. About 70 percent of foundations are private, supported by individuals and the general public, 25 percent are corporate foundations, and the remainder are government-linked foundations.

Exhibit 3.14 categorizes foundations in Taiwan by mission and purpose. The number of those involved in culture and education top the list at 2,126 (70.6%). Charitable and social welfare-oriented foundations follow at 479 (15.9%), then medical and health care foundations at 119 (4.0%), agriculture at 43 (1.4%), and transportation at 41 (1.4%). Bringing up the rear are foundations concerned with economic development, media, and environmental protection. The missions and purposes of Taiwan's foundations are highly concentrated in the fields of culture, education, charity, and social welfare.

Government-related foundations consist of those foundations established entirely by government agencies. They are subordinate to government departments and assigned particular government functions. A total of 86 foundations are in this category.

Mission and Purpose	Number	% of Total
Cultural and educational	2,126	70.6%
Social welfare and charitable	479	15.9%
Medical and health care	119	4.0%
Agriculture	43	1.4%
Transportation	41	1.4%
Economical development	33	1.1%
Media	30	1.0%
Environment protection	29	1.0%
Others	114	3.8%
Total	3,014	

Source: Himalaya Foundation

Exhibit 3.14   Taiwan Foundations Categorized by Mission and Purpose

The total endowment of Taiwan's 300 largest foundations in 2000 amounted to NT$50.8 billion, rising 37.3 percent from NT$37 billion in 1999. The Buddhist Compassion Relief Tzu-Chi Foundation, one of the largest Taiwan foundations, had an endowment that exceeded NT$12 billion. Seven other foundations exceeded NT$1 billion each.

One of the most critical issues facing Taiwan's foundations today is the lack of a unified procedure for the registration and supervision of foundations. Foundations are currently regulated by different judicial and administrative bodies. At present, each of 20 ministries and bureaus has issued its own regulations for establishing and supervising foundations, with associated legal and administrative guidelines. Provincial, county, and municipal governments in Taiwan can also approve and supervise local foundations. To establish a foundation, an endowment varying in size from NT$500,000 to NT$30 million is required, depending on the supervising government agency, with different regulations regarding the composition of those assets, including cash, real estate, and securities. Efforts are currently underway to streamline these procedures and reduce administrative overlap and inconsistencies among supervising government agencies.

PHILIPPINES

The Philippines has the most developed philanthropic infrastructure in Southeast Asia. Contemporary philanthropy dates back to corporate and Church response to social and political unrest in the 1960s, but there are of course philanthropic traditions and institutions dating back to the Spanish and American colonial periods. Philippine Business for Social Progress (PBSP) was founded in 1970 as a vehicle for corporations to contribute to social and economic development through professional services provided by PSBP staff. Originally, member corporations pledged to contribute 1 percent of their net profits into a pooled fund managed by PBSP, although in later years the percentage declined as corporations began to implement their own community development programs directly even as they continued to contribute to PBSP.[23] The Bishop-Businessmen's Conference for Human Development was founded in 1971, and the Association of Foundations in 1972. The Corporate Network for Disaster Response was founded in 1990 and in 1992, the League of Corporate Foundations was established with 12 members (rising to 45 by August 1999).[24] A Philanthropy Steering Committee, consisting of representatives of major Philippine corporate and independent foundations, local and international development NGOs, and official development assistance agencies, meets monthly to share information and collaborate on projects. PBSP and other organizations, such as the recently founded Venture for Fundraising, provide sophisticated training and consulting services to nonprofit organizations, foundations, and corporations on all aspects of fundraising as well as community development project design and implementation.[25]

Despite the sophistication of the infrastructure, little hard data are currently available on actual giving by individual foundations and corporations.[26] Philippine Business for Social Progress produced two annual surveys reporting on corporate giving in 1992 and 1993, and the Asian Institute of Management resumed the series in 2001, reporting data for 1999. According to those reports, 249 companies were reported to have made cash grants of Peso 261 million in 1992 (approximately U.S.$10.2 million), while 204 companies reported cash grants of Peso 309 million in 1993 (approximately U.S.$11.4 million).[27] In 1999, 122 companies reported total cash contributions of Peso 195 million (approximately U.S.$5 million at the depressed exchange rates prevailing in 1999).[28] In all three years, approximately two-thirds of the company respondents reported less than Peso 1 million in cash grants. In 1992, nine companies reported more than Peso 10 million in grants, accounting for 50 percent of total cash contributions. In 1993, eight companies accounted for 50 percent of all cash contributions, while in 1999, seven companies accounted for 81.5 percent of total cash contributions. In each year, education, health, social services, and disaster assistance were the most popular causes for corporate giving.

Other indicators of the approximate level of corporate giving are provided by 1996–1998 data from the League of Corporate Foundations (LCF). The LCF has a membership of 42 corporate foundations and eight corporations with social development programs. During this two-year period, the LCF reported a combined asset base of Peso 4 billion among its members. Close to Peso 1 billion was spent on programs in education (engaged in by 82% of LCF members), entrepreneurship development (38%), community development (35%), environmental protection (33%) and in housing and related services (33%), as well as other programs in health, arts and culture, disaster relief management, advocacy, rural development, cooperative development, institutional development and communications development.[29]

In mid-2001, the LCF Subcommittee on Education published the results of its March 2000 survey on giving to various educational causes by LCF members. Twenty-one of the 50 member firms set aside a total of Peso 71.64 million ($1.8 million) for scholarship grants for the 1999–2000 school year. The survey also revealed that while LCF members reported having been affected by the 1997 Asian financial crisis, most of these companies increased their 1998 budgets for scholarship grants by as much as 75 percent over 1996 levels. Furthermore, six companies started seven new scholarship programs worth Peso 4.8 million during the economic crunch. Most of the scholarship recipients were beneficiaries (dependents) of employees.[30]

CHINA

Chinese foundations and social organizations (NGOs) have attracted a good deal of attention in recent years. While these institutions share some structural characteristics with their nominal counterparts elsewhere in Asia, upon closer examination they turn out to be qualitatively different in character and purpose. Many Chinese foundations were created at the initiative of government or Communist Party agencies as part of the policy of "opening and reform" that began in the late 1970s. Under this broad program of reform, China began to move away from its command economy to a mixed market economy; the central government began to decentralize some of its functions to lower levels of government (with a concomitant decline in central tax revenues), and social services, academic research, and some other functions previously financed by the government began to receive less funding under the slogan "small government, big society." In this context, foundations and social organizations began to emerge in China in the early 1980s, under close government sponsorship and supervision, with missions variously described as supporting, assisting, partnering, and supplementing the activities and funding of government agencies in their respective fields. Fundamentally, foundations have been viewed by the Chinese leadership as vehicles to attract funds to supplement declining government budgets—from the public, from corporations and, above all, from ethnic Chinese living abroad.[31]

The first Chinese foundation established at the start of the reform era was the China Children and Teenagers Fund, established in 1981 under the auspices of the All-China Women's Federation. It was followed by the Soong Ching Ling Foundation in 1982, under the auspices of the General Office of the State Council, China's cabinet. Exhibit 3.15 shows the year of establishment, the sponsoring government agency, and the principal activities of 17 Chinese foundations operating at the national level.[32]

Based on data from 1995, one unpublished research paper reported that approximately 1,000 foundations had been created between 1984 and 1995,[33] while a more recent paper reports the

Foundation (Year Established)	Major Activities	Sponsoring Government Organization
Amity Foundation (1985)	Within the Christian mission of the foundation, to provide a broad range of social service, disaster relief, educational, social development, and related assistance to China's rural poor	Not GO sponsored: registered with the Ministry of Civil Affairs
China Association of Science Foundations (1992)	To promote the effective management of foundations devoted to the advancement of science and technology	State Science and Technology Commission
China Cancer Research Foundation (1984)	To promote effective approach to cancer treatment and cure through scientific research; to provide financial support for the Foundation's numerous cancer research and treatment centers	Chinese Academy of Medical Sciences, Institute of Cancer Research
China Charity Federation (1994)	To provide comprehensive social and economic support for impoverished urban and rural families; social assistance for the aged and orphans; disaster relief; financial support for community organizations	Ministry of Civil Affairs
China Consumer Protection Foundation (1989)	Monitors quality, safety, and effectiveness of new products coming into the Chinese economy; engages in consumer education; awards prizes annually for safe and effective new products	China Light Industry Federation
China Children and Teenagers Fund (1981)	To provide broad-based social, educational, and economic support for impoverished children and their families; disaster relief; support for institutions and organizations serving children.	All China Women's Federation
China Disabled Persons' Welfare Foundation (1984)	To promote the integration of disabled persons into the mainstream of society, especially in education and employment	Ministry of Civil Affairs
China Environmental Protection Foundation (1993)	Environmental protection; promotion of technical exchange; and cooperation with other countries on environmental matters	National Environmental Protection Agency of China
China Film Foundation (1989)	To promote the development of the Chinese film industry; to promote international exchanges and cooperation; and to contribute to the training of film professionals	Ministry of Broadcast, Film, and Television

Foundation	Major Activities	Sponsoring GO
China Literature Foundation (1986)	To advance the social welfare of Chinese writers; to promote international literary exchanges; and to foster the development of literary creations and young authors	Chinese Writers Association
China Medical Foundation (1984)	To promote medical education, research, and treatment with a focus on cancer treatment and cure; to promote academic exchange and international cooperation on a broad range of issues of concern to medical professionals	China International Promotion Committee for Friendship
China Population Welfare Foundation (1987)	To promote population stabilization in China and elsewhere; to promote the economic status of the rural poor, especially that of village women; and to promote international exchange and cooperation on a broad range of population stabilization matters	State Commission on Family Planning
Chinese Red Cross Foundation (1993)	To promote the general welfare; to assist with disaster relief; and to promote careers in areas and fields traditionally served by Red Cross and Red Crescent Societies around the world	China Red Cross Federation
China Science and Technology Museum Development Fund (1994)	To promote the popularization of science and technology; to promote financial support for museum-based education in science and technology	National Museum of Science and Technology
China Trade Unionist's Development Foundation (1988)	To promote the social welfare of trade unionists and their families; to give assistance to enterprises and workers in difficulty	All China Federation of Trade Unionists
China Youth Development Foundation (1989)	To promote the general welfare of children and youth, with a special concern for the educational needs of the rural poor; to promote research into problems of children and youth; to promote international cooperation among persons concerned with the special needs of youth	All China Youth Federation
National Natural Science Foundation of China (1990)	To promote the quality of research and research education in the natural sciences	State Science and Technology Commission

Exhibit 3.15 Major Activities, Sponsoring Government Organizations (GOs), and Year Established for Selected Chinese Foundations

existence of 1,081 foundations at the end of 1999.[34] The 1998 paper showed the distribution of foundation interests shown in Exhibit 3.16.

There are also several federated funding bodies, the largest of which is the China Charities Federation, created in 1994 and supervised by the Ministry of Civil Affairs, which raises funds from the public and from abroad for disaster relief and social welfare programs and operates through a network of affiliates in major cities throughout China.

Most Chinese foundations are fundraising and operational, rather than grantmaking. They make few grants at home, let alone overseas. The legal framework governing Chinese foundations and other nonprofit organizations has been revised in recent years and is currently embodied in three regulations and one law. The revised Regulations on the Registration and Administration of Social Organizations and the Provisional Regulations on the Registration and Administration of Private Non-Enterprise Institutions were both promulgated by the State Council in November 1998.[35] In 1999, the National Peoples Congress enacted the Public Benefit Donations Law, intended to provide a broad framework under which subsequent implementation regulations would clarify the terms under which donations, particularly from abroad, may be made and the accountability and reporting requirements of recipient organizations and responsible government agencies. Those implementing regulations have yet to be fully developed and promulgated. In addition, a new Regulation

Foundation Type	Number	Percentage
Social welfare	307	30.3%
Culture and education	257	24.6
Literature and arts	107	15.4
Scientific research	92	8.5
Sports and health care	86	7.7
Environmental protection	16	1.3
Other fields	130	12.2
Totals	995	100.00

Exhibit 3.16 Distribution of Chinese Foundations by Field of Interest, 1997

on the Administration of Foundations is currently circulating in draft and is expected to be promulgated sometime in 2002 or 2003.

Registering and operating a nonprofit organization in China involves a two-tier process. The Ministry of Civil Affairs at the national, provincial, or municipal levels is the *registration* authority, with the power to grant or deny registration applications; while functional government ministries and bureaus are the *supervising* authorities for nonprofits operating in their areas of specialization (such as health, education, science, etc.). For foundations, there is the additional requirement of obtaining approval from the Non-Financial Institutions Division of the People's Bank of China. There are strict regulations regarding government supervision, the size of initial endowments, geographical distribution, membership, and a general rule limiting the number of similar purpose foundations (or associations) in any given administrative region or province.[36]

Although the regulatory framework is very strict, the definition and organizational form of Chinese foundations is very vague:

> . . . a Chinese foundation can be an organization that looks for funding, instead of one that dispenses an existing fund; it can be an organization that relies on government funding to implement certain programs preset by the government; it can be a company which provides some kind of public service on behalf of a government agency or an enterprise; it can also be a very flexible and loosely organized group that tries to cater to miscellaneous purposes, depending on time and circumstances.[37]

Chinese foundations may be further classified into government-funded agencies, such as the National Science Foundation and the National Social Science Fund, created and financed by the Ministry of Science and Technology and the Central Committee of the Communist Party, respectively. Other foundations are self-defined as "non-governmental," but continue to receive financial or in-kind subsidies from their sponsoring government agencies for their administration and in some cases their programs, and in many cases foundation staff continue to receive their salaries, housing, and other benefits from their official government employers. Only a few smaller foundations rely largely on public contributions, such as the Beijing Philharmonic Orchestra Foundation and some municipal arts associations.[38]

It is difficult to obtain detailed financial or programmatic information about Chinese foundations. Although they are required to submit financial reports to their sponsoring government agencies, there is no requirement for public disclosure of financial (or program) data. Sponsoring ministries typically treat the reports as confidential material. On the other hand, as some Chinese foundations have grown more sophisticated in their fundraising from the public and from international sources, they have begun to publish financial reports in the national and local newspapers. In mid-2000, the China Charities Federation published its first detailed "annual" report, covering the period 1998–1999, containing both project descriptions and financial tables audited by Peat Marwick Huazhen.

Despite this highly restrictive operating environment, Chinese foundation and social organization (NGO) leaders see promise for the future, arguing that given China's recent history, it is natural that the government continues to play a leading role in the organization and supervision of the nonprofit sector. But they also believe that the emergence of more autonomous Chinese foundations and NGOs is inevitable as economic reform deepens.[39]

DONOR SUPPORT FOR THE CREATION OF ENDOWED GRANTMAKING FOUNDATIONS

One of the most interesting and potentially important trends in recent years has been support from the official development community to create new kinds of endowed grantmaking foundations that are at the interface of the public and private domains: endowed with public funds but managed by at least semiprivate governing boards.

These new publicly endowed foundations differ from traditional modes of project support in at least three critical ways: (1) they are funded from the income earned on endowments intended to provide a secure and steady stream of income; (2) the endowment is typically created from public funds or from a mix of public and private funds; and (3), they are governed by semiautonomous boards of trustees composed at least in part of private citizens which have the authority and responsibility to oversee the endowment and the distribution of grants.

More than 80 such funds currently exist around the world, and others are in various stages of development, mostly in environmental fields, such as the Foundation for the Philippine Environment and the Indonesian Biodiversity Foundation.[40] In addition, the Foundation for Sustainable Society (FSSI) was established in the Philippines through a Swiss debt swap.[41] The Ford and Rockefeller Foundations provided initial endowment support for the National Foundation for India and the Indian Foundation for the Arts, and the Ford Foundation has been instrumental in the creation of the Bangladesh Freedom Foundation.

Endowments have been created by a variety of innovative mechanisms, including the local currency proceeds of debt swaps, proceeds from the sale of donated food commodities, endowment grants from bilateral donors, corporate donations of blocked local currencies, as well as cash contributions from American foundations. The endowments thus created can be quite substantial, ranging up to tens of millions of dollars.

Several bilateral donors, including the United States, Canada, the Netherlands, Norway, and Switzerland, have participated in this type of financing, and major support has also come from the Global Environment Facility of the United Nations Development Program.[42]

In the very complicated process of swapping debt for local funds that can be used for development purposes, donor funds are used to purchase discounted debt currently owed by a developing country to a foreign creditor. The debt paper is then exchanged for local currency at face value and invested, typically in host country bonds or other secure financial instruments. At the end of the process, the interest earned by the endowment is available to the endowed NGO or foundation for the purposes specified in an agreement between the NGO or foundation, the donor, and the host government.

The legal and programmatic stewardship of the endowed foundation is usually vested in a board of trustees, which serves in a fiduciary role and is legally obligated and accountable for managing and protecting the endowment in accordance with the terms specified in the founding agreement. Frequently the founding agreement will require the appointment of a qualified securities firm to manage the portfolio of endowment investments and the appointment of an accounting firm to conduct regular audits.

CONCLUSION: CRITICAL CHALLENGES FACING FOUNDATIONS IN EAST ASIA

At their best, private foundations in the United States have served as catalysts, facilitators, and incubators of positive social change in fields as diverse as education, urban development, science and technology, poverty alleviation, social welfare policy, community asset creation, and voter education, among others. On the international scene, American private foundations were the venture capitalists of the Green Revolution and contributed intellectual leadership and initial financing for successful efforts in disease eradication, innovation in medical education and public health, family planning, foreign language training and area studies, among other innovations. The (usually idealized) perception of American private foundations as social entrepreneurs and innovators of important social policy, is widely shared in East Asia. Equally prevalent, however, is the belief that private foundations do not, and for the foreseeable future, cannot play such a role in East Asia.

Limited Public Awareness and Expectation

Emerging foundations in East Asia operate in historical, political, and social contexts very different from the United States. Throughout the region, the centralized state has historically played the dominant role in defining the public interest, closely controlling the provision of public goods and services, and setting the permissible limits of public participation in policy making and implementation.[43] It is often remarked in Japan, for example, that if "something is worth doing, the state should do it." Consequently, in most of East Asia, popular views of the relative roles of the public and private spheres—and their relationship—differ significantly from the United States. The concept of privately funded and privately managed public interest organizations whose scope extends beyond traditional limited mandates (such as providing charitable assistance to widows, students, the poor, the sick, or to disaster victims) is neither well-understood nor widely appreciated. The legitimate scope for private participation in resolving social issues or in the formulation of public policy is generally perceived to be rather limited, while the state is expected to provide basic services. Indeed, private nonprofit organizations are often treated with suspicion as to their motives and intentions. In most of the region, government bureaucrats, in particular, invariably believe that they alone have the right to define and protect the public interest and often reject the notion that private foundations or other nonprofits have a legitimate right to participate in the making of public policy or the implementation of public programs.

In addition, foundations are sometimes viewed as tax havens for the very wealthy and, in some Asian countries, have the unfortunate legacy of being associated with political corruption. The recent effort to place ex-president Suharto on trial for corruption in Indonesia, for example, centered on his alleged misuse of over $600 million collected through seven charitable foundations which he, his family, or his political party established and to which corporations (and civil servants) wishing to do business with the state had been required to contribute. The charges stemmed not from this method of charitable fund-raising, which is unfortunately common throughout the region, but from Suharto's alleged misuse of the funds so collected to support his children's business ventures. Even more recently, some of the charges against former President Estrada in the Philippines included his alleged misuse of charitable foundations to launder illegal gambling contributions and to provide cover for direct bribes. In Korea, government efforts to extort funds from corporations in the 1970s and 1980s under the guise of charitable contributions were widely referred to as "quasi-taxes" and routinely budgeted in corporate planning estimates. Unfortunately, even more examples of the misuse of foundations from elsewhere in the region abound.

This historical context affects the formation and role of private and corporate foundations in many ways, most immediately in terms of the legal and regulatory environments in which they operate and in the absence of strong local traditions of autonomous governance of philanthropic entities.

Restrictive Legal and Regulatory Environments

In 1999, the Asia Pacific Philanthropy Consortium published *Philanthropy and Law in Asia*, a comparative study of nonprofit law in 10 East Asian countries.[44] The study covered the nonprofit sector as a whole, but many of the findings also apply to philanthropic foundations. Overall, the study found that nonprofit law is incomplete and still evolving in the region.[45] In a few countries, the absence of explicit law provides some political space for the sector, but more frequently, within the dominant civil law tradition of East Asia, the absence of explicit law creates a legal limbo that makes it difficult for nonprofits to formally organize, to raise money, or to advocate on public policy issues.

Moreover, nonprofit law in Asia is evolving out of a national security context rather than a civil liberties context. Existing laws and regulations throughout the region reflect the security concerns of former colonial regimes, the social control orientation of various types of authoritarian regimes, and the historical tradition in East Asia of state dominance over the economy and society. Although it is generally much easier throughout the region to register and operate a foundation, which is a collection of assets, than it is to register an association, which is a collection of people, nonprofit organizations throughout the region are generally more heavily regulated than commercial firms.

Where explicit laws and regulations do exist, they are often vague, inconsistent, and are administered by multiple overlapping jurisdictions. Often, several different ministries will have the de facto authority to register and supervise a new foundation, depending on the foundation's field of interest and geographic scope. Often, several different ministries will have the authority to register and supervise nonprofit organizations, each applying its own set of rules and regulations. There is typically a *registration* authority in the form of a Home Ministry, Ministry of the Interior, Ministry of Civil Affairs, or a National Cultural Commission that has the authority to grant or deny formal registration for foundations or other nonprofits. In addition, *supervisory* authority is typically vested in functional ministries operating in the same field as the foundation, such as ministries of health, social welfare, education, religion, environment, or foreign affairs. Foundations often require additional approval from a central bank or Ministry of Finance. Each of these authorities may impose its own rules and requirements, which may contradict each other. Foundations that operate at a national level typically face more complicated registration requirements than foundations that operate at subnational or municipal levels, where approval may be more easily obtained and "founding endowments" are usually smaller. In addition, the limits of ministerial jurisdiction often make it difficult for multipurpose foundations to register. In Japan and Taiwan, for example, multipurpose foundations are effectively impossible to create, since to do so requires crossing ministerial jurisdictions.

The net result is that throughout the region, the registration and supervision of foundations and other nonprofit organizations is characterized by enormous scope for bureaucratic discretion and the added cost of multiple registration requirements.

The tax treatment of foundations and other nonprofits varies within the region but in general is not as favorable as in the United States or Western Europe. In most cases, formal incorporation and registration of a foundation automatically provides tax *exemption*, but the process of obtaining tax *deductibility* for donors is much more complicated and restrictive.

Capital accumulation is another area of tight government control—not usually through formal laws and regulations, but more often through what the Japanese call "administrative guidance," the close oversight and supervision provided by bureaucrats in the ministries to which foundations are responsible. Out of a misguided sense of protecting NPO assets, foundations in many counties are prohibited from investing their assets in equities or commercial paper. They are required to keep their assets in secure local currency savings accounts or government bonds. In practice, this means that in recessionary periods—as in the current post–economic crisis period—endowments earn very low rates of return, frequently less than needed to cover both administrative and program costs.

Finally, in some countries foundations are required to obtain prior approval of proposed grants from their supervising ministries and are required to submit to the supervising ministry the minutes of board meetings. Throughout the region, governments retain the right to dissolve foundations and other nonprofits for vague and politically determined reasons, such as "engaging in acts that harm the public interest" (Korea); "engaging in activities detrimental to the national interest" (China); for "operating against the interests of the state" (Vietnam); "for being managed in a manner contrary to public order, good morals, or the security of the state" (Thailand); or "being used for purposes prejudicial to public peace, welfare, or good order" (Singapore).

Weak Internal Governance

One consequence of such close government supervision is that the internal governance of Asian foundations and nonprofit organizations is generally weak and seldom autonomous. All countries in East Asia require that foundations have the equivalent of governing boards and, often, audit and management committees. Boards usually consist of prominent individuals who lend their names but are not usually expected to exercise close supervision of program activities or to independently determine foundation policy. These governance functions are in practice performed by supervising government agencies. In the case of corporate foundations, corporate officers typically set foundation policy, again with close ministerial oversight.

Developing stronger internal governance mechanisms (and reducing the direct intervention of government agencies) is therefore a critical task facing Asia foundations (and other nonprofits).

There have been very few formal studies of the international governance of foundations and other nonprofits in Asia. One of the first such studies, an effort to explore how nonprofit governance is defined in various countries and to identify "best practice," has recently been launched by the Center for Community Organizations and Management at the University of Technology in Sydney, Australia, with a report anticipated in 2003.

Developing Staff Competence

The lack of professional staff is often cited as another weakness of foundations in East Asia and a barrier to their future development. This is not surprising given the infancy of most foundations in the region. Most conferences on the status of the sector usually produce a standard litany of professional development needs: for staff training at universities or in management training programs; internships at established foundations in the United States or Europe; short-term staff exchanges; and opportunities for informal networking. An informal network of younger foundation staff has begun to emerge in the form of CAFO, the Conference of Asian Foundation Officers, in which program experience in the arts and culture, civil society, and other fields can be shared. In addition, academic centers for the study of philanthropy and the nonprofit sector have begun to emerge in Japan, Korea, the Philippines, Thailand, Taiwan, and elsewhere, which will contribute over time to the enhanced professionalization of foundation staff in Asia.

The more fundamental need of course, is to create environments in which it is possible and desirable to have a career in the nonprofit sector, with appropriate social recognition and financial compensation. That time may not be too far off in some countries—Japan, Korea, and Taiwan, for example—as the sector matures and public attitudes and expectations about the legitimate right of private actors to operate in the public domain evolve in the years ahead.

NOTES

1. The reports of the three conferences constituted the first comparative and most comprehensive overview of the philanthropic sector in Asia then available. See Barnett F. Baron (Ed.), *Philanthropy and the Dynamics of Change in East and Southeast Asia* (New York, East Asian Institute, Columbia University, 1991); Ku-Hyun Jung (Ed.)., *Evolving Patterns of Asia Pacific Philanthropy* (Seoul: Institute of East and West Studies, Yonsei University, 1994); and Tadashi Yamamoto (Ed.), *Emerging Civil Society in the Asia Pacific Community* (Tokyo and Singapore: Japan Center for International Exchange and the Institute of Southeast Asian Studies, 1995).

2. World Bank, *The East Asian Miracle: Economic Growth and Public Policy* (New York: Oxford University Press, 1993). China was not included in the World Bank's study because of the significant differences between it and the other countries in terms of state ownership and control of the economy, the nature of corporate governance and decision-making, and China's then limited reliance on markets. Despite these differences, China's annual economic growth averaged 5.8 percent during the 1980s.

3. These points are further elaborated in Barnett F. Baron (Ed.), *Philanthropy and the Dynamics of Change in East and Southeast Asia* (New York: East Asian Institute, Columbia University, 1991); Tadashi Yamamoto (Ed.), *Emerging Civil Society in the Asia Pacific Community* (Tokyo and Singapore: Japan Center for International Exchange and the Institute of Southeast Asian Studies, 1995); James W. Morley (Ed.), *Driven by Growth: Political Change in the Asia-Pacific Region* (Armonk, NY: M.E. Sharpe, 1993 and 1998); and Lori Vacek, *International Conference on Supporting the Nonprofit Sector in Asia* (San Francisco: The Asia Foundation, 1998).

4. Tadashi Yamamoto and Hitomi Komatsu, "Japan's Philanthropic Development in the Asia Pacific Context," in Yamamoto (Ed.), see note 3, pp. 561–582; see also Tae-Kyu Park, "Corporate Foundations in Korea," in Yamamoto (Ed.), *id.*, pp. 583–590; and Nancy R. London, *Japanese Corporate Philanthropy* (New York: Oxford University Press, 1991).

5. For an explication of the business rationale and illustrative case studies from Asia and elsewhere, see for example, Lori Vacek, *Corporate Citizenship in Asia Pacific: Conference Report* (Washington, D.C.: Council on Foundations, 1997); Tadashi Yamamoto and Kim Gould Ashizawa (Eds.), *Corporate-NGO Partnership in Asia Pacific* (Tokyo: Japan Center for International Exchange, 1999). Also Jane Nelson, *Business as Partners in Development* (Prince of Wales Business Lead-

ers Forum in cooperation with the World Bank and UNDP, 1996); David Logan, Delwin Roy, and Laurie Regelbrugge, *Global Corporate Citizenship: Rationale and Strategies* (Washington, D.C.: The Hitachi Foundation, 1997); World Bank, *Business Partners for Development: Discussion Paper* (Washington, D.C.: January 1998); Laurie Regelbrugge, "Engaging Corporations in Strengthening Civil Society," in Leslie Fox and S. Bruce Shearer (Eds.), *Sustaining Civil Society: Strategies for Resource Mobilization* (Washington, D.C.: CIVICUS, 1997); Craig Smith, "The Promotion of Corporate Citizenship" (Bloomington: Indiana University Center on Philanthropy, *Essays on Philanthropy*, No. 26, 1997); *An Introductory Guide to Corporate Partnerships in India* (Washington, D.C.: US-India Business Council, December 1997); and Simon Zadek, *Doing Good and Doing Well: Making the Business Case for Corporate Citizenship* (New York: The Conference Board, Research Report 1282-00-RR, 2000). See also Ros Tennyson, *Managing Partnerships: Tools for Mobilizing the Public Sector, Business and Civil Society as Partners in Development* (London: Prince of Wales Business Leaders Forum, 1998).

6. The Synergos Institute's recently published *Foundation Building Sourcebook: A Practitioner's Guide Based on Experience from Africa, Asia, and Latin America* (New York: Synergos Institute, 2000) notes that the "sourcebook uses the term 'grantmaking foundation' largely because it is readily understood to most people working in this field. It should be noted, however, that there is no universal consensus on the use of the term. It is used here for the sake of consistency but could as well be replaced with other terms including 'grantmaking trusts,' 'grantmaking NGOs,' or even 'civil society resource organizations.' Even the meaning of the word 'foundation' differs between regions of the world because legal, philanthropic, cultural and historical contexts vary significantly between countries." For more information on Synergos' project on "civil society resource organizations and development in Southeast Asia," which reports on a survey of 77 operating/funding organizations with budgets primarily in the $100,000 to $1 million range, see the Synergos Web site at *www.synergos.org/globalphilanthropy*.

7. The most recent and comprehensive review of corporate philanthropy in Hong Kong is provided in *The Role of Companies in the Development of a Vibrant Third Sector in Hong Kong*, a consultant's report commissioned by the Government of Hong Kong in 2001, accessible at *www.info.gov.hk/cpu/english/papers/*.

8. See Chang-Soon Hwang, background paper on Korea prepared for the International Conference on Strengthening Philanthropy in Asia Pacific: An Agenda for Action, Asia Pacific Philanthropy Consortium, Bali, Indonesia, July 2001. Available at the APPC Web site, *www.asianphilanthropy.org*.

9. See Darwin Chen, background paper on Hong Kong prepared for the APPC Bali conference cited in note 8; available at APPC Web site, *www.asianphilanthropy.org*.

10. *Directory of Grant-Making Foundation in Japan 2000* (Tokyo: Japan Foundation Center, Japanese edition published in May 2000; English-language edition anticipated in December 2000). Not all foundations responded to each question in the survey, however, so that the number of respondents varies by question. For a general overview of the nonprofit sector in Japan, including

foundations, see Tadashi Yamamoto (Ed.), *The Nonprofit Sector in Japan* (Manchester University Press, 1998).

11. Under the complex Japanese civil law system, two of the largest grantmaking entities with international programs, the Nippon Foundation and the Center for Global Partnership of the Japan Foundation, are not included in the *Directory*'s analysis. Owing to their formation by statute and their public sources of funding, 3.3 percent of the proceeds of motorboat racing in the case of the Nippon Foundation, and funding through the Diet and the Ministry of Foreign Affairs in the case of the Japan Foundation, both of these entities are classified as "special public interest corporations" rather than foundations. For a detailed analysis of the applicable laws and regulations, see Takako Amemiya, "Japan," in Thomas Silk (Ed.), *Philanthropy and Law in Asia* (San Francisco: Jossey Bass 1999), pp. 131–162; and "The Nonprofit Sector: Legal Background," in Tadashi Yamamoto (Ed.), *The Nonprofit Sector in Japan*, Johns Hopkins Nonprofit Sector Series Number 7 (Manchester: Manchester University Press, 1998), pp. 59–98.

12. Detailed information about the four largest Japanese "foundations" with international interests may be found on their Web sites: The Nippon Foundation at *www.nippon-foundation.or.jp*; Toyota Foundation at *www.toyotafoundation.or.jp*; Sasakawa Peace Foundation at *www.spf.org*; and the Center for Global Partnership of the Japan Foundation at *www.cgp.org*.

13. See Keidanren, *White Paper on Corporate Philanthropy in Japan 1999* (September 1999) and *Synopsis of the Survey of Corporate Philanthropic Activities in Fiscal 1998* (December 14, 1999).

14. 1999 data reported in Tadashi Yamamoto, background paper on Japan for the APPC conference in Bali, July 2001, available at *www.asianphilanthropy.org*.

15. See the chapters on Japan by Takako Amemiya and Yoshinori Yamaoka in Thomas Silk (Ed.), *Philanthropy and Law in Asia* (San Francisco: Jossey Bass, 1999), pp. 131–162 and 163–198.

16. For details, see note 14, Yamamoto, background paper for Japan prepared for the APPC Bali conference; and Japan Center for International Exchange *Civil Society Monitor*, Numbers 4 (1999) and 6 (2001), both available at *www.jcie.or.jp*.

17. See note 11, Amemiya, pp. 146–147.

18. Federation of Korean Industry, *Corporate Community Relations White Book*, 2000, in Korean. All data presented in this section are taken from the *White Book*.

19. Ku-Hyun Jung et al., "Korea," in Silk, *Philanthropy and Law in Asia*, see note 11, p. 224.

20. Park Tae-Kyu, "Corporate Foundations in Korea," in Yamamoto, *Emerging Civil Society in the Asia Pacific Community*, see note 3, pp. 583–590.

21. The database (in Chinese) is accessible at *www.npo.org.tw*; the English-language version is under construction at *www.tpic.org.tw*. The directory of 300 foundations will be available at *www.foundations.org.tw*.

22. The following data are derived from Andy Y.H. Kao, background paper on Taiwan prepared for the APPC Bali conference, July 2001, available at *www.asianphilanthropy.org*.

Notes

23. Victor E. Tan and Maurino P. Bolante, *Philippine Business for Social Progress* (New York: Synergos Institute, 1997).
24. For an overview, see Gisela T. Velasco, "Overview of Organized Philanthropy in the Philippines," in Yamamoto, *Emerging Civil Society,* see note 3, pp. 591–608.
25. See Aurora Tolentino, background paper on the Philippines prepared for the APPC Bali conference, July 2001, available at *www.asianphilanthropy.org.*
26. The most recent effort to analyze trends in donor support aggregated data across all types of donors and is most useful as a directory of donor contact information rather than a source of information about philanthropic donations. See Association of Foundations, *Donor Trends: A Resource Book of Development Assistance in the Philippines* (Manila, 2000). See also Bishop-Businessmen's Conference, *Directory of Foreign and Local Development Assistance Agencies,* 3rd Edition (Manila, 1998); and the *1999 Directory of the League of Corporate Foundations,* which provides contact information for its 45 current members. On case studies of corporate giving programs, see Juan Miguel Luz and Teodoro Montelibano, *Corporations and Communities in a Developing Country* (Manila: PBSP, 1993) and Christina V. Pavia, "Cebu Hillyland Development Program," in Tadashi Yamamoto and Kim Gould Ashizawa, *Corporate-NGO Partnership in Asia Pacific* (Tokyo: JCIE, 1999), pp. 81–94.
27. Gisela T. Velasco et al., *Annual Report on Corporate Giving* (Manila: Center for Corporate Citizenship, Philippine Business for Social Progress, July 1993 and January 1995). The exchange rates are the average exchange rates for the respective years reported in IMF, *International Financial Statistics Yearbook 2000.* Also see Velasco's "Corporate Philanthropy in Asia: The Philippines Case," *Working Paper #1* (New York: Center for the Study of Philanthropy, City University of New York, Winter 1996).
28. Asian Institute of Management, Center for Corporate Responsibility, *Report on Corporate Giving Philippines 2001.* Reflecting the economic downturn post-1997, the average exchange rate for 1999 had fallen from the 25–27 range prevailing in 1992–93 to Peso 39.089 = $1.
29. Tolentino, see note 25.
30. *Id.*
31. For further background, see Zhao LiQing, background paper prepared for the APPC Bali conference, July 200, available at *www.asianphilanthropy.org.* See also Zhao LiQing (Ed.) [Qinghua conference book]; Nick Young with Anthony Wu, *China: An Introduction to the Nonprofit Sector,* (Kent: Charities Aid Foundation, 2000); Vivienne Shue, "State Power and the Philanthropic Impulse in China," in Warren F. Ilchman, Stanley N. Katz, and Edward Queen (Eds.), *Philanthropy in the World's Traditions* (Bloomington: Indiana University Press, 1998), pp. 332–354; and Zhang Ye, "Foundations in China: A Survey Report," in Tadashi Yamamoto (Ed.), *Emerging Civil Society in the Asia Pacific Region* (Tokyo: Japan Center for International Exchange, 1995), pp. 523–532.
32. Zhao, APPC conference paper, see note 31.

33. Zhu Chuanyi, "Foundations and Their Development in China," Chinese Academy of Social Sciences, unpublished manuscript, January 1998.

34. Shang Yusheng, "China's NPO Development and Strategic Thinking," unpublished paper presented at the Conference on Corporations and Public Welfare, Shanghai, October 2000. For a report on the conference and examples of Chinese corporate philanthropy, see *Chinabrief* (Beijing), Volume III, Number 3, Autumn 2000.

35. English translations of these regulations may be found in the online *International Journal of Nonprofit Law* at *www.icnl.org/journal*. For a balanced review of the new regulations and how some Chinese NGOs view them, see *Chinabrief*, "New Rules for the Nonprofit Sector," February 1999.

36. For details, see Xin Chunying and Zhang Ye, "China," in Thomas Silk (Ed.), *Philanthropy and Law in Asia* (San Francisco: Jossey Bass, 1999), pp. 85–124. A new Regulation on the Administration of Foundations is circulating in draft form as this is being written.

37. Zhang Ye, "Foundations in China," in Yamamoto, see note 31, p. 525.

38. Zhang Ye, "Foundations in China, see note 31.

39. Zhao LiQing, see note 31, and forthcoming report of the July 1998 Beijing conference.

40. For details on organizational structures, funding modalities, and operational issues encountered to date, see the report of the *First Asia-Pacific Forum on Environmental Funds*, Cebu, Philippines, February 16–21, 1997, available from the Nature Conservancy. For case studies of the Foundation for the Philippine Environment see Teresita C. Rosario, *Foundation for the Philippine Environment: A Case Study* (New York: Synergos Institute, 1997); Antonio B. Quizon and Maria Theresa Lingan-Debuque, *The Creation of the Foundation for the Philippine Environment: A Case Study of Cooperation Between the US Agency for International Development and FPE* (New York: Synergos Institute, 1999).

41. See Alan de Guzman Alegre, *The Creation of Foundation for a Sustainable Society, Inc.: A Case Study of Cooperation Between the Government of Switzerland and FSSI* (New York, Synergos Institute, 1999); and CODE-NGO, Helvetas, and the Swiss Coalition of Debt Organizations, *Building the Foundations of a Sustainable Society; The Philippine Experience at Creative Debt Relief* (Geneva, 1997).

42. See Global Environment Facility Secretariat, *Evaluation of Experience with Conservation Trust Funds* (New York; UNDP, 1998).

43. The literature on these issues is vast. For an excellent discussion of the Japanese context, see Tadashi Yamamoto (Ed.), *Deciding the Public Good: Governance and Civil Society in Japan* (Tokyo: Japan Center for International Exchange, 1999), especially Yoshida Shin'ichi, "Rethinking the Public Interest in Japan: Civil Society in the Making," pp. 13–50.

44. Thomas Silk (Ed.), see note 15.

45. For a summary of the main findings, see Barnett F. Baron, "The Institutional Context for Civil Society Development in Asia," *International Journal of Nonprofit Law*, Vol. 3, Issue 2, February 2001, available at *www.icnl.org/journal/*.

CHAPTER 4

Bolstering Border Philanthropy: United States and Mexico Join Forces to Combat an Array of Problems

By Grant Williams

PERSPECTIVES

The past decade has been transformational for U.S.–Mexico relations. With the North American Free Trade Agreement and new presidential administrations in both countries, we seem to be continually redefining the potential of cross-border relations. How is that potential manifested in philanthropic work? Several foundations in the United States have expressed interest in the growing movement of organized philanthropy in Mexico. In cross-border relationships such as that between El Paso, Texas and Juárez, Mexico, we are discovering traditions of cooperation that may serve as models for partnerships in the future.

Reporter Grant Williams provides a basis of understanding for exploring cross-border partnerships. This chapter, which was first published as an article, is reprinted here with permission of the *Chronicle of Philanthropy, http://philanthropy.com.*

Over the past decade, the U.S.–Mexico border has been home to unprecedented economic good times. For the next decade, it may be poised for a philanthropic bonanza.

Since the landmark North American Free Trade Agreement (NAFTA) was enacted nearly eight years ago, the 2,000-mile border from Texas to California has drawn thousands of businesses in search of new markets and hundreds of thousands of workers in search of a more prosperous life, particularly on the Mexican side. But the influx of capital and labor has left in its wake a dramatic array of environmental and social problems—problems that have strained governments and nonprofit organizations and left organized philanthropy on both sides of the border looking for more ambitious and coordinated ways to respond.

Encouraged by what many see as fresh enthusiasm on the part of newly elected presidents on both sides of the border, grantmakers, nonprofit leaders, and government officials are redoubling their efforts to ameliorate the detrimental side effects of economic growth, which include pollution, poverty, water shortages, inadequate housing, and the rape or murder of hundreds of women.

Among the priorities of foundation and government officials are the following tasks:

- *Assess what works.* Next month, the Ford and Meadows Foundations will hold a two-day meeting in Dallas with a number of other grantmakers to discuss ways to step up philanthropy efforts along the border. Among items on the agenda are expanding the role of community foundations and creating an organization that could serve as a clearinghouse for nonprofit groups to share information and ideas. The Dallas meeting follows a Border Summit on philanthropy and other matters held last month near the border town of McAllen, Texas, by the University of Texas—Pan American, at which foundation officials emphasized the need for increased collaboration among organizations.
- *Ease regulations.* In Mexico, President Vicente Fox has ordered that complicated rules be simplified for gifts of property,

food, and other in-kind goods from donors in the United States to Mexican charities. In the United States, the Council on Foundations recently secured an Internal Revenue Service statement clarifying that U.S. grantmakers need not fully investigate overseas charities to make sure that they meet all the standards required for U.S. charity status. Instead, foundations in the United States need only obtain detailed accounts from the grantees of how the award of money is to be used.

- *Build civil society.* A critical challenge, say foundation officials, will be to shore up the financial and management structures of small, locally rooted nonprofit groups, and to inculcate a "culture of giving" in Mexico, a country that some say has lacked a strong philanthropic tradition.

"Foundations that used to work on Mexico spent a lot of time working on strategic relationships between the United States and Mexico," observes David Lorey, a program officer handling U.S.–Latin American relations for the William and Flora Hewlett Foundation, in Menlo Park, California, which is in the process of spending $10 million in grants for border projects. "There is a very appropriate turn now toward engagement with real issues on the ground that have to do with poverty and justice and environmental degradation."

Philanthropic efforts along the border are not new. Some grantmakers in the United States, such as the Ford and Meadows Foundations and the El Paso Community Foundation, have been involved for two decades or more. Since NAFTA went into effect in January 1994, a growing number of community foundations have also sprung up on the Mexico side of the border, including the Fundación Internacional de la Comunidad, in Tijuana; the Fondo del Empresariado Sonorense, in Nogales; and the Fundación del Empresariado Chihuahuense, in Ciudad Juárez.

One just-announced high-profile effort: a new foundation, being created by the first lady of Mexico, Marta Sahagún de Fox, that will try to reduce poverty and improve health care in Mexico and Latin America.

Although there are no comprehensive tallies of "border philanthropy" year by year, experts agree that it has been growing by leaps and bounds. A Foundation Center study found that a subset of such grants—those from U.S. foundations to Mexican nonprofit groups—increased by 60 percent from 1994 to 1998, to $24 million. That sum made Mexico the fourth leading recipient of U.S. philanthropic funds, behind England, South Africa, and Canada.

AN INTEGRATED REGION

The growth in border philanthropy stems in part from an agreement, reached in conjunction with NAFTA, that eased cross-border giving by making Mexican charities the legal equals of U.S. charities for purposes of U.S. law, and likewise recognizing U.S. charities under Mexican law.

But increased interest in the border has been driven by more than mere legal changes. It has been propelled by a growing recognition that, just as the economic fates of the United States and Mexico have become increasingly linked, so too has the welfare of the people living on both sides of the border.

Experts say this recognition is long overdue. The border has traditionally been a sort of netherworld, often neglected by faraway national governments, multinational corporations, and organized philanthropy. With the recognition that the border increasingly exists in name only, foundation and nonprofit leaders are creating cross-national institutions that will treat the area along the border as an integrated philanthropic region.

The Paso del Norte Health Foundation, a $211 million fund created in 1995 with proceeds from the sale of a nonprofit hospital to a health care corporation, runs public health programs in southern Texas, southern New Mexico, and Ciudad Juárez. The foundation works closely with government health agencies, charities, and universities on both sides of the border to tackle common problems such as diabetes, poor nutrition, and teenage pregnancy.

"When I can stand up and look across the border and see Juárez, it's easy to see that there really is no border," says Ann G. Pauli, the foundation president, speaking of the view from her El Paso offices. "We are all one country down here."

LEGAL BARRIERS

Although promising experiments in cross-border philanthropy have begun, nonprofit and government officials from both countries agree that steps must be taken to remove lingering barriers to international giving and to increase Mexico's capacity to build and sustain its own nonprofit organizations.

"There are still rough spots in the Mexican law that they have not worked out on their own," says Janice Woods Windle, president of the El Paso Community Foundation, whose $100 million in assets make it one of the largest grantmakers along the border. "We keep hoping that, as time goes by and we do more and more work together, that the laws in both countries will become more reflective of each other so that it is very easy to work in either country."

Legislators in Mexico are considering relaxing regulations, put in place several years ago following reported cases of charity fraud, that will make it easier for U.S. foundations to support Mexican charities. Likewise, the Mexican government has taken steps to make it easier for U.S. companies to donate goods to Mexico.

Strengthening border nonprofit groups has also gained increased support. Shortly after NAFTA was enacted, the Meadows and Levi Strauss Foundations and the Houston Endowment created the Southwest Border Nonprofit Management Resource Center, based at the University of Texas–Pan American in the border town of Edinburg, Texas.

In addition, working with the Texas Historical Commission along different parts of the border, foundations have been supporting the development of a "heritage corridor" that will draw tourists and economic development to historically significant sites. The Meadows

Foundation, which has made an estimated 300 border-related grants totaling nearly $26 million over the past two decades, has supported the Los Caminos del Río corridor in the area of Brownsville and Laredo, Texas. The El Paso Community and Hewlett Foundations have together given $300,000 to support the Pass of the North Heritage Corridor in the area of El Paso, Juárez, and Las Cruces, New Mexico.

"For any of the problems on the border, the key missing actor is a set of strong institutions," says Mr. Lorey of the Hewlett Foundation. "This is true across a whole range of issues. There aren't university research programs, there aren't nonprofit activist organizations."

BUILDING ASSETS

Another strategy for bolstering Mexican nonprofit groups is to broaden and deepen their sources of financial support. For example, the El Paso Community Foundation and the Fundación Margarita Miranda de Mascareñas in Juárez have created a binational foundation that has also received $1 million from the Hewlett Foundation to make environmental grants along the border. The new fund will redistribute some of the money in grants to smaller charities and use the rest to develop its own management and governance-assistance programs for nonprofit groups.

Within the next few weeks, the Ford Foundation, which has supported border work since the early 1980s, is expected to announce a new program to increase the number and assets of community foundations on both sides of the border.

Six of the nine community funds along the U.S. side of the border are young and only modestly endowed, with less than $1 million apiece. On the Mexican side, there are four border grantmakers, and three more in formation, but none has an appreciable endowment, according to David Winder, director of global philanthropy and foundation building for the Synergos Institute, in New York, which is advising Ford on the community foundation project.

Richard Kiy, president of the International Community Foundation, a San Diego grantmaker that has given nearly $240,000 to border projects since its creation a decade ago, argues not only that there must be more foundations, with larger endowments, but also that they should work more closely together in the border region. At the philanthropy border summit last month, he called for the creation of a "binational regional association of grantmakers," whose role would include coordinating joint foundation projects, serving as a forum for foundations to share lessons learned, and "educating major national, corporate, and specific individual donors about the unique needs of the U.S.–Mexico border."

George V. Grainger, a grant officer at the Houston Endowment, which has increased its border philanthropy over the past five years, observes: "Everybody recognizes that one of the fundamental problems with philanthropy along the border is that there are no philanthropic assets—huge needs, a lot of public charities, but little in the way of dollars available from local sources."

Mr. Grainger also notes that Mexican nonprofit groups, even more than their U.S. counterparts, sometimes find it difficult to work with foundations, which prefer to make grants for specific projects as opposed to providing operating support of electricity, rent, salaries, and other basic expenses. "That ought to be a priority," he says.

GIVING TRADITIONS

Officials on both sides of the border argue that it will be difficult to strengthen nonprofit groups without first inculcating a "culture of giving" among Mexican individuals. Mexican nonprofit groups received 6 percent of their income in 1995 through donations from private sources, compared with 21 percent for U.S. nonprofit groups, according to the most recent research by Johns Hopkins University's Comparative Nonprofit Sector Project.

"It is increasingly clear to me that there is a need to promote and stimulate generosity and social responsibility among citizens and businesses, and it is also evident that, although we have moved forward in this regard, we still have a long road ahead," Jorge Villalobos, president of the Mexican Center for Philanthropy, told the border philanthropy conference. "There is a continued scarcity of people who systematically give a share of their income in their local community. There isn't that culture," he observed.

Mexican companies and multinational corporations that have operations along the border represent major untapped sources of funds. Many of these companies, with headquarters far away from where they do business, are roundly criticized for failing to do enough to support the people and places that produce the profits.

"It's not like Dallas, Monterrey, Mexico City, or Houston," says Mr. Kiy of the International Community Foundation. "The border tends to be somewhat out of the loop on corporate foundation support."

At the Border Summit, Bruce H. Esterline, a vice president at the Meadows fund, said that among the most pressing challenges for grantmakers is to convince corporate chief executives, who have authority over assembly plants located hundreds or thousands of miles away from company headquarters, "to invest in the quality of life issues, on both sides of the border."

Mr. Lorey of the Hewlett Foundation says such work is tricky but rewarding. "Measuring outcomes is difficult," he concedes. "But the bottom line is, you have a better idea if you have made a difference doing this kind of work compared to funding some kind of theoretical policy study on the future of the U.S.–Mexico relationship."

Section Two

More Than Sitting on Money: The Gentle Balance of Prudence, Growth, and Mission

CHAPTER 5

The Process of Investment: Stakeholder Negotiations

By Russell T. Hill and Craig T. Cross

PERSPECTIVES

Fiduciary responsibility lies at the heart of governing and operating foundations and nonprofit organizations. Many foundations see this as the ultimate obligation driving investment, management, and board activities. Yet in terms of investment, most foundations turn over much of their responsibility and control to a financial advisor or consultant. Where does the board's responsibility stop and the investment advisor's or service provider's begin? How does the board engage in a process of both understanding its responsibility and initiating a relationship with a trusted investment advisor?

In this chapter, Russell Hill and Craig Cross draw from their many years of experience working with individuals, families, nonprofit organizations, and foundations to offer a framework for clarifying, documenting, and implementing an investment plan. Russell T. Hill is president of Halbert, Hargrove/Russell LLC in Long Beach, California. Craig T. Cross is a principal, officer, and co-founder of the firm.

How are foundations different from other institutional investors? In what ways are they similar: What can we usefully take from our standard institutional investing toolbox and apply to the foundation area? Is there some benefit to be gained in applying a more rigorous standard of analysis, oversight, and communication in the investment of foundation funds?

In this chapter, we hope to provide some answers to the questions asked above. Our writing is inspired by the explosion of new foundations and endowments created by the enormous increases in wealth over the past few years and anticipated in the next several decades to come.

For purposes of our exposition, we use the word *foundation* generically, although of course there are many permutations as examples. What we really mean to discuss are the essentially permanent funds whose basic purpose is to support the mission of a foundation defined by an eleemosynary charter.

Because of the proliferation of charitable giving, family foundations, and other foundation assets, many capital pools are being created on an ongoing basis that have limited professional staff to service them, as well as limited staff that are rigorously trained in investment management. Investment committees may or may not have the fiduciary and investment background necessary to meet the standards we'll discuss further.

We hope to contribute some useful tools for and approaches to this relatively new growth area to enlarge the vocabulary, understanding, and, by extension, the practices of stakeholders and investment professionals alike. In the not-for-profit world generally, the concept of *stakeholders* is a useful analog of the ultimate shareholder of the for-profit world. Those who have, or may have, an interest or stake in the ultimate outcome of a foundation's investment management process might include board members, staff, founding donors, prospective donors, other funding sources, organizations, beneficiaries, the larger community, and referring professionals such as CPAs and attorneys. Explicit recognition of the interests of each party can lead to the process we call *stakeholder negotiation*, and, ultimately, to a better overall outcome from the investment process, defined in the institution's own terms.

To answer the questions we posed previously, we'll follow a structure of three simple ideas:

1. Investment activities of foundations, whether individual trusts, private, or public foundations, and their endowing funds must be anchored to the realities of the financial environment and the necessary responsibilities undertaken by fiduciaries. Investment of funds by a fiduciary is a process, not an end point to be reached.
2. Financial professionals can use tools to create a language or vocabulary for discussion among the various stakeholders of a foundation and to memorialize decisions reached. Financial markets and the codification of fiduciary rules provide a framework for negotiation.
3. Finally, while the process of reaching consensus among various stakeholders is usually messy, the process itself has several organizational benefits, in addition to providing a disciplined investment policy agreement.

Larger foundations generally have well-defined investment processes, but in these cases their board members tend to be removed from the tradeoffs necessarily made in investment management. Particularly in smaller foundations, we view the process of reaching consensus itself to be an opportunity to engage board members more directly.

HOW ARE FOUNDATION FUNDS DIFFERENT FROM OTHER INSTITUTIONAL FUNDS?

What sets foundations apart? The trustees of a foundation are in an extraordinary position to determine what their liabilities are: many of their liabilities are actually contingent on the decisions they make.

The trustees of a charitable organization generally have some ability to define who their stakeholders are and what the stakeholders' interests may be in addition to fundamental fiduciary responsibility; the trustees then have the responsibility of balancing those interests.

Subject to legal requirements such as the minimum 5% payout and excise tax, or others, which also tend to be contingent in nature, such as some percentage of an account balance on a certain date, the trustees have the ability to determine the following:

- The discretionary status of the funds, which rests with the trustees in grantmaking foundations.
- The balance between future and current expenditures, and a baseline for what constitutes stability. This tends to be a delicate balance between current operations and the proposed growth rate of operations in an operating foundation.
- The tradeoffs to be made between operating expenses versus capital expenditures. These typically can be reallocated and either slowed or accelerated at the trustees' discretion, at least within limits.

By way of contrast, the largest institutional funds, at least in the United States, can be broken down between defined benefit plans and defined contribution plans. Both are retirement benefit structures governed by the Employee Retirement Income Security Act (ERISA).

Defined benefit plans have liabilities determined by several factors, such as compensation, ages of employees, longevity, and so on. These liabilities are determined and reviewed under relatively well-defined actuarial rules.

Defined contribution plans face only the liability of providing funds equal to ending balances. But these ending balances in terms of amounts and timing are largely determined by external factors that are not under a sponsor's control.

THE FIDUCIARY OBLIGATIONS OF FOUNDATIONS

In organizing our understanding of the fiduciary obligation of foundations, some codified guiding rules for fiduciary investing provide direction and stability to an organization: the Uniform Prudent Investor Act (UPIA). In the following discussion, we will extract from the UPIA information relevant for a fiduciary trustee and attempt to develop a framework for oversight responsibilities.

After this brief discussion, we'll describe some of the investment tools used by institutional investors that can serve as an investing vocabulary. In our context, we hope it provides a language for negotiation among stakeholders; to give one example: "We are willing to accept X percentage more volatility to attempt to reach Y goal, but we also expect full effective diversification." By the end of this chapter, our hope is that the previous sentence will be intelligible.

UNIFORM PRUDENT INVESTOR ACT (UPIA)

To begin with, we must note that the various enactments of the UPIA do not specifically refer to foundations; however, they seem to argue for similar treatment in the statement that follows: "In making investments of trust funds the trustee of a Charitable Trust is under a duty similar to that of the trustee of a private trust" [Restatement of Trust, second paragraph 389, 1959].

Even though the UPIA applies to private trusts and not to charitable corporations, the 1992 Restatement observes, "the duties of the members of the governing board of a charitable corporation are generally similar to the duties of a trustee or Charitable Trust" [Restatement of Trust, third Prudent Investor Rule paragraph 379]. How does the UPIA relate to the investment of funds for a charitable organization or corporation? As previously stated, it is "expected to inform" the trustees. Ignoring its provisions is probably not wise for a trustee.

The more relevant provisions of the UPIA for a charitable trustee are included in the following sections.

Section 2: Standard of Care, Portfolio Strategy, Risk and Return Objectives

Although this section is somewhat complicated, the relevant portion reads: "A trustee's investment management decisions respecting individual assets must be evaluated not in isolation but in the context of the trust portfolio as a whole and as a part of an overall investment strategy having risk and return objectives reasonably suited to the trust."

Implication for trustees. As part of the reporting process, rather than discussions about individual stocks, or theories of the economy, investment managers should report on how a particular asset or asset class impacted the returns and the expected risk, how they measured up to the risk expectations adopted *a priori*, and devote some time to developing and understanding, at the board level, whether expectations have changed and what expectations should be for the future. For those experienced in hearing investment reports, this will sound very different from discussions about why one company or another rose or fell in value during the reporting period or why a particular style of investing is in or out of favor.

Section 3: Diversification

"A trustee shall diversify the investments of the trust unless the trustee reasonably determines that, because of special circumstances, the purposes of a trust are better served without diversifying."

Implication for trustees. This section of the UPIA develops the idea of compensated and uncompensated risk. A risk is compensated if it results in the opportunity for an increased return; financial markets, however, do not compensate risk in the case of a failure to diversify. Therefore, a trustee's failure to diversify effectively involves an unjustifiable risk (and, thus, probably a breach of duty) because there is no expected or consistent compensation for assuming that risk (see Exhibit 5.1).

Lesser Importance

Greater Importance

Liquidity Risk

Credit Risk

Interest Rate Risk

Volatility Risk

Higher Risk For Mis-Estimation Of Time Horizon Or Risk Tolerance

Company Risk

Sector Risk

Asset Class Risk

Investment Style Risk

Investment Manager Risk

Compensated Risks: Risks deliberately accepted in the expectation of higher returns.

Liquidity Risk: CD's, GIC's, direct real estate investment, private equity, venture capital.

Credit Risk: High yield securities expected to return more over time after credit losses ("junk bonds").

Interest Rate Risk: Longer duration bonds normally return more than shorter maturity instruments.

Volatility Risks: Equities (stocks) generally have more variability of return than, say, Tbills over shorter time horizons.

Uncompensated Risks: Risks often mistakenly accepted in the quest for higher returns but which could be diversified away. Modern Portfolio Theory says reasonably efficient markets will not consistently reward the acceptance of diversifiable risk.

Company Risk: The risk that a specific company stock may do extremely well or poorly; this is the most widely understood uncompensated risk.

Sector Risk: The dominant element of stock returns is often its capital market sector, communications for example, in which a company is represented. Owning twenty telephone stocks does not avoid this hazard.

Asset Class Risk: Avoidance of, or simply missing, a major asset class such as real estate, international stocks, emerging markets, etc., means elimination of a powerful risk reduction mechanism.

Investment Style Risk: Each manager seeks to achieve high returns through an approach to the capital markets that will strongly influence and group returns. Over shorter time horizons, style group returns can and will diverge strongly from "the market" and each other, though they will converge over long enough periods.

Investment Manager Risk: The risk that a specific organization will not continue to perform well relative to its style grouping or other performance benchmark for personnel, technical, or managerial reasons.

Exhibit 5.1 Investment Risks and the U.P.I.A.

Section 5: Loyalty

"A trustee shall invest and manage the trust assets solely in the interest of the beneficiaries. No form of 'social investing' is consistent with the duty of loyalty if the investment activity entails sacrifice in the interest of trust beneficiaries—for example, by accepting below-market returns in favor of the interest of the person supposedly benefited by pursuing the particular social cause. People who are in favor of socially directed investing bear the burden of demonstrating that a particular method of social investing does not or may not result in below-market returns."

Implications for trustees. If a particular foundation desires to veer from the best economic interests of its beneficiaries, as part of its mission or for other fundamental reasons relating to its eleemosynary charter, then the controlling language must have specific enabling language to override the UPIA concept. The UPIA serves as default, which is always subject to being overwritten by specific language. Note also that it is generally unlikely that the organization—and thus the organization's current and future employees—are specific beneficiaries of the foundation. So is it true that the staff are specific stakeholders for purposes of beneficiary analysis? Perhaps yes; perhaps no. What's best is if an explicit analysis is undertaken.

Section 6: Impartiality

"If a trust has two or more beneficiaries, the trustee should act impartially in investing and managing the trust assets, taking into account any differing interest in the beneficiaries."

Implication for trustees. This is the primary area where current versus future expenditures need to be taken into account. Are currently unnamed beneficiaries actually stakeholders? How much emphasis should be given to organizational stability versus program growth? Who are our stakeholders, and where do their interests coincide or conflict? These debates are covered further under our discussion of spending policy agreements.

Section 9: Delegation of Investment and Management Functions

"A trustee may delegate investment and management functions that a prudent trustee of comparable skills could properly delegate under the circumstances. Among other things, the trustee shall exercise reasonable care, skill, and caution in selecting an agent and periodically reviewing the agent's actions in order to monitor the agent's performance and compliance with the terms of the delegation."

Implication for trustees. The same standards for reporting that are necessary under the standard of care are necessary to fulfill obligations under the delegation sections of the UPIA.

UNDERSTANDING FINANCIAL MARKETS

With the basic knowledge of fiduciary obligation in hand, an equally basic level of understanding of investment markets seems to us to be necessary for trustees to fulfill their fiduciary obligations.

For most, needed general knowledge of the market tends to be somewhat philosophical in nature. The fiduciaries' concern with prudence, and prudence in this context, seems to apply particular focus on portfolio structure, including diversification. What are the acceptable risks of a downturn? What should be traded for higher future expected returns? How much return do we need to meet our organizational objectives?

We'll begin by showing how various asset mixes have performed since World War II. This is not, of course, a full set of asset classes, but it includes the critical classes of stocks, bonds, and cash and is the best form we know that shows the tradeoffs between expected risk and expected return, primary and absolute return (see Exhibit 5.2).

As we'll discuss later, these are major asset classes used in any asset allocation, although not a complete listing. A rather distinct implication of Exhibit 5.2 is that any selected portfolio requires periodic rebalancing or rebalancing under some set of discipline rules.

One Year Returns
January 1950 - June 2001

Legend: Largest Loss | Average Return | Largest Gain

Portfolio Mix:	Year Ending 6/01	Largest Loss	Average Loss	Average Return	Average Gain	Largest Gain	Percent Negative	Percent Positive	Percent of Returns Greater Than Inflation
90% Stocks No Bonds 10% Cash	-12.8%	-34.3%	-7.1%	13.2%	18.2%	55.9%	20%	80%	73%
80% Stocks 10% Bonds 10% Cash	-10.3%	-30.2%	-6.1%	12.4%	16.7%	52.5%	18%	82%	73%
70% Stocks 20% Bonds 10% Cash	-7.8%	-26.2%	-5.4%	11.7%	15.0%	49.1%	16%	84%	73%
60% Stocks 30% Bonds 10% Cash	-5.3%	-22.2%	-4.4%	10.9%	13.5%	45.7%	15%	85%	73%
50% Stocks 40% Bonds 10% Cash	-2.8%	-18.2%	-3.5%	10.1%	12.1%	42.3%	13%	87%	72%
40% Stocks 50% Bonds 10% Cash	-0.2%	-14.1%	-2.9%	9.3%	10.7%	38.9%	10%	90%	72%
30% Stocks 60% Bonds 10% Cash	2.3%	-10.1%	-2.3%	8.5%	9.4%	35.5%	8%	92%	72%
20% Stocks 70% Bonds 10% Cash	4.8%	-6.1%	-1.9%	7.8%	8.3%	32.1%	5%	95%	71%
10% Stocks 80% Bonds 10% Cash	7.3%	-3.9%	-1.3%	7.0%	7.4%	28.9%	5%	95%	69%
No Stocks 90% Bonds 10% Cash	9.8%	-4.2%	-1.4%	6.2%	7.1%	30.2%	11%	89%	63%

The Consumer Price Index for June 2001 is preliminary.

Data: Rolling 1 year returns using monthly data (606 Observations).

Stocks: Standard & Poor's 500 Stock Index • Bonds: 5 Year Treasury Bonds • Cash: 90-Day Treasury Bills • Inflation: Consumer Price Index

Sources: Standard & Poor's Corporation; Ryan Labs, Inc.; Lehman Brothers; Bureau u of Labor Statistics; Copyright © 2001 Crandall, Pierce & Company • All rights reserved.

238S-1   Copyright © 2001 CRANDALL, PIERCE & COMPANY • All rights reserved • 14047 West Petronella Drive #103 • Libertyville, Illinois 60048 • 1-800-272-6355 • Internet: www.crandallpierce.com   -CLXXXIV-

Exhibit 5.2   Asset Allocation—Risk & Reward

Each asset class grows at a different rate; a balanced asset allocation at one point is highly unlikely to remain so for more than a year or so at a time. This drift from one allocation to another can expose a portfolio to unwanted risks that are not appropriate to the level of expected return chosen. To explore this topic further, we'll add additional asset classes. Because some asset classes are not easily measured, the time series is somewhat shorter than our previous graphic (see Exhibit 5.3).

As opposed to Exhibit 5.2, Exhibit 5.3 shows another, more academic way of looking at risk. We'll discuss this a bit further as follows, where risk is viewed as the standard deviation of expected returns. Although we believe this formulation is useful—and it is widely used by institutional investors—we do not think it is entirely relevant to many investment decisions.

One can easily see how difficult it is to determine the top-performing asset class in advance. Even though the calendar year is an artificial period of time, significant variation exists from one asset class to another. It is also constructive to note how well a straightforward, strategic asset allocation does in comparison by smoothing investment returns and allowing a constant investment posture.

THE LANGUAGE OF MODERN PORTFOLIO THEORY

Early on, we promised you a language for stakeholder negotiations: the language of modern portfolio theory (MPT). What we will attempt to provide next is the equivalent of an abridged but straightforward introduction to a language: a beginning lesson in conversation, not one that aims for the fluency of a native speaker. Delegated investment advisors should be able to provide an investment committee with the full complement of terms and concepts, explain each in more depth, and describe how each fits into the foundation trustee's fiduciary obligation. The order of definition is somewhat difficult because many of the definitions are intertwined. We ask for your patience; hopefully all will be clear by the end of our discussion.

Year	S&P 500 Growth	S&P 500 Value	Small Cap	Bonds	International	Real Estate	Emerging Markets	Equity Aggressive Strategy Mix	Aggressive Strategy Mix	Balanced Strategy Mix
1979	15.72	21.16	43.09	4.97	6.18	35.86	-	24.25	16.66	12.94
1980	39.40	23.59	38.58	5.51	24.43	24.36	-	33.07	26.68	20.79
1981	-9.81	0.02	2.03	8.95	-1.03	6.02	-	-1.96	-0.56	1.52
1982	22.03	21.04	24.95	28.87	-0.86	21.60	-	20.82	18.38	20.83
1983	16.24	28.89	29.13	9.01	24.61	30.64	-	25.19	22.24	18.64
1984	2.33	10.52	-7.30	14.74	7.86	20.93	-	2.62	6.39	9.33
1985	33.31	29.68	31.05	19.79	58.73	19.07	-	32.30	33.37	29.65
1986	14.50	21.67	5.68	13.32	69.94	19.17	-	18.78	27.02	24.27
1987	6.50	3.68	-8.77	3.86	24.93	-3.65	-	3.25	8.51	7.77
1988	11.95	21.67	24.89	7.38	28.59	13.47	-	20.01	20.14	17.18
1989	36.40	26.13	16.24	13.64	10.80	8.84	61.51	26.98	23.01	20.26
1990	0.20	-6.85	-19.51	9.75	-23.20	-15.34	-2.20	-8.26	-6.63	-2.06
1991	38.37	22.56	46.05	14.96	12.50	35.54	39.54	33.81	27.17	23.13
1992	5.07	10.53	18.41	7.10	-11.85	14.52	3.29	9.40	6.21	6.24
1993	1.68	18.60	18.91	8.07	32.94	19.67	79.61	17.73	18.60	14.97
1994	3.14	-0.64	-1.82	-1.76	8.06	3.17	-12.00	-0.52	-0.15	-0.27
1995	38.13	37.00	28.44	15.83	11.55	15.25	-8.42	29.45	24.20	22.41
1996	23.97	21.99	16.49	4.54	6.36	35.26	9.38	20.81	17.30	14.63
1997	36.54	29.99	22.36	8.46	2.06	20.29	-14.74	26.81	21.68	19.24
1998	42.15	14.68	-2.55	7.85	20.33	-17.51	-22.01	17.86	17.16	15.96
1999	28.25	12.73	21.26	0.99	27.30	-4.62	67.11	21.70	20.02	15.96
2000	-22.08	6.08	-3.02	10.63	-13.96	26.35	-31.76	-8.15	-7.19	-4.00
Average Annual Returns	17.45	17.03	15.66	9.84	14.74	14.95	14.11	10.91	9.24	7.37
Growth of $100.00 1979-2000	$2,559.46	$2,871.74	$1,892.57	$769.67	$1442.52	$1,757.40	$273.33*	$2,556.78	$2,123.60	$1,685.35
Annualized Returns 1979-2000	16.08	16.49	14.30	9.65	12.90	13.92	8.74*	15.87	14.90	13.70
Annualized Std. Dev. 1979-2000	16.59	14.44	19.48	5.36	17.04	12.93	23.02*	14.72	12.15	9.75

Individual asset classes represented by the following indices: S&P 500 Growth; S&P 500 Value : Small Cap = Russell 2000; Bonds=Lehman Brothers Intermediate Aggregate Bond; International = MSCI EAFE; Real Estate = NAREIT Equity; Emerging Markets = S&P/IFC Composite. Asset Allocated mixes are represented by the following: Equity Aggressive = 60% S&P 500, 25% Russell 2000, 5% MSCI EAFE, 5% NAREIT Equity, 5% S&P/IFC Composite; Aggressive = 42% S&P 500, 11% Russell 2000, 18% Lehman Brothers Intermediate Aggregate Bond, 5% NAREIT Equity, 19% MSCI EAFE, 5% S&P/IFC Composite; Balanced = 32% S&P 500, 41% Lehman Brothers Intermediate Aggregate Bond, 5% Russell 2000, 14% MSCI EAFE, 5% NAREIT Equity, 3% S&P/IFC Composite. Prior to 1985, S&P/IFC Composite allocation were placed in the MSCI EAFE. Mixes are rebalanced annually. Indexes are unmanaged and cannot be invested in directly. Copyright © 2001 Halbert, Hargrove/Russell LLC. All rights reserved.

*1989-2000

Exhibit 5.3 Single Asset vs. Multi-Asset Portfolios: Best Performing Asset Class by Year—Multi-Asset Strategy Performance

The essence of MPT is that the overall portfolio is more important than any individual component. One can describe a portfolio by analyzing the expected return of each asset class, determining the correlation among asset classes, and then evaluating and understanding the variance in returns period to period in each asset class.

MPT is not very "modern" in the sense that it was first developed by Harry Markowitz in the early 1950s; further developments and derivatives ensued over the next 30 years or so, which earned Markowitz, William Sharpe, and Merton Miller a shared Nobel Prize in Economics.

The structure of MPT allows investors to use computer analysis to estimate tradeoffs between risk and return. Critically, the inputs to a computer model can come from various sources: they can be historical actual numbers, estimated long-term numbers, or short-term forecasts that are continually modified based on any number of systems. Trustees should be comfortable with the source of the inputs to the computer models being used by their advisors. Models are extraordinarily sensitive to changes in input, particularly so with expected returns.

In fact, MPT is a workable description of reasonably efficient capital markets over time. Its most important contribution is its global focus on portfolio risk and return—rather than on component parts. Modern portfolio theory has had value beyond its predictive applications. From the outset, it provided a language for discussion among investment professionals (although many may call it a language for arguing among investment professionals).

Let us first, in a reasonably nontechnical fashion, attempt to define some of the critical terms. We can then see how MPT can aid in portfolio construction, evaluation of portfolio performance, and dialogue among stakeholders.

- *Expected return.* This is in fact exactly what it says: The amount one would expect, over some time horizon, that a particular asset class would deliver in relation to a risk-free return such as Treasury Bills.

The last few years of investment history are likely not a reliable guide to the future. Equity returns have been so far above historic norms that they are probably not sustainable. The most useful analysis of recent historical patterns is provided by another tool that we will discuss, Monte Carlo simulation.

- *Variance ("risk")*. This is the academic's definition of risk. Risk is defined as the variability of returns that fall around the expected return of any particular asset type. Originally, due to limitations in computing power, variance was measured by the standard deviation of returns. Using standard deviation assumes a particular distribution of returns around the expected return, called a *normal distribution* (the "bell curve" of past dreaded statistics classes). There has been a great deal of discussion about this distribution, but in fact, for most asset classes, the returns are close enough to make it a useful description (see Exhibits 5.4 and 5.5).

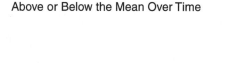

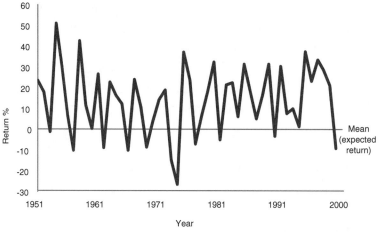

Exhibit 5.4   Expected Risk Concept

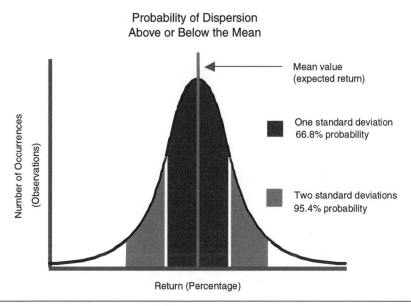

Exhibit 5.5   Expected Risk Measurement

This academic measure of risk, standard deviation, which is accepted because of its ease of computation regarding statistics of normal distributions, leaves many with an apparent logical inconsistency: Who really cares about volatility above the mean expected return? That is, most of us look at risk as the possibility or probability of losing money, not the probability of making more than we expected.

- *Correlation.* Correlation describes the relationship among discrete asset classes. In investment management, correlations indicate whether asset classes move virtually in tandem or do not have much relation to each other in their movement—or whether there is an inverse relationship, in which they tend to move in opposite directions in a fairly predictable fashion (see Exhibit 5.6).

- *Asset class.* This concept refers to a group of investments that have statistically similar expected return, variance, and correlation characteristics. Thus, one can statistically determine an

Relationship Between Two Quantities
Such That When One Changes, the Other Does as Well

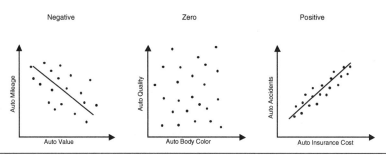

Exhibit 5.6   Expected Correlation Concept

asset class by simply looking at the pattern of returns of large pools of investments over time and then categorizing them. We normally think of asset classes as U.S. Equity (Large Cap), Non-U.S. Equity, U.S. Equity (Small Cap), Emerging Markets, U.S. Bonds (Fixed Income), U.S. Cash (Money Markets or Treasury Bills), and Real Estate. Other types of asset classes are now emerging, such as hedge funds and private equity, for which we have less knowledge of benchmarks (see Exhibit 5.7).

It must be apparent by now that we are coming close to an explanation of the thrust of the UPIA's cautionary guiding rules for investing; mixing assets with low or negative correlations dampens risk (see Exhibit 5.8).

The proper asset class allocation question for a trustee is: Did we receive enough risk control benefits to offset the return reductions from diversifying? As fiduciaries, we have to diversify, so we won't do as well as if we had picked the best asset class or as poorly as if we had picked the worst asset class. In our case, risk control might mean raising the level of accepted

Coefficient of Correlation
Measures Strength & Direction of Correlation

Asset Class

	1	2	3	4	5	6	7
1: US Equity(Large Cap)	1						
2: Non-US Equity	0.5	1					
3: US Equity Small Cap	0.9	0.4	1				
4: Emerging Markets	0.3	0.3	0.3	1			
5: US Bonds	0.4	0.2	0.3	0	1		
6: US Cash	0	0	0	0	0.2	1	
7: Real Estate	0.1	0.1	0.1	0	0	0.3	1

Exhibit 5.7   Expected Correlation Measurement

Mixing Partially Uncorrelated Assets
Can Reduce a Portfolio's Overall Risk

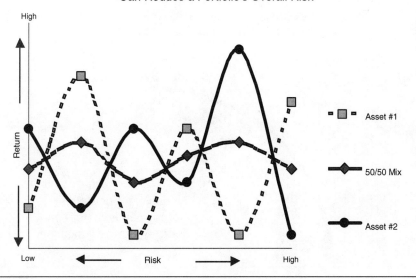

Exhibit 5.8   Risk Dampening

risk to meet our goals or lowering it to lower our risk to appropriate levels. Getting to this point is our fundamental approach and our fundamental question.

- *Efficient frontier*. The efficient frontier is a graphical construct that displays the historical or expected performances of different asset classes over time. At any level of risk one would always want mixes to achieve the highest level of expected return. At any level of expected return, one would always want to have the lowest level of risk. "Efficient" portfolios are those whose combination of assets displayed these optimal levels of risk versus return. What is often lost in discussion is that the efficient frontier is used to display asset allocations based on expected returns and correlations and cannot be known until after the fact (see Exhibit 5.9).

Investment advisors are often asked whether the best portfolio is "A," "B," or "C" in Exhibit 5.9. The answer in a fidu-

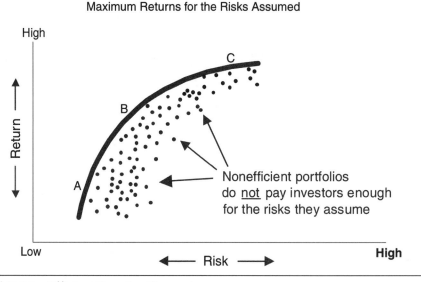

Exhibit 5.9 Efficient Frontier Concept

ciary sense is that one should have a portfolio on the efficient frontier to fulfill UPIA guidelines. Which portfolio should be selected becomes an issue of what expected return is required.

- *Efficient market theory, strong form.* This theory states that all the information contained in security prices is reflected immediately. Everyone knows everything at the same time, and price patterns are random and unpredictable. Those who believe in the strong form of efficient market theory tend to practice rigorous passive investing, utilizing index funds or exchange-traded funds.

- *Efficient market theory, weak form.* This form of efficient market theory also predicates that price and volume information have no predictive value, and agrees that no automatic trading rules can be established that can "beat the averages." Those who subscribe to this theory believe that active managers can develop sources of information that will enable them to forecast returns that are different from general market expectations. For these proponents, the mix of active and passive investments is a function of how far one is willing to vary from a benchmark (known as *residual risk*).

Weak form theorists tend to be less dogmatic in their beliefs. They state several reasons why markets are not perfectly efficient, although they are mostly efficient most of the time:

- Investors engage in nonrational behavior; this is generally studied under the heading of behavioral finance.
- There are differences in the interpretation of economic events and market activities that cause investors to behave differently, to the profit of some more than others.
- There are clientele effects in investments. The most notable of these is the fact that retail mutual funds and fixed-income investments compete in the marketplace based on current yield, which is often counterproductive to total returns. The retail clientele demands an attribute that is not in their best economic interests.

EFFECTIVE DIVERSIFICATION

Another useful definition that we will add, although it is not part of the lexicon of MPT, is the idea of effective diversification. We have graphically displayed the concept of a strategic allocation in Exhibit 5.9, but such an allocation requires true diversification, not just a high number of securities. The year 2000 offered a prime example of why holding 50 different technology stocks didn't constitute effective diversification.

We believe that a fiduciary must include all of the major asset classes unless there is an explicit reason not to include them in the controlling charter. The markets have taught us that it is not possible to know in advance which asset classes will do better or worse—at least on a consistent basis.

We also believe, as is true with most institutional investors, that multiple specialists and managers, multiple investment styles, and the addition of both active and passive management are all appropriate to achieve effective diversification.

Why do we think effective diversification is so important? After all, isn't it true that stocks always win in the long run? The true answer to this question is that stocks usually win in the long run, but that not all of us will survive to reach that long-run target.

The two exhibits that follow really tell the story. Returns from any particular asset class do tend to narrow over time. As Exhibit 5.10 shows, in Year One the expected return from U.S. Equities might be about 11 percent, but, in order not to have violated your expectations, you would have had to take on an acceptable range of return of between about minus 20 and plus 55 percent (two standard deviations). Yet, over 10 years or so, the range narrows rather dramatically, as can be seen at the right end of the graphic.

What is true historically for returns, however, is not indicative of what happens to ending wealth. Ending wealth actually diverges over time, which is the subject of much confusion in investment literature.

Exhibit 5.11 shows that, over long periods, relatively small differences in annual return can make huge differences in ending wealth. When this reality is coupled with the twin megaliths of asset allocation

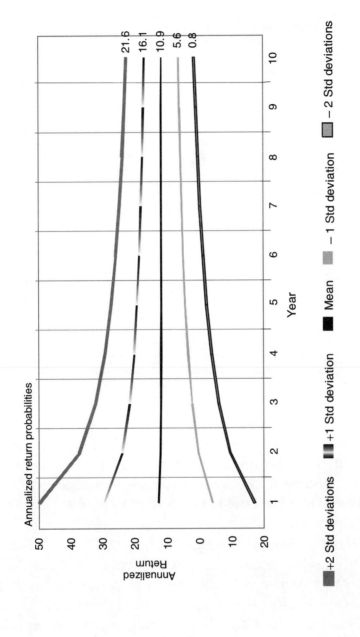

Exhibit 5.10 Effect of Time on "Risk"

149

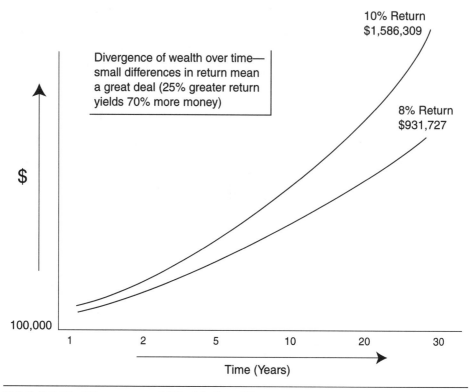

Exhibit 5.11   Divergence of Wealth Over Time

decisions and spending policy for draw down, one aspect of stake-holders' consensus becomes resoundingly clear. One can see why we believe that the central function of the trustee—making these tradeoffs—is critical to the foundation, and why nonparticipation tends to disenfranchise those trustees who are not involved in these decisions.

MPT is not a perfect description of the way the world works, but it is a highly useful mechanism and vocabulary for discussing explicit tradeoffs between risk and return. It is not terribly useful to couch a discussion from the perspective of "I don't want to risk . . ." There will always be the risk that some outcome or another is in danger; the central decision is which set of outcomes are most important and which we are willing to take the most risk to achieve.

BEHAVIORAL FINANCE

Our review of modern portfolio theory leads us to believe that a foundation should hold a portfolio that is efficient; that is, it lies somewhere on the efficient frontier. It should also be appropriate in that it has the right level of risk for the level of expected return that the foundation's goals and objectives require. As a practical matter, the portfolio should also be relatively stable. In other words, we should not have to change our investments every short while based on new information. We know from investment theory that new information is as likely as not to be counterproductive, because historically it has had relatively little bearing on long-term outcomes.

When we actually view investor behavior in action, however, it seems more accurate to say that investors act in the following ways:

- They make bold forecasts about the future.
- They make timid decisions to actually invest.
- They are liable to reverse their decisions or make inconsistent decisions at different times or under otherwise similar circumstances.

Many cognitive researchers suggest that there appears to be substantial evidence that the decisions we make are actually made unconsciously in specialized parts of the brain. Once the decision is made, it is relayed to the conscious mind, which proceeds to build a rationale for the decision. Such unconscious behavior is necessary for speed in relatively primitive situations, which is explained by its evolutionary roots; it is problematic, though, in the complex world of financial decision making.

The field of behavioral finance draws on the research of many academic disciplines, including cognitive psychology, in theorizing why investors often make poor investment decisions: Why can't they seem to learn from past mistakes? Why do they ignore a plethora of information that argues against certain investment moves?

There are four characteristics of investor behavior that are particularly applicable to trustees and foundations:

- *Loss aversion.* We know that, in general, people find losses approximately 2 to 2.5 times as unpleasant as gains are pleasant. This is what we refer to when we call people loss averse. A highly explicit risk and return tradeoff is required to get many, or even most, people to accept an appropriate level of risk in either their own investments or an investment pool for which they bear responsibility.
- *The "do-something" impulse.* The media around all of us are information peddlers. They want to get investors to take their subscription, buy their magazine, listen to their news show, hit their Web site. But data, and even information that is flowing in, do not necessarily carry any importance for investment decisions and are in fact normally just noise. Again, as human beings, we have a disposition to act when we hear information. A key benefit of both an investment policy agreement and the delegation of investment decisions to a separate committee of more sophisticated investors, is that the do-something impulse can be tempered by good judgment and a disciplined investment process.
- *Herding.* The tendency, when faced with uncertainty or complexity, to want to know what "they" are doing, since "they" must know something, coupled with the fear of straying too far from what "they" are doing.
- *Reputation risk.* This is the concept of agency risk. That is, either those trustees who may have a relatively short remaining tenure or staff members who may be rotating in function decide that it is not in their best interests to take on risk in return for long-term return benefits to the foundation. The refrain "not on my watch" has been heard in many a boardroom. John Maynard Keynes said it best: "Worldly wisdom teaches that it is better for reputation to fail conventionally than to succeed unconventionally."

The effects of what behavioral finance has observed, however, are far from trivial. As a central proposition, a foundation should attempt to reduce such effects wherever possible. Our experience has been that simple knowledge of these effects is not sufficient; we like to use the eyeglass analogy. Suppose that I have weak vision. I can try to memorize my environment, so I'll know what to anticipate as I move through it, but the better solution would be either surgery or eyeglasses. In the same manner, we think building a structure around the human propensity to make errors of decision or implementation is far superior to simple education.

In Exhibit 5.12, we can look at retail mutual fund investors to see the rather horrifying magnitude of errors largely introduced by investor financial behavior considerations. Dalbar analyzed mutual fund flows versus stated performance to determine industrywide effects from the widespread tendency to "chase performance." If, as

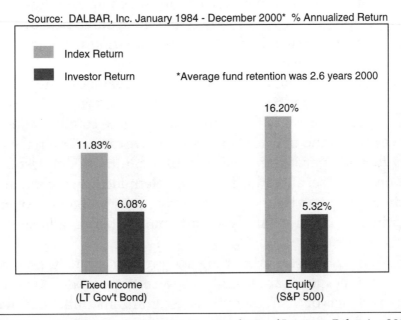

Source: DALBAR, Inc. January 1984 - December 2000* % Annualized Return

Index Return

Investor Return   *Average fund retention was 2.6 years 2000

16.20%

11.83%

6.08%   5.32%

Fixed Income   Equity
(LT Gov't Bond)   (S&P 500)

Exhibit 5.12   DALBAR, Inc. Quantitative Analysis of Investor Behavior 2001

some commentators believe, the next decade is likely to see much lower gross market returns, perhaps in the 6 to 8 percent annual range, what will our trend-following retail investors earn?

MONTE CARLO SIMULATION

As powerful as MPT and its means/variance optimizers are, even when we apply them in combination with our knowledge of the anomalies that stem from behavioral finance, our arsenal still lacks a method of dealing with issues concerning the pattern of returns and the timing of losses and/or withdrawals. These are critical to understanding investment portfolios and are in fact crucial to the long-term retention and growth of a foundation's fund assets.

The timing of losses and gains, and withdrawals and contributions, is extremely important. Obscured by averages and expectations, real dollars go into and come out of a portfolio as contributions or foundation-designated spending. Markets go up and down with lack of predictability, except that they will in fact go up and down.

The graph in Exhibit 5.13 shows how small differences in average returns impacted by the timing of losses or distributions can make an enormous difference in ending wealth.

A Monte Carlo simulation provides, organizes, and analyzes possible scenarios for combinations of asset class returns, generally drawn from historical data. From running these combinations over and over again, and developing scenarios, we can ascertain the probability that any particular scenario will occur. In its simplest framework, once an asset allocation has been determined, an accompanying spending policy can be analyzed to arrive at its probability of eating into principal or successfully maintaining inflation-adjusted purchasing power.

Even though scenario building and probability analysis are powerful techniques that can usefully supplement a model constructed within the tenets of MPT, there are still significant limitations. Part of the reason we believe so strongly in diversification is that all of our economic history is simply that: our economic history.

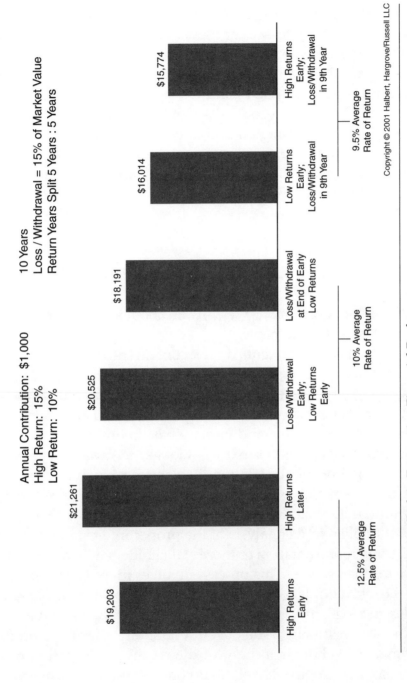

Annual Contribution: $1,000
High Return: 15%
Low Return: 10%

10 Years
Loss / Withdrawal = 15% of Market Value
Return Years Split 5 Years : 5 Years

$19,203 — High Returns Early
$21,261 — High Returns Later
$20,525 — Loss/Withdrawal Early; Low Returns Early
$18,191 — Loss/Withdrawal at End of Early Low Returns
$16,014 — Low Returns Early; Loss/Withdrawal in 9th Year
$15,774 — High Returns Early; Loss/Withdrawal in 9th Year

12.5% Average Rate of Return
10% Average Rate of Return
9.5% Average Rate of Return

Copyright © 2001 Halbert, Hargrove/Russell LLC

Exhibit 5.13 Timing Risk in Forecasting Financial Performance

Without needing to explore alternative universes in the science fiction sense, it's easy to see that several world events might have turned out differently. A simple example should suffice to make this point. Around 1900, Japan accounted for some 3 percent of world gross domestic product (GDP) and Germany roughly 5 percent. Investments made in those economies would have done well for a significant period, but passing through the destruction of World War II would have left an investor's fortune in tatters. On the flip side of that coin, of course, are the positive developments of the United States, but what if this had been reversed?

SPENDING AND INVESTMENT POLICY AGREEMENTS

In the following few sections we will talk about spending policy and investment policy agreements.

Usually, these documents do not contain the word *agreement* in the name. If anything, they are referred to as a *statement*. Perhaps this is a small thing, but we think semantics are important in reminding all parties about how a foundation originally arrived at a policy, how the policy can be changed, and under what circumstances.

The word *policy* implies that it is a longer-term and more fundamental decision of the foundation. It is changeable, but in order to change the policy, a designated process must be followed rather than daily whim or fluctuations in the current market. Likewise, the term *agreement* implies some analysis of the proper interest of stakeholders and some representation of those stakeholders who do not speak directly for themselves. This process involves identifying the possible pool of stakeholders and then applying their interests alongside the rules and logic of the UPIA. Not everyone who may have an interest in the investment results of a foundation's charitable funds is a legitimate stakeholder in light of the fiduciary obligation of the trustees; similarly, some less obvious considerations may need to be explicitly recognized, as we have discussed previously.

We suggest the use of the tools we have described, especially using mean variance optimizers to come up with an asset allocation expressing the constraints and the goals of the investment policy agreement. At the same time, we would suggest the use of Monte Carlo analysis to determine whether spending policy is likely to be viable in the light of financial market realities. It should be immediately obvious that these processes are interactive. Clearly, a more aggressive spending policy requires a more aggressive investment policy, or a more aggressive development policy, or both.

The duties of loyalty and impartiality set forth by the UPIA will most likely place some limits on how aggressive an appropriate portfolio strategy can be, and properly force efforts toward the development side of the ledger. Financial professionals can help with modeling on both asset allocation and spending policy. But modeling is not decision making; this role is a proper function of the trustees.

SPENDING POLICY AGREEMENT

The creation of a viable spending policy should provoke varying viewpoints and values regarding these questions: How much should be spent on current versus future programs? Should the foundation spend more than the required 5 percent? How much risk of development success is warranted? How much does/should the organization rely on endowment distributions versus other revenue sources? How do we deal with the possible instability of distributions? There are some relatively standard rules of thumb that can be applied, but these tend to be dangerous in that they rely more heavily than is often realized on specific investment market experience. We recommend the use of all available analytical tools in our toolbox, including multi-period probability-based modeling, mean/variance analysis, and Monte Carlo analysis. We also recommend expert systems analysis to determine practical ranges of spending and to give solid, grounded guidance to staff and present and future board members. In the following section, we'll detail the various counterbalancing issues and decisions that all trustees face.

Issues and Opportunities

Conflicts among goals and policies can create ongoing tension between board and staff members when creating an endowment spending policy.

Potential economic and institutional objectives that may result in tradeoffs include the following:

- *Maximize long-term total return*. Implies smaller distributions for current institutional objectives and a higher-risk investment policy.
- *Maximize annual spending*. Implies penalizing future generations and growth of programs that may be unacceptable to the board and/or staff.
- *Maximize present value of spending*. This could be read as the same as annual spending, but it really is a balancing act between total return and annual spending.
- *Preserve wealth and purchasing power*. This places maximum restraints on distributions, which are limited to long-term, real (inflation-adjusted) earnings.
- *Maximize or optimize stability and predictability of spending*. Typically, long-term total return should be moderated in order to optimize stability and predictability.

In addition to internal conflicts, the capital markets themselves cause some tradeoff-related tensions:

- *The level of expected return is inversely correlated with the predictability of that return*. Long-term returns to stocks are much higher than most other basic asset classes, but the volatility of those returns is also higher than most other asset classes.

- *Purchasing power vs. stability.* When one is primarily concerned with stability, then annual return variability is increased by adding the variability of the current inflation rate.
- *Annual spending vs. long-run wealth.* Whether this is a discretionary spending policy or simply spending as in the case of an individual, anything not reinvested will negatively impact wealth in the long run.

These decisions are inherently difficult, interactive, and relatively continuous in nature.

Spending Policy Alternatives

The basic differences in spending policies may be described as follows:

- *Market driven.* This position means that whatever is earned in the current year will be spent, or perhaps can be smoothed out over a several-year period. This growth pattern does not assist in stability, but it may be inflation adjusted.
- *Constant growth.* This position implies that some relatively conservative number will be withdrawn each year. Any shortfalls must be made up by development policy or new funding sources.
- *"Snake in the tunnel."* This position is a combination of an expected growth rate and anticipated spending adjusted year by year depending on inflation adjustments, smoothing, and other factors that are agreed to in advance.
- *Dynamic.* This position is a forward-looking spending policy that continually adjusts for past performance, past development success, inflation, and expected returns on some conservative and disciplined basis. The most common policies use a rolling 12-quarter valuation against a stated percentage, usually 4.5 or 5.0 percent. Some policies use exponential calculations to overweight recent performance.

- *Discretionary.* The board can elect to remove funds at any time under any circumstances. The result of this type of policy is somewhat predictable.

Risks Associated with Policy Shortfalls

Specifically, what are the risks associated with policy shortfalls? They may include the following:

- *Permanent erosion of capital.* Funds spent in excess of earnings cannot earn future returns for future needs.
- *Budget shortfall.* This might be an interim operating shortfall, which may or may not be financeable by other sources.
- *Inflation.* Clearly, purchasing power risk for a permanent endowment is a critical consideration at all times.
- *Subpar performance of endowment.* This is the most likely outcome because lack of a disciplined and informed approach usually results in inefficient capital allocation and returns.

Budget Politics

What about what we call "budget politics"—and the appetite for spending? Some of the difficult issues in this area include the following:

- *Sticky costs.* As new programs are adopted, they tend to have ongoing funding needs that are difficult to cut off in midstream. Without stable funding, new programs are at risk.
- *Permanence of windfall.* Organizations often look at a windfall as if it were going to be repeated and start new programs that generate their own sticky costs as above.
- *Restricted vs. unrestricted funds.* Difficult issues arise for many foundations when restricted funds actually cause the incurrence of new operating costs and do not relieve other budget items.

- *Squirreling.* There is a tendency on the part of both staff and board members to hide reserve funds against future contingencies. While this reaction is normal and human, it must be analyzed and maintained as a reserve—not a management panacea.
- *Trustee resistance.* Trustees, normally volunteers, resist taking risks because the returns to those risks may well be "not on their watch" and not worth the risk to their reputations.

Additional potential stressors under the heading of budget politics include unrealistic capital market expectations, fluctuating government spending programs, the difficulty of maintaining inflation-adjusted fees for services, and an always-changing U.S. tax policy.

INVESTMENT POLICY AGREEMENT

As we move from spending policy agreements to investment policy agreements, we must always bear in mind that an investment policy agreement is not an asset allocation. It is often best to include an asset allocation within an investment policy, but they are truly different creations.

We should try to avoid generalities as much as possible when creating an investment policy agreement, although some are occasionally useful. If we use generalities, then we should define their parameters within the investment policy. By this, as an example, we mean defining aggressive as within the boundaries of a stated standard deviation of return, as the percentage of assets held in equities, or some other objective measurement. Typically, an investment policy agreement will have multiple goals. These might include the following:

- Creation of a policy that is clear to the board, the staff, and any advisors who are delegated to implement investment decisions.

- Serving as the basis for reporting and oversight. This is a basic function of the trustees, but it's usually shortchanged in traditional investment manager reports. The trustee should want to know whether performance has been within the bounds described in the investment policy. If performance falls outside the bounds—whether too high or too low—then questions should be raised on the portfolio level in terms of specific asset classes. Adherence to the known investment policy agreement and performance within its boundaries constitute a key evaluation point for review of investment managers.
- The investment policy agreement is a living document. It must be revisited on no less than an annual basis to see if circumstances have changed. Risk tolerance, for example, seems to shift in response to market action, even though, in all probability, the spending needs of the foundation have not shifted in that regard. We believe it is constructive to add discussions in terms of dollars as well as percentages because many stakeholders respond better to one form of information over another.

The following is an example of a summary investment policy agreement, which includes data on actual asset allocation and the way in which it will be reviewed.

INVESTMENT POLICY AGREEMENT
EXECUTIVE SUMMARY

Account Number:	5255555
Type of Account:	0
Taxable Account?	Yes
Current Market Value:	$4,107,776
Anticipated Annual Net Cash Flow:	($100,000)
Expected Investment Time Horizon:	15 Years
Client's Risk Tolerance:	Moderate

Investment Policy Agreement

Asset Allocation	Target Percentage	Permitted Range	Expected Return
US Stocks:			
Large Company	32%	29 to 35%	11.5%
Small Company	4%	1 to 7%	12.4%
International Stocks:			
Developed Markets	14%	11 to 17%	11.5%
Emerging Markets	3%	0 to 6%	13.0%
Real Estate:			
Real Estate Investment Trusts	5%	2 to 8%	9.7%
Fixed Income:			
Short-Term	0%	0 to 0%	6.7%
Intermediate-Term	40%	37 to 43%	8.2%
Long-Term	0%	0 to 0%	8.5%
Cash Equivalents:	2%	0 to 4%	5.5%
Total:	**100%**		

See Exhibit 5.14 for a target asset allocation chart and Exhibit 5.15 for a graphical representation of an efficient frontier.

Expected Portfolio Return and Volatility:

1-Year Expectations

Expected Annual Return	9.9%	$406,957
Expected Variability of Return (Standard Deviation)	10.2%	
68% confidence range (2 out of 3 yrs.)	–0.2% to 20.1%	($10,237)
95% confidence range (19 out of 20 yrs.)	–10.4% to 30.2%	($427,431)
Probability of annual return falling below:		
5.00%	31.6%	
0.00%	16.6%	
–5.00%	7.2%	($205,389)

15-Year Expectations

Expected Annual Compound Return	9.5%
Expected Variability of Return (Standard Deviation)	2.6%
68% confidence range	6.9% to 12.1%
95% confidence range	4.3% to 14.7%

See Exhibit 5.16 for the one-year holding period at a 95 percent confidence level.

This Investment Policy Agreement is used to illustrate the potential performance of a portfolio of assets based on client-specific time horizon, needs, and risk tolerance level. The standardized investment results presented are calculated using historical rates of return for each asset class. Expected return is a statistical concept, not a projection or estimate of future results. Further, this investment policy agreement is not intended to illustrate the expected results of any particular investment or combination of particular investments.

Overview

The purpose of this investment policy agreement is to assist the client and investment advisor in agreeing on an asset allocation, implementing portfolio investments, and providing a framework for evaluation of results.

Risk Tolerance

After analysis of goals and objectives, the client and investment advisor have determined that a moderate stance is appropriate. In establishing client's risk tolerance, the ability to withstand short- and intermediate-term variability was compared to various levels of expected return. Client's prospects for the future, current financial condition, future goals and objectives, and other factors suggest that some interim fluctuation in market value and rates of return must be tolerated in order to reach client's targets. The primary method of risk control will be effective diversification.

Time Horizon

The recommended investment strategy is based on an investment horizon of 15 years or more. Over the short term, both stocks and bond markets can be expected to be volatile. Historical one-year returns for the U.S. stock market have varied from positive 53 percent to negative 43 percent. One-year returns for U.S. bonds have varied from positive 44 percent to negative 8 percent. Client understands volatility of returns in the short term and has agreed to view cyclical fluctuations with appropriate perspective.

Asset Class Restrictions

A full range of asset classes may be utilized.

Portfolio Rebalancing

Over time, each asset class may build up to the maximum point within the permitted asset allocation range. At least quarterly, portfolio allocations will be checked to assure that asset class proportions remain within the permitted range. Corrective action will be taken as needed. Generally, nontaxable portfolios are rebalanced within a narrow band; taxable portfolios attempt to account for taxation as well.

Performance Measurement

Time-weighted rate of return measurements will be made at quarterly intervals for the portfolio as a whole and for each separate asset class. Rates of return will be compared to relative indexes for each asset class to assure that performance remains within acceptable ranges.

Investment Policy Agreement

Evaluation benchmarks for each asset class are as follows:

U.S. large company stocks
U.S. small company stocks
Non–U.S. stocks—developed markets
Non–U.S. stocks—emerging markets
Real estate investment trusts
Short-term bonds
Intermediate-term bonds
Cash equivalents

Duties and Responsibilities

Investment advisor will reach agreement with client about an appropriate asset allocation for client's investment portfolio. Investment advisor is then responsible for implementation of investment decisions, reporting on performance, being available to answer questions, and reviewing client needs as they may change, but no less than annually on a formal basis. All investment advisor responsibilities will be performed in accordance with published *Services and Standards*.

Client is responsible for providing investment advisor all relevant information on client financial conditions, goal and objective modifications, and/or changes in risk tolerance that may affect asset allocation decisions. Client agrees to read this investment policy agreement carefully and ask questions, as appropriate, to fully understand its provisions.

Adoption of Investment Policy Agreement

I (we) have agreed to the provisions outlined in this IPA. We agree that this document should be reviewed no less than annually and that modifications, if any, should be made in writing.

_____
Client Signature

_____
Client Signature

_____
Investment Advisor Signature

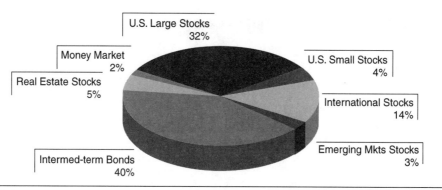

Exhibit 5.14   Target Asset Allocation

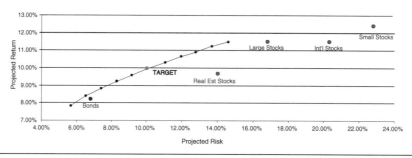

Exhibit 5.15   Efficient Frontier

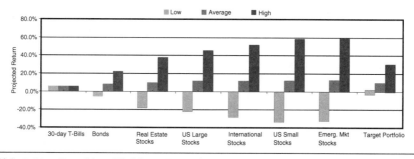

Exhibit 5.16   One-Year Holding Period @ 95% Confidence Level

What should trustee boards, and staff, take away from any discussion of investment or spending policy?

- The most important element for trustees is to have highly realistic return expectations in terms of the capital markets, and in terms of the possibilities and probabilities of actual results and timing from development activities.
- An efficient portfolio at the maximum risk comfortable for the institution, with a disciplined total return objective, will most likely optimize overall results in conjunction with spending policy.
- The institution should buffer windfalls from the pitfalls of creating permanent spending obligations and constantly balance market-driven and constant-growth strategies.
- One of the most important actions is to create an informed political and investment forum among the groups charged with investment and spending decisions and the group charged with overall control, typically the full board. This approach has the effect of stabilizing policy and reducing the unwanted risk of changing policy in midstream.

In traditional foundations, investment concerns are delegated to an investment committee that is quite possibly also charged with developing a spending policy to bring back to the full board. The investment committee frequently consists of either the wealthiest members of the board or those board members considered to have some special investment expertise. In any event, we do not think this is the optimal path for many foundations. Although it may be seen as avoiding the easy path, we view the stakeholder negotiation process as planting seeds of learning for both the board and staff. The resulting trees can bear fruit for many years to come. The process itself is not without an enormous commitment of energy and effort; it is unlikely to be successfully pursued in some small portion of a normal board meeting.

One of the reasons for these difficulties is that board members have different learning styles and certainly learn at a different pace.

Fortunately, learning theory abounds, consultants are available, and even donated services can assist the smallest foundation in many undertakings.

WHAT ARE THE BENEFITS OF STAKEHOLDER NEGOTIATION?

If it is true that "the central concern of a fiduciary is the tradeoff of all investing between risk and return" (UPIA), then perhaps the primary benefit of stakeholder negotiation can be seen as making that tradeoff explicit. Changing goals from unstated and implied to specific and stated is often a painful process. Further, it may require the rejection of some noncore opportunities that otherwise seem like a "good thing to do."

But the balance between risk and return may require even further definition. Making an explicit risk versus return tradeoff the central concern of a trustee requires explicit goals and objectives. The trustee must be able to reject noncore opportunities and focus on development activities whether they are aggressive or passive in nature.

To create specific goals and objectives, all stakeholders need to be identified, and the duty of impartiality requires balancing benefits among the appropriate beneficiaries (see Exhibit 5.17).

The informed exercise of fiduciary obligation can help to engage members of the board and become a very real benefit of serving on the board as members learn specific roles and obligations within their fiduciary duty. If an investment committee cannot articulate the goals and objectives and the explicit risk-versus-return tradeoffs, then a foundation board probably should not delegate these duties to that committee.

In many foundations, the board and the staff are chosen for their compatibility with the organizational mission—or perhaps their ability to raise funds. Neither of these qualities is necessarily a good indication of their ability to fulfill their fiduciary obligations under the UPIA. In addition, boards frequently face significant turnover, and it becomes necessary to reinvent the wheel each time this significant amount of turnover takes place. The formalized creation of and ad-

What Are the Benefits of Stakeholder Negotiation?

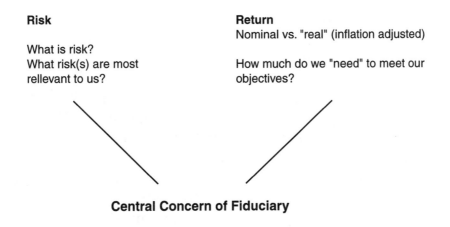

Risk

What is risk?
What risk(s) are most
rellevant to us?

Return
Nominal vs. "real" (inflation adjusted)

How much do we "need" to meet our
objectives?

Central Concern of Fiduciary

Exhibit 5.17   Explicit Risk/Return

herence to investment policy can provide an objective baseline for new members.

Advance discussion can make both reporting on investment results and oversight of outside investment managers much more meaningful. All too often, the managers' reports consist of talking about different companies and weaving stories about how the economy is behaving, what is going to happen in the future, and the like. It is certainly questionable whether this discussion has any meaning in terms of actual value in predicting the future, but in any event the reporting should be goal focused and not focused on outside benchmarks. Such focus allows for the inclusion of absolute return strategies. Assuming the organization has a worthwhile mission, effective and responsible stewardship of funds that is well articulated and apparent to the outside observer can provide significant benefits. These benefits include promoting donor comfort and attracting split-interest gifts that can provide interim income or residual beneficiary benefits.

SOME CONCLUSIONS

Three straightforward ideas can be concluded:

- Foundations need to operate within the constraints imposed by both fiduciary rules and financial markets.
- Stakeholders can use tools to better understand each other's interests and resolve differences.
- The process of reaching consensus, while it might be painful, gets much better buy-in from all stakeholders and offers a better understanding of the foundation's mission.

The process described in this chapter is well summarized by Exhibit 5.18.

Objectives
Investment Policy
Spending Policy
Development Policy

Plan

Review

Analysis of Results
Compliance With Plan

Do
Implementation
Capital Placement

Objectives Include:
Preservation of Capital
Hedge Against Inflation
Maintain Stability of Program
Increase Contribution to Program Development
Each Board Needs to Rank Importance of
Competing Objectives

Proper exercise of fiduciary responsibility requires an ongoing process of planning, implementation, and review/evaluation. Regular scheduling of reviews can help eliminate inadvertent oversights.

Copyright © 2001 Halbert, Hargrove/Russell LLC

Exhibit 5.18   The Fiduciary Cycle

We hope the information we have shared is useful to those responsible for carrying forward and implementing the missions of the many worthwhile foundations throughout the United States and the world. A great deal of information is available to supplement the brief comments we've made; among the best sources, including bibliographic information, is David F. Swensen's *Pioneering Portfolio Management* (New York: The Free Press, 2000).

CHAPTER 6

Assets, Investment, and Prudence

Interview with Joseph Kearns

PERSPECTIVES

You have just been given the financial stewardship of a $1 billion trust. What are your issues and priorities? How do you balance the programmatic goals of the institution with prudent investment policies? How does the chief investment and financial officer foster a healthy working relationship with his or her key constituencies—investment counsel, fellow foundation staff, and the board? What are the emerging issues affecting long-term budget planning?

This chapter documents an interview with Joe Kearns, former chief financial officer of the Getty Trust in Los Angeles. Kearns, who is semiretired, spoke to the editors from his ranch in Oregon, where he raises cattle while advising private foundations on how best to accomplish their goals and fulfill their fiduciary responsibilities. He recounts personal experiences from his years at the Getty Trust and other foundations, highlighting the challenges of bringing wisdom and prudent practice to bear on the stated intentions of the founder.

Joe Kearns: That's a typical situation where, as we do this interview you'll pick up comments reflecting my strong views about investment committees and their responsibilities. I had a recent experience attending my first investment committee where there were 20 people sitting around the table. I have my concerns that a committee of this size can be effective.

Frank Ellsworth: Sounds like they might be using the committee as a fundraising vehicle.

JK: When you bring a manager in to be interviewed and there's 22 people sitting there that meet only a couple times a year, it is not very effective and it is certainly not fair to the manager. These are all experiences I've had over my lifetime, and I think I've honed it down to a structure that can operate efficiently.

FE: Well, maybe on that note, let's just sort of shift slightly here and move into the interview.

JK: Did you get my e-mail?

FE: Yes, I did. You know, Joe, you bring to this task an extraordinary background; sort of investment dean at large. The theme of this interview deals with the fiduciary responsibilities that go with foundations. And knowing your background, I think you are uniquely positioned to help us out here. Why don't we, as a context for this interview, set up the following situation? Let's put into this scenario an individual, who has a net worth of $50 million, who is thinking about setting up a foundation. Now this individual does not know anything about the investment process. This is an individual who (to sort of spice up the situation) has a large block of family company stock that has been in the family for many years. So, using this as the base model, a way to get to some fiduciary issues and the investment process, please start.

JK: Sure. I don't want to jump ahead of you here—but from my experience with that situation, these individuals who have created the wealth are very good at creating it as entrepreneurs, but when it comes to setting up the foundation, and the investment program of a foundation, that is a field totally foreign to them. They look to someone for advice and counsel on that area. As you know, there are lots of people who love to give it, but many of them, in my judgment, are not that qualified to do it, and most of them are selling some investment product. That's how they make their living; therefore, they do not give an unbiased view of how this process should really work. Many times they turn to their lawyers or accountants who they trust but may not have foundation experience.

FE: Do you find that people who have been very successful, in the sense of taking risks to accumulate the fortunes they have, do you find that these individuals can move rather quickly into another world of risk, as in investment risks?

JK: Once they understand how it works, my experience has been that yes they are fairly amenable to moving the process along. A lot of it has to do with age. If someone's at the latter stage of their life and/or has health issues, they want to get this done, obviously it's going to move more quickly. If they are just now getting around to the process, I have found that they are ready to move along and get it set up. They just need someone with my background who is willing to sit down with them and say, "Listen, you've got this X number of shares of the company's stock and it doesn't pay a dividend. The foundation will have a minimum distribution requirement each year, and your portfolio is not diversified. Your risk levels of the portfolio are very concentrated. You are going to be forced to sell and distribute under the IRS guidelines, which could be ill-timed, both in the marketplace or in the family situation. So those are things that I have run across specifically that I think they need to address and develop a plan for an orderly divestment of their company holdings.

FE: Your reference to total return I think is an important one to look at for at least a moment. How do you find it most effective to communicate the concept of total return to such an individual or to any board?

JK: I think they should start on the spending side. What will be my level of spending each year? Am I going to spend the minimum required for distribution? Or in some cases, no, I want to spend more than that while I am alive because I have got all these projects I want to support. I try very hard to get them to think through the spending side. Okay, for example, we are going to spend 6 percent of the corpus. Or we are going to spend 4.75 percent plus expenses and just barely cover the minimum distribution requirement. Then I try to get them to think through the diversification of their assets. I discuss at length the various asset class alternatives. Without getting too technical, I add expected returns into the mix on these asset classes and develop a long-range inflation assumption. I then work it back to show them that over time if they are going to spend 5 percent or 6 percent with expenses, this asset mix with these various asset classes and expected returns will provide them with the income on a total return concept basis. This will also protect the corpus from inflation—I am a big believer that it should not only be the minimum spending requirement that they agree upon, but also plus a long-range inflation assumption. There are those who don't want the foundation to exist in perpetuity. They believe you ought to distribute the assets in a much shorter period of time. I don't necessarily subscribe to that view. I believe that if you have foundation, the benefits can go on forever if properly managed.

FE: *Let me, if I could, ask another question about the spending. And I understand the importance of getting the donor, the founder, or the board to look at spending early on. Do you see the 5 percent required payout, Joe, as a maximum or a minimum?*

JK: Well, in my experiences in both large and small foundations, I see it as the maximum. Now there can be lots of other parameters that enter into the picture, one of which I mentioned before, the founder may want to spend more at the end of his or her lifetime, for example, on specific projects that could raise the level for a specific period. But I think if you want the foundation to be in existence in perpetuity, which is usually the goal of most of the people that I have dealt with, I think it is very important to manage the spending level close to the minimum distribution requirement.

Joe Lumarda: Just a follow-up on that in terms of spending policy, Joe: when they get the gist of what the spending policy is, and you're talking about a number, is that a short conversation or a long one? If it's a hundred million dollars and they haven't been philanthropic throughout their life, and they have this wonderful opportunity and they realize they have to give away five million dollars, do they get hung up on that before determining a figure?

JK: It's a little bit surprising to them I guess. And it is a major dialog back and forth before that can be resolved. When I first started doing this, I did not realize the thought process of individuals like this. If they have a hundred million dollars, and even if they have been somewhat philanthropic, it's been on a case-by-case basis where somebody has called them and said, "I'm supporting this XYZ charity and would you help out?" And they say, "Yes, that sounds good," they write them a check. Even if it's at a small foundation and it's been operated on a pass-through basis, that is what they have been doing. Now you're talking about a more structured organization that's going to have to spend five million dollars a year. And some of them haven't thought it through that way and it sounds like something that has just hit them for the first time. But, I think with several progressive discussions, in most of the cases that I've been involved with recently, they have come to the conclusion that yes, that is really what I want to do. It has also got them to think a lot more about the philanthropic side and the guidelines for the next generation of the foundation. If the founder is active and he or she runs the foundation and suddenly they are gone, the foundation can take different turns on the philanthropic side without well-defined guidelines and disciplines. Whereas, I stress you think through this spending policy initially and you also think through the objectives of what you're all about.

JL: Let me step back again, to the creation of this foundation and the dilemma or the opportunity of the founders. Now you're talking in very specialized terms, spending policy, total return, for someone who may have been working all their life to make this money they have in a large block of stock because they've been building this company all their life. And I would imagine—and you're a specialist in the industry—what have you seen in terms of their selection of an advisor? What is the tendency for a person like that to go through an endowment investment specialist? Or do they usually go to their buddies?

JK: Usually their banker, their accountant, or their lawyer who they have worked with for 30 years because they have a lot of confidence in them. Sometimes their broker, or maybe somebody that has done some M&A [mergers and acquisitions] work for them. The M&A guys always think that they've got the inside track. And I've seen that firsthand where maybe they led the secondary offering where they have sold a portion of the family stock. So they think they are right there, they can advise this person on how to set up an investment program. They have a conflict of interest. Their approach is to manage assets in a brokerage account. I am totally opposed to that, having actually been through one of those cases.

JL: Can you talk about that a little bit?

JK: Yes, they have a totally different agenda. They see this large amount of money that is generated in this case through a secondary offering, and they were the leader or were listed. So therefore, they felt they had an automatic in to help the individual invest it. They know nothing about foundations in most cases. They know nothing about how to structure the spending policy and relating it to how you invest the assets, nothing about the tax reporting, and nothing about any of the fiduciary or regulatory responsibilities. Yet, sometimes they get their foot in the door and I think they do a terrible disservice to the individual when this happens.

JL: Do you have a "for instance" story without mentioning any names?

JK: In one case I was brought in right when this process had started; that is, all the names on the secondary offering were lined up to meet this individual and tell him how to invest his money. He invited me to sit in on these meetings. They were very matter of fact that they deserved this business and that they were in the best position to do it and that they had a plan to do it. In my opinion, they were high-powered brokers. And they were going to invest his assets accordingly. I convinced him to pull back, sit back, and of course I did not become very popular with these major names for doing that. But I said there's a large enough amount of money here that we can put together a very professionally diversified portfolio using the best money managers in the world. And the client said, "Well, I didn't think I could do that with a couple of hundred million dollars." I said, "Absolutely you can! And then I can bring them to the selection process independently, not getting paid on the basis of bringing them to the table and let you look at them." And the client said, "Yes, let's take a look at that." We did it very professionally and got it set up and operating. And not one of those investment banking houses got a piece of the business, not by my choice, it's just they weren't competitive.

JL: *A few minutes ago you alluded to a very important concept—fiduciary responsibility. Unfortunately with a lot of these situations it's after the fact of getting in trouble that they are introduced to this vital concept for their foundation. How do you introduce the philosophy to an individual who it's come before?*

JK: Well, it takes time and usually I try to relate it to some of the things they've done in their entrepreneurial past. That is how they best relate to this. And that's how I've been most successful with sitting down and saying, "It's like when you formed your company, when you took over this company, or when you did this, or you sold that, this is how we have to think about the foundation. This is here forever, this money is set aside under your objectives when you are still here and your board and subsequent boards will take into the future." I would like to circle back to another example that I got involved with more recently. This individual, in setting up the foundation, didn't know who to turn to. The client lived in a more remote area of the country and had a big business operation with union pension plans. They had hired a regional consultant for these funds over the years and he got to know them. So he thought, well, I'll talk to him about it. Well, unfortunately, the consultant the client talked to didn't have foundation experience and really had set his consulting business up after being a broker and still operated in a similar mode. So they were off on a whole different tangent when I got involved and I had to convince them to pull back and go a little bit slower. If you are going to add more assets to this foundation, this is the time we can put together a more diversified portfolio. That consultant is no longer involved with the foundation. I felt it was my responsibility to lay out the options for this individual. Fortunately, he listened.

FE: Joe, your first hypothetical example, as you were summarizing what happened, you indicated that the original folks who were on the table didn't get the business, not by your choice, but because they weren't competitive. Let's look for a minute at the cost. What do you think is a fair expense, if you will, for the investment process and investments in a foundation?

JK: Well, if you think of overall costs, the larger the assets, the more economies to scale there are in fees, although that's changing somewhat as the years go by. But I always tell my clients that we ought to be able to do all of this, including the custodian part of it, for 100 basic points or less. That ought to be our objective.

FE: Do you have any idea how that relates to costs in a generic way, let's say nationally?

JK: It's low, because some of the situations I have gotten involved with recently, I am very surprised to see what they haven't negotiated, basically they have just accepted, what people have put forth in the way of fees. They are much higher than what I think they should be. Some of them will go as far as setting up the equivalent of what I call a wrap account, where the fees are 1.5 to 2 percent or higher in some cases. It is not necessary to accept these high fees if someone is advising them that really understands what the options are there and how the marketplace works.

FE: Do you think that that's because those shadows and mirrors when it comes to communicating costs, do you think that is just because often a board doesn't understand the costs? Why is it that there's such a range?

JK: I think it is because a board or a chairman of the investment committee doesn't have a broad background on what the marketplace really is for quality investment and support services. I think they just listen when they are sitting there on the couch and these people come in—most of them are pretty good at presenting—and they listen and in their mind it sounds good so they think it must be the going rate, when it is not necessarily so. And a lot of them get stuck in brokerage situations where the big brokerage houses get to manage their money in a brokerage account. And they have no idea what the true costs of the account are.

FE: Do you find that foundations that are working with a financial advisor/ broker are understanding more commission recapture programs?

JK: Not necessarily so. Some do, and some don't.

FE: Perhaps it would be helpful if you just for a moment defined what a recapture program is and the possible role it could play with a foundation.

JK: It's allowable from a fiduciary and legal standpoint to have a commission recapture program, which is really a portion of the commissions that are paid on the transactions in the foundation account directed to a third party. They are available to the foundation to be used for expenses that are legitimately related to the operation of the endowment. You could use them to pay for fees for research or measurement services. Over recent years there have been some severe criticisms of this program because of abuse. In my opinion, the criticism is totally justifiable with the way some people misuse the recapture commissions. But if it is properly accounted for and used to offset the investment costs of the foundation directly, all audits I've been involved with for the past years have stood up fine. It is a good way to reduce the investment expenses.

On the other hand, you have got to stress to the committee, or whoever is running this, that commission recapture can be very inefficient and expensive. It is great that you get 25 percent of the commissions flowing back to the foundation, but if you're paying ten cents a share instead of five on all your transactions to get that, then it is not cost efficient. I think that is the one thing people don't truly understand. You need to monitor execution and efficiency of the program at the same time; and sometimes if you really cut the amount of your commission cost, commission recapture is not as easy or as efficient as if you are paying more per share.

FE: *If you were a CFO of a private foundation and you were wondering whether you should be pursuing of recapture program, what questions would you ask? And do you see any guidelines that might be helpful to the CFO asking those questions?*

JK: Yes, I think the basic guideline that you have to start with is the level of recapture you think can be accomplished. Where does this level become a hindrance to the manager? In other words, the manager has to deal with certain brokers for the recapture program, and it limits their flexibility. But if they are a small shop that does buy most of their research from the street; for example, I've seen one manager who just said, "No, I don't have many analysts on my staff and I buy most of my research. I cannot afford to have a quarter of it recaptured. It interferes with the ability to do my research." In that case, we step back. But I think the size of the recapture program is number one. Number two, who does it for you and what do they charge to do it? There are various ranges of fees for the service. And thirdly, what kind of reputation does the third party that is going to do it for you have? Other than that, it's a decision of the committee. If the CFO recommended to a committee that, yes, we can save $200,000 per year, then it should be considered.

JL: *Is it fair to say, depending on the consultant you have or the advice that you're receiving and the professional that you're working with, that that may not even get on the radar screen?*

JK: That is very true.

JL: *Based on—because if they're brokers, they're looking for a commission, therefore . . .*

JK: Most of the consultants have a brokerage relationship, and the pure consulting business has low margins and they are getting squeezed. Although the big consultants have done well, you look at where their income comes from, most of it is not coming from consulting, it's coming from other fee businesses with higher margins. Those who have just stayed in the true consulting business are struggling and raising fees in recent years.

FE: *How common is it, Joe, for a consultant to a foundation to charge both a fee as well as then recommend investments that go into funds where there is a 12b-1 fee and they pick up the 12b-1 fee as well as a fee? How common is that?*

JK: I don't see it much in the larger foundations. Where I have seen it is in the smaller-sized foundations. In my travels and speaking to groups, I see very little of that in the large foundations.

FE: *How can a CFO guard against that situation?*

JK: Well, I think that when you look for a consultant, their reputation is number one. Do your research and negotiate a flat fee. If it is a large enough account, most of the investment managers use separate accounts, not funds, so there is no 12b-1 issue. But there is always the concern of whether they are getting a kickback. We have seen over the last few years, a few cases where there have actually been proven kickbacks to the consultant for bringing certain money managers to the table. That is part of our business that we all have to work very hard on, and any CFO or committee that is looking at hiring a consultant has to keep that in mind.

FE: We've been talking here about consultants, understandably. Why should a foundation use a consultant? Should a foundation always have a consultant? And if you could talk a bit about the upside and downside of consultants.

JK: I think that a foundation should always have a consultant, even if they have someone with extensive experience on their board that has been in the foundation world. I think you need, from a fiduciary standpoint, to have someone else out there who you can bounce ideas off of. Maybe they don't play as large a role in the case where you have a strong investment committee chair or investment committee in general. Maybe the consultant is more in the background grinding out numbers, doing projects and so forth and is not totally in charge like they are in some other situations. I would like to come back to the subject of investment committees' roles, but the consultants should be there and should have a defined role. In some cases, I think they have too large of a role. As you work with some of these consultants, that is the kind of role they like because they make all the decisions and just kind of tell the chairman of the committee what they are doing and away they go. It is the easiest way for them to operate. I don't believe in that at all. I think the investment committee chair has to be strong, experienced, knowledgeable, and able to deal with these issues and use the consultant on a project basis, reporting basis, or analytical basis or portions of the above. But not let them be in the total driver's seat when it comes to managing selection and fees. Yet, I do see the whole spectrum out there. I do see some relationships where they just advocate totally to a third party, and whatever they do is fine. I do not think that is fulfilling your total fiduciary responsibility.

JL: So with fiduciary responsibility in the role of consultant—let me just pursue a little bit exactly where they all sit. You're saying that a con-

sultant helps you in the realm of fiduciary responsibility as that third-party independent eye between the board and the managers themselves, and you referred to if the consultant is also a manager, that's where you get into trouble?

JK: That is right. I think that if consultants are also managers, I don't think that they should be on the top of the list. There is just too much of a conflict there.

FE: *I think I also, Joe, hear you saying that the role of a consultant with a particular foundation can vary in terms of where the particular foundation investment committee is in their investment life. In other words, more active in some situations, as the investment committee matures or board matures, it may be a less significant role. Is that true?*

JK: Yes, and they should be compensated accordingly. For example, if you have a strong CFO with investment background versus a CFO that just came out of the accounting world and is very good at controller-type functions but investments really are not his strong point, I think the consultant there would play a much stronger role. But if the CFO is very strong and if the investment committee's chair's experienced—has chaired these kinds of committees before—I think the consultant has a lesser role. But I still think he ought to be there because the chairman of the committee and/or the CFO don't always have the time to deal with some of the issues that come up that consultants are very experienced in working with. For example, if they are having trouble when the ownership of a firm changes, whether it be a custodian bank or whether it be an investment manager, the consultant can provide additional insight. You need to do research on what is happening, and they have the tools to do that and are quick to come back with information. I think that is very important. If you didn't have them there, you would have to go out and find someone to get that information.

FE: *Assuming that the consultant has an obligation to tell a committee or board if they are breaching fiduciary responsibility or might be putting* *themselves in a position where they are getting close to doing that, how often do you think a consultant is equipped in that situation? Have you seen it in your experience?*

JK: I've seen it over time. The problem is, like with any vendor, they do not want to lose the contract. So if they speak up or are too harsh or are too quick to point something out to the chairman or to a CFO in some cases, they could be without a contract.

FE: *Can you think of a couple of examples where the foundation board breached fiduciary responsibility?*

JK: None comes to mind at the moment. I tend to stay away from those kinds of things. The way I manage in my career and organizations I have been involved with, I really haven't gotten into situations like that.

FE: *Let me tell you of a recent example in my experience where a member of an investment committee involved in the investment business—when the foundation was looking for yet another asset allocation or another money manager—insisted that his company not only be considered but his company be used.*

JK: That is way beyond the limits of anything that I think is appropriate. I would never tolerate or recommend that. I think, when someone is invited to an investment committee as a member, it is clear (and in one case I have seen it in writing) that they agree that the firm that they represent (or maybe they are retired now but they still have the loyalty to that firm), cannot be considered for a position in the portfolio.

FE: *So, if I understand what you're saying, in terms of conflict of interest, it's your view that foundations should not allow a board member to get any material gain, at least in terms of investment possibilities?*

JK: Absolutely. If the consultant that they have, and I have had this happen—actually, we were going to hire a specialty equity manager and I instructed the consultant to go out and find me the best five managers in that area. Well, when they came back, one of the five was a company that one of my investment committee members had an affiliation with, but I wrestled with this and I talked to lawyers. This came up totally independent of the investment committee member. He did not have any say or comment in the matter, and we ended up bringing that name forward in the final. Obviously he didn't vote, but since it came up from a totally independent entity, we went ahead with it. So I think I'm comfortable with that kind of thing. But the other side of it is when they are pushing it or they are recommending it, or, "I played golf with Fred on Saturday and he's got this great company that manages equities or whatever, and you ought to take a look at it." It is one thing to say you ought to take a look at it versus they ought to be hired. There is a line there that can be drawn.

JL: From your experience can you describe the attributes and aspects of an ideal consultant?

JK: An ideal consultant quickly develops a good understanding of what the organization is all about. What is the mission, the objective of the foundation? What is their spending plan? How are they going to accomplish it? They are an extension of the foundation staff or, in some cases, where you do not have a CFO or a strong CIO, they fulfill that role. That is the full capacity experience that I talked about earlier. The biggest weakness that I find with these firms, even though they've been in a relationship for years, is that they didn't comprehend where the organization is going on the investment side. They trip on that once in a while, and I think that is embarrassing. But again, that comes to the point where maybe the consultant has 20 or 30 relationships and it is hard to keep the players straight. I think that is the biggest weakness that they have to deal with.

FE: Let me shift gears only slightly. The days of investment with diversification, let me just put it simply, 60 percent equity and 40 percent fixed income seem to be shifting. We've seen a lot of change, evolution recently, particularly in the area of alternative investments. The hedge funds, the private equity, the stressed debt, and so forth. What is your view of the role of alternative investments in a foundation portfolio?

JK: I am a big supporter of including alternatives as an asset class. I refer to it as the nonpublicly traded asset class. But I say it with some conditions. There is a very wide range of opportunities out there, everything from timberlands like I'm looking at out of my window now to very sophisticated arbitrage strategies. It also includes hedge funds, private equity, venture capital, and others. I am certainly in the camp of the more defined arena, as I call it. That would be private equity, venture capital, and hedge funds if properly structured. But again, that is an area where a committee or chairman probably has the least amount of knowledge. Not that you are going to go out and put 40 percent or 50 percent of your assets in this class like some college endowments are doing, which I'm very critical of from the liquidity standpoint. In a foundation world, I can see it is totally appropriate to do 15 percent in this combined arena if you take the extreme edges off it. I don't see you buying timberland; I don't see you buying farmland; I don't see you buying those kinds of things because they are so specialized, so few people know anything about. How do you select a consultant that can advise in those areas? Whereas venture capital, private equity, hedge funds are certainly more defined.

FE: *So is it appropriate to say that the real issue, if you look at publicly traded verses nonpublicly traded, is somewhat of an artificial one? The real issue is what is the research that's gone behind whatever vehicle is being recommended?*

JK: That's right. For example, I got involved recently with one proposed investment where the firm was recommended by a friend of my client that delivered tremendous returns, in the year 2000. I said, with those returns it must be a hedge fund. That is the only way you could get numbers like that. So he said, "And by the way, what do you think of a manager that told you that he won't tell you what he does?" Well, I could never recommend someone who doesn't tell you what they do and how they do it. I think that it is your fiduciary responsibility to understand what they do and then make a decision. If they flatly refuse to tell you about how they do it, not only do you have an illiquid investment, you don't know what is going on. Whether it is a pyramid scheme or anything else, I don't know. I cannot in good conscience recommend those kinds of investments. There are those kinds of things going on out there as we speak and believe it or not because of some of the numbers they purportedly report as performance, they are selling well! But I think we, or foundations in general, have to be totally alert.

FE: What criteria should an investment committee, a foundation board, use in selecting and investment? In other words, when you're helping a CFO or a board, say, look there are 4,000 different opportunities out here and here are ones I think, board, you should consider. Sort of walk through how you think a board should evaluate what investments to select.

JL: And I guess that gets us down to criteria as an offshoot of stated investment policy.

JK: Right.

JL: How do you develop that from beginning to where you feel comfortable with where you are?

JK: You have to have policy that defines asset classes. You can have ranges; there are lots of ways to do it, but everybody has to agree. You go charging off in that direction and hopefully you won't vary from that direction too much over time. Now within the policy, then you say, "Okay, I'm going to have 40 percent in U.S. equity." And then you break that down into a couple of different categories of large cap growth, large cap value, mid cap, small cap, for example. Then it is the CFO's responsibility and/or the consultant to bring you qualified candidates within these areas. In other words, you do not try to look at everything. You divide it up and you break it down into the components of the asset mix and the policy that you're trying to operate with. Then, looking at managers, obviously somebody has to do the due diligence first, usually that's the consultant and/or the CFO sorting the names, performance records, etc. The committee itself, when they get involved, usually has a large amount of material in front of them in advance. Then they get a short face-to-face meeting with them and if the CFO and/or the consultant hasn't been in the manager's office, they should not receive further consideration. So let's assume that they have done that, they have been there, they have interviewed, they have updated everything, and then the manager comes and presents to the board. One thing you really have got to watch for in a situation like that are presentation skills. Money managers in general, actual portfolio managers (which is who I like to talk to, not the marketing rep), are not known in general for good presentation skills. I want the guy who is going to actually manage my money to come to the committee to propose. Usually the marketing representative comes and the portfolio manager attends who will actually manage their money. So when it is his or her turn to talk, any time they do not do very well, the committees tend to weigh their decision on their presentation skills. They say, "Well, I had three here this afternoon, and that individual gave a terrible presentation." Well, many portfolio managers didn't become portfolio managers because of their political or presentation skills, we know that. I think that is one of the big downfalls that has to be dealt with by committees over time. Once you hire a manager, you have them come in once a year to report, and the committee changes over time. I've seen some very tragic situations where someone has done reasonably well, but they just make a terrible presentation. They do not have good presentation skills, no matter how much they have been trained, but they are good at analyzing numbers, sitting in the corner picking companies, that's what you hired them for. Yet, when they come to your meeting, they walk out and the committee says, "That was terrible!" Well, no, that is not why they are here. A good CFO or a good consultant can really earn their money in that area and say, "Listen, you hired them to be, say, a small cap manager. They are one of the best in the country. The portfolio manager just is not good at presentations."

FE: *Um, Joe, let me just peel that back another layer. You said that the role of the CFO and/or consultant is to bring to the table qualified candidates. How do you qualify the candidates?*

JK: I think there are several criteria, but managers have to have a proven record. They have to have been around three to five years. That does eliminate some people who are just starting out, but I tend to eliminate those, unless they have brought a team from another firm that has been together for many years and now they are striking out on their own. I want proven three- to five-year track records in this business with the same team. A lot of times records are created by other people than the people you're talking with. Ownership of the firm is important—understanding the ownership. I used to have a rule that I only recommended independently owned companies—those owned by the partners. Well, in the last 20 years that has cut the list almost to nothing because most of these have become either part of another firm or owned by someone else. That used to be an automatic for me to get rid of them in the early 1980s if they were sold to someone. I had to change my tune on that over time because that is the trend of the business. When they are sold, you have to look at the ownership, what are their intentions, incentives to keep the key people that have created the record that you're buying, etc. When people leave after you have hired them, that should be a yellow flag for review. The CFO should be bringing that to the committee and/or the consultant. You should not be reading about it in the paper.

FE: *Looking at the proven record, I know that that gets into questions of results and performance. I'm wondering what your views are on the role of benchmarks and even more particularly, let's say, how valid is the S&P, if you will, as a benchmark? Do you think benchmarks—does this mean that short-term emphasis becomes more important than long-term results?*

JK: Well, let me just talk generically first about benchmarks. In the foundation world, let's face it, we need a real rate of return because we have to spend money every year. If you have to spend 5 percent every year and inflation projections are 3.5 percent, I have to lay out a plan that can give me 8.5 percent compounded over time as a minimum just to stay even with inflation. If you become very benchmark oriented, which of course many organizations have, on the ERISA side and since many of the managers in the foundation world are also ERISA managers, that is what they want to talk about. That is when they come in and say, "Well, the S&P was down 19 percent in this period and we were only down 17 percent. Therefore, we are doing a good job." Well, I think boards get lulled into hearing that, particularly in the last few years, and I think it is dangerous to accept that. We need to think about what foundations are trying to accomplish and what the spending requirements are, and this is not an ERISA account. We have to spend money every year! And we have to spend a certain amount every year. And if the markets are down and yes we were down 17 percent instead of 19 percent, how does that help the foundation meet its spending requirement? I think too much emphasis is put on that. I would rather see more emphasis put on what the actual earnings requirements are for this organization and report relative to that. Now having said that, I do report benchmarks now to most of my clients because everybody wants to see how they have done, but I try to keep the emphasis off of that and talk about what our long-term objectives are, what our long-term earning requirements are, and what these managers are doing relative to that. If you have a large cap value equity manager that did quite well in 2000 relative to other managers, but how did they do relative to other large cap value managers? I think that is a very valid comparison. But within that you have to be extremely careful because a lot of value managers have been beat up for so long, a lot of them in my opinion have changed their stripes. They own certain stocks that are difficult to justify as value-type investments. That came from just getting beat up for so long that a few of these things kind of sneaked across the line. So there are two levels to look at in that case: how they did relative to other managers of the same category and, within that, have they stuck to their original discipline.

FE: I know with the issues involved with the S&P we've seen a movement to other types of benchmarks, if you will, and certainly in the mutual funds side of the world we have Lipper. Do you think we are fine-tuning? Do you think we are going in the right directions to try to come up with benchmarks that we think are better benchmarks?

JK: Yes, I think that is just a natural outcome of how we have classified and broken down the assets into finer asset categories. We used to talk about just stocks. Now we're talking about five or six categories of stocks or sometimes more. Benchmarks are becoming totally not only manager driven, but also client driven. I have seen RFPs where the client picks a certain benchmark and a certain sector allocation within that benchmark, and he only wants plus or minus 2 percent from that at any given time. Well, that drives a manager to manage a whole different way in finding the best stocks. If you are a small cap manager, say, find me the best small cap stocks. I don't care about tracking error. That type of benchmark pressure drives them away from picking the best stocks and produces index-like performance. The consultant, the CFO, and the committee has to be alert to that. In the foundation world, where we basically pay no taxes on our investment gains and we know what our spending requirements are, I don't think you need to manage to an index.

FE: Let's talk a bit more about the role of the CFO. Do you see the role of a CFO as a facilitator, an advocate, a leader? Have you seen changes in the role of a CFO during your career, and do you have any thoughts about what that CFO five years hence is going to look like and act like?

JK: I have seen many changes in my career of the CFO role in a foundation, the biggest of which is they have become much more professional. They have come from the corporate side over time with broad experience in all aspects of CFO responsibilities and they've brought those applications to the nonprofit and the foundation world. I think that has been a tremendous boost. If you look at the CFOs in the major foundations out there over the last five or ten years, say, they have become much stronger, much more professional, and I think the product that they produce is reflective of that. I relate it to the students that I speak to at UCLA Anderson's school every fall. They say, "I would really like to have a financial career in the nonprofit area." And Joe, you have had a lot of experience in the nonprofit sector and you may not agree with me on this, but I tell them to go out and get some true financial experience. I don't care if that is working in the bank trust department. Then bring that experience to a nonprofit, and I think everyone benefits. Whereas if you grow up in that area from the day you graduate from college, I don't know that you can be the same broad-based CFO that I think these large organizations need.

FE: What is the role of a CFO on a management team of a foundation?

JK: Although they have an overall financial role, I think the important responsibility is in the investment side. Now granted they usually have the controllership responsibilities, budgeting, and insurance, and those are important, but what makes the engine run? The endowment of the foundation, the investments of the foundation are the income stream. They are basically responsible for that directly day to day, but within that they have an investment committee to report to in most cases. There is the larger foundation example where the CFO reports almost directly to the investment committee. Although the CEO is involved, the CFO or CIO usually has the wealth of financial and investment experience. It is their responsibility to work with the chairman of the committee monitoring the portfolio, making recommendations and changes and strategy.

JL: Let's see, there's a lot of chiefs that are being created in foundations. There's what's traditionally known as chief financial officer, then—and I believe in the past at least 10 to 15 years—a chief investment officer. Legally before I think paving the way there. And then recently I've seen job descriptions quoted out there for chief administrative officer. What's your perspective on these new careers?

JK: If you think about career development, those of us in my generation were trained to be total CFOs, including the administrative side. We got all those experiences early in our careers. As I mentioned back in my Bell System days, having investment experience as well as heavy treasury, controller experience groomed me someday to be the treasurer and a chief financial officer. Now today career paths are much different, very specialized. You grow up in an accounting organization, you become a controller. You grow up in an investment organization, you are an investment type. That has driven a lot of the organizations to have separate CFO and CIO positions because there are not as many people around that have both experiences at a senior level as there used to be. That is also the same with chief administrative officers.

FE: *The last decade, Joe, that I suspected goes back prior to that, in fact I'm recalling my days at the University of Chicago when the South Shore Bank and Jesse Jackson was getting started up, which leads to the question of the increased interest in SRI or socially responsible investment. And there's quite a range of vehicles out there that fall into that category. What is the role of socially responsible investment for a foundation?*

JK: I think it depends on the organization. For example, if it is a religious organization, it has certain objectives. I think that certain socially responsible investments might be appropriate. For the average person setting up a family foundation, it would take a lot of effort to convince the founder that this is something that ought to be done unless the founder was already involved in something like that, which they normally are not. That is not how they made their money. That is not in a sector of where they have traveled. So I think it is a much bigger discussion at that point. Whether it should be a part of all organizations, I reserve judgment on that to some degree, certainly understanding that in certain organizations just by their very nature, this would be more appropriate. But as a taxpayer in the state of California, reading about what CALPERS and CALSTERS are doing, I'm wondering if they are not pushing their fiduciary responsibility to the limit.

FE: Let me just push that question a little bit further. As I listen to you, I think I hear two different aspects of the questions about the role of socially responsible investment. The first involves values and the value of the family, organization that is funding a foundation, the values that might be in place. The second thing I'm hearing deals more strictly with investment and whether it is prudent to be using socially responsible investment from an investment point of view. Now I know that the last number of years has been a good time for the market, so lots of vehicles look good if you're looking at a five-year record, any type of vehicle I'm talking about here, not just socially responsible investment. But do you have more thoughts as to whether socially responsible investment for the purely investment point of view makes sense?

JK: Well, I think you have to be able to look at an investment and be convinced that it has a reasonable probability to meet the organization's objectives. I think that is something that you cannot back away from. If some of these investments in specialized categories do not meet that criteria, I have difficulty recommending them to my client.

JL: Let me guess what your strategy is and you can respond. You wait and see if it comes to the floor, and if it doesn't and it is not something that is brought up and if it is, it is something that you respond to and probably have some managers there that are capable of executing it.

JK: That is correct.

JL: Are you finding more and more that it is now becoming a part of the first question you ask as opposed to being responsive?

JK: Somewhat. It is certainly not in the startup organizations that I've been involved with. That is not something that comes up high on the list. You can understand why.

FE: Isn't part of that issue one of costs?

JK: That is important, and familiarity and all those issues that go with it.

JL: *You mentioned a few times that you have some pretty strong views on the makeup and the role of the investment committee. I'm not sure if you had a chance to follow that through.*

JK: No, I didn't really get to. Let's start with the chairman of the investment committee. I don't care if it is a committee of two or three or six. The chairman should absolutely be an experienced financial person. If it is the only financial person on the total board, that ought to be the position that they recruit for. I have seen several cases where the chairman of the investment committee was handed to them as an honor or seniority, etc. And it was a terrible disservice to the whole investment side of the foundation because he didn't have any experience, or very little, or if it was, it was not applicable and that kind of thing. I think if you look at the major foundations around the country, the successful ones have very strong investment committees in total, but particularly the chairman. That is a very critical role, the chairman of the investment committee. They have the experience and understand how the foundation segment works and how the investment segment within that foundation is applicable. And as far as membership of the committee, again, I would prefer that they be experienced investment types. And some foundations say, well, we can't find the people, we are an art organization, or a music organization, or whatever, and these people do not have any investment experience. Well, you have got to find one that maybe likes music or likes art; there are people like that, and bring them in. Short of that, I have seen a situation which has worked extremely well where they have brought people on the investment committee who are not board members, who had specific experience or investment experience. I highly recommend it if that is the case. If you cannot find directors or trustees that meet the criteria of your main mission that have financial experience, I think you have to look to bringing in people specifically for that function at the investment committee level.

FE: *Joe, in addition to having experienced people chair as well as on the board, what other characteristics do you think make for a good investment committee?*

JK: I think as much as I want experience and it is part of my criteria, the other big issue with that is they have to be able to take their firm hat off and bring to the committee table their generic experience. That is the toughest challenge you'll find. You'll bring in somebody with 30 years of experience at a big name organization, and some of them cannot take that hat off in the sense of the company itself. And that is when we get back to some of those things: "You ought to look at so and so and you ought to hire so and so" and that kind of thing, versus, let's talk about it in a committee structure where they share their experiences, they share their knowledge of their area where others can learn from it.

FE: *How do you evaluate the effectiveness of an investment committee? And should a foundation board have guidelines for evaluating effectiveness?*

JK: I think they should have some written guidelines, including a committee charter, but it is a difficult area, and I think that in the end it comes down to how well the investment area has done relative to their formal objectives. The committee is responsible for that directly. The board is also, but the committee on a more specific basis and the CFO on an ongoing basis. And if they are constantly jumping around, for example, from index funds to active managers, and changing their overall long-term strategy, over time they are not going to do that well. I think that criteria in itself has to be evaluated by the full board.

FE: *How can a board do that? I'm imagining a board where there may be two or three people who really understand investment and they are on the investment committee. I mean, how can you evaluate an investment committee? Or is that a role of the consultant?*

JK: That is partly the role of the consultant, but if you have a strong investment committee, the consultant is not going to contribute too much in that area. The chairman of the overall board has to have the ability to evaluate how effective the investment committee chairman and/or the committee is doing. It is relative. It is easy to pick out the cases where they are always changing directions or bringing some nonstandard idea to the table. It is the ones that don't change much and not much happens. How do you evaluate the effectiveness of that? The only criteria in the end is the pre-agreed-upon overall strategy and performance objectives. How are you doing relative to that?

JL: *With the natural evolution or the rotation of chairs, how do you get away from change based on personal preference? As you said, one chair may be more index oriented to one chair being more active-manager oriented?*

JK: Well, in my 17 years of experience as CFO of a major foundation, I went through four chairmen and I don't know how many committee members in that period, but I felt that it was my main objective to keep the ship on course within the agreed-upon strategy. That is a constant conflict in some cases because you get committee member rotation. All of a sudden someone says let's get rid of all of these active managers, let's replace them with index funds. Sometimes CFOs lose their jobs over changes like that. You have to be able to hang in there for a market cycle. Hopefully you have a strong enough CFO that has some influence with the CEO and chairman of the board as to who they select as committee chair so they don't get someone that has a very different viewpoint.

FE: *What kinds of strategies or techniques, Joe, have you observed or used over the years with regard to orienting an investment committee and a board about responsibilities in order to keep the ship heading in the right direction?*

JK: I always kept the major strategy papers that we had written and been approved by the board, for example on assets, manager selection, and performance reports. I always had an updated package to give the new investment committee member to read. Now some read it and some don't. But then I would follow up with them and say, "Listen, I'd like to have lunch with you, talk about this, go through it, get you to understand why we have done what we have done over the years, why we think it's been successful, and why we have operated within these written criteria that we have given you." And then, if you would like to meet with a money manager to get an idea of who these people are. I don't bring them all in for a new board member, but I have brought in specific managers to give him an idea that further strengthens what I have said. These managers are carefully selected. I think that has been effective. Some people respond to it better than others. Some people think they know it all. You get the whole gamut. The majority want to learn as much as they can so that when they go to that first meeting they are as informed as they can be.

FE: *As we wind down the interview, Joe, I'm thinking as I reflect on what we've talked about that we've covered a lot of questions, policies, and so forth. What questions and issues are absent from discussion these days? Now whether these are absent at a board meeting, whether these are issues that aren't being discussed professionally, are there any— another way I guess of putting this question—are there any surprises that may be in store because we don't have our eye on the right ball, if you will, with regard to stuff that could be pretty fundamental?*

JK: The thought I have is I just feel that boards do not pay enough attention to recommendations that are major changes of strategy. They do not fully analyze them and realize what they are looking at and what they are voting on. Take the simple one of active management versus indexing; there are always periods of time when index funds look a lot more attractive because the active managers just have not done as well. And then there are periods when it is the other way around. Foundations are in business for the long haul, in perpetuity in most cases. I think if you set your strategy and you go that direction, you may make variations in that strategy, but basically you stick with it. Those organizations that have done that for 15 or 20 years have outperformed and been more successful than those that are constantly changing the whole way they do things. I think boards need to be cognizant of that, and many of them are not, or they do not want to be.

FE: *One final question: You are certainly very highly regarded in the profession, and as you probably know and if not I'll say it bluntly, you've been a mentor, a role model for many, many CFOs. As you reflect on your career, was there anyone who served as a model or a mentor for you?*

JK: Adrian Cassidy, who was the Senior Vice President of Finance when I was appointed Director of Pensions at Pacific Telephone, was an early mentor. He was a seasoned regulatory attorney that took me under his wing and taught me how to interview and select investment managers. Later I had the good fortune of working with John English. John recently passed away. He was in charge of the pension fund at AT&T when I was just taking over the California Bell Company pension job. He was one of my mentors. He went on to the Ford Foundation in New York and headed that up for 15 years. I went on to a major foundation shortly thereafter, so our careers tracked. We were best friends, and I really admired how he approached money managers and how he viewed the entire investment business with candor, honesty and integrity. He stuck to what he did best and didn't change course, and his results were very good.

FE: *Well, I think on that note, appreciation from both of us at this end of the interview, Joe. Thank you!*

Section Three

The Trusted Counsel: The Changing Rules and Roles of Advisors

CHAPTER 7

The Role of Counsel in Foundations: Choices, Beginnings, and Service

By Reynolds Cafferata, Esq.

PERSPECTIVES

When one thinks of setting up a foundation, nine times out of ten the first person called is the attorney. From that point on, the attorney becomes a key advisor during the various life stages of a foundation—the application process, organizational structuring, plans for succession, and so on. From day one, the trusted attorney keeps the foundation from running afoul of ever-changing regulations. What is the scope of this integral relationship? What are the important questions or issues to be kept in mind when examining the work done by an attorney? In terms of service, what should a foundation client expect? Is there a road map of best practices for this relationship?

Estate planning and tax attorney Reynolds Cafferata uses both experience and conventional wisdom to answer these key questions. Cafferata, a partner with Riordan & McKinzie in Los Angeles, advises charitable organizations and individuals on the structure of large charitable gifts using charitable remainder trusts, charitable lead trusts, private foundations, support organizations, and other gift structures. Cafferata's estate planning clients include officers of high-tech companies, business owners, and individuals who work in the entertainment industry.

The role of the foundation[1] lawyer is much like the role of the lawyer for a business. The lawyer is a vital part of the team in forming and operating the foundation. Just as business cannot succeed if it is dominated by its lawyer, however, a foundation will not be effective if its operations are dominated by its lawyer. To be effective, foundation managers[2] should understand the role of the lawyer and how to work with the lawyer to achieve the foundation's goals.

The foundation managers must understand the services, role, and limitations of the lawyer to use his or her services for the benefit of the foundation. Foundation managers who fail to call on a lawyer at the proper times or who do not understand the lawyer's services, role, and limits may waste foundation resources or put the foundation at legal risk. The lawyer may have a role in almost every aspect of a foundation's operations. At the inception of the foundation, this means guidance regarding the choice of entity and structure. Thereafter, the new foundation needs assistance in obtaining tax and regulatory approvals. The foundation managers may require advice regarding internal governance and duties. As an active business entity, the foundation will need risk management guidance and may need representation in litigation. The foundation will often need guidance in its contractual and employment relationships. Finally, the foundation must be counseled regarding maintenance of its tax-exempt status.

FORMATION ISSUES

In most instances, a lawyer will be, and should be, consulted at the formation of a foundation. Just as the legal discussion for a business starts with an analysis of the choice of entity, the discussion regarding the formation of a foundation also starts with an analysis of the choice of entity. A client will often start a discussion regarding private philanthropy by asking a lawyer to form a private foundation.[3] Often, however, the private foundation will not be the best entity to meet the client's objectives.[4] The lawyer must elicit from the client his or her purposes in forming the entity and the activities that the client expects for the foundation. Based on this information, the lawyer can recommend to the client the best choice of entity for his or her private philanthropy.

For the lawyer to be effective, the client must have a clear understanding of the expected activities of the foundation. Will it make grants to other charities only? Will it award scholarships or operate a soup kitchen? Obviously, the foundation activities may change over time. The more detailed an understanding of future activities that the client provides to the lawyer, the better the lawyer will be able to identify the best structure for the foundation. Certain structures work well for one type of activity but not for others. To avoid an inappropriate structure, the lawyer must be aware of all likely activities.

Like a business, the analysis of choice of entity for a foundation comprises tax structure, legal structure, and choice of jurisdiction. The lawyer must work with the information from the client to develop the best tax and legal structure and to form it in the appropriate jurisdiction.

Choice of Tax Entity

A foundation can be one of three entities under the tax code: (1) a part of an existing charity (not an entity at all), (2) a private foundation, or (3) a public charity. The lawyer must be familiar with all of these alternatives to properly advise a client forming a foundation.

The first choice of a tax entity may be no entity at all. Perhaps a restricted fund with an existing charity or a donor-advised fund[5] at a community foundation would meet the donor's objectives.[6] The restricted fund would allow a client to focus support on an existing program at a charity that is of interest to the client. The donor-advised fund allows the client to deposit funds with a community foundation or other charity and recommend distributions to other charities or for charitable purposes. Some lawyers do not readily suggest restricted funds or donor-advised funds because they do not involve significant work for the lawyer or an ongoing relationship with a foundation that will have regular legal needs. If one of these alternatives meets the client's objectives, however, the lawyer should recommend it to the client.

When people think of a private philanthropic entity, they generally think of the private foundation. The private foundation, however, is subject to several disadvantages under the Internal Revenue Code.[7] The income tax deduction for contributions of most forms of appreciated property to a private foundation is limited to the donor's tax basis in that property.[8] The percentage of a donor's adjusted gross income that can be offset by a deduction for a contribution to a private foundation is more limited than in the case of a contribution to a public charity.[9] Private foundations are subject to a tax on their investment income and are subject to rigorous reporting requirements in the form of the 990-PF tax return.[10] Private foundations must distribute 5 percent of the value of the private foundation's assets annually.[11] Certain types of distributions from private foundations require prior IRS approval or additional reporting and record keeping.[12]

The primary benefit of a private foundation is that the client can have total legal control over the private foundation's operations. For clients for whom absolute control is an essential requirement, a private foundation may be the appropriate entity. If a client intends to form a private foundation, the lawyer must be fully familiar with the limitations of private foundations and must analyze the expected activities of the foundation to be certain they are compatible with the private foundation limits.

Private philanthropy is often carried on through a private foundation, but there are a number of public charity alternatives that a client should consider. The lawyer for the client forming a foundation should explore these alternatives with the client. The most flexible public charity alternative is the support organization.[13] A charitable support organization's operations are linked to those of an existing public charity (or charities) in such a way that the support organization is treated as a public charity rather than a private foundation.[14] The link to the public charities is achieved either by allowing the public charities to appoint a majority of the governing body of the organization or by structuring the distributions from the support organization of the public charities to ensure that the public charities will be attentive to its operations.[15] In any event, the majority of the governing body of the support organization may not be family members of the creator of the support organization or persons under the creator's control, such as employees.[16] The lawyer should be able to explain the legal and practical aspects of the support organization relationship to a client. The lawyer also may need to be able to explain the structure to the supported charities if they have not previously participated in a support organization. Making grants from a support organization can be more complicated than from a private foundation. The lawyer should minimize the limits on support organization grants at the formation by helping select appropriate supported charities. Charities with broad purposes will allow the support organization to fund a wide variety of charitable activities.

In addition to providing tax advantages, the support organization offers other potential advantages over the private foundation. The relationship of the support organization to the public charities can assure succession of management and that the support organization is always dedicated to the causes and issues that are important to its founder. Close relationships to public charities also makes their expertise available to the support organization to maximize the effectiveness of the programs of the support organization. The lawyer should help the client consider these benefits and use them to the maximum advantage for the foundation's operations.

Often the choice of tax entity involves tradeoffs. The lawyer should help the client understand all of the options available, and the benefits and limits of each entity. Sometimes expected operations will be wholly incompatible with one or more options, in which case the lawyer will direct the client to the only suitable structure. Often, however, more than one entity will accommodate the client's interests. In this case, the lawyer must help the client understand the tradeoffs, but the client must decide which tradeoffs are acceptable.

Choice of Legal Entity

In addition to selecting the tax structure that will be used as discussed previously, the lawyer must advise the creator of a foundation regarding the choice of legal entity. Although the client should be the primary decision maker regarding tax entity tradeoffs, the lawyer can be relied on to select the suitable legal structure. Typically, foundations are structured as either a trust or a corporation. The lawyer should review with the client the details of each structure and help select the one best suited to the client's needs and the expected foundation activities.

The corporate structure is most helpful if the foundation will have active operations and significant and complex interactions with other persons or entities. The corporation provides a clear liability shield for its creators, officers, and directors. The duties and obligations of corporate officers and directors are set forth in a well-developed body of law. Finally, the requirements for a corporation to contract and engage in other transactions are clearly understood. This well-developed body of law for corporations is helpful in analyzing complex operations and relationships.

The advantage of a trust is the flexibility that it affords in structuring its governance and operations. There are few mandatory provisions under most state laws for the governance of a trust. Within the trust instrument, the creator of a trust is generally free to create the rules for its governance. Trust operations are more private than those of a corporation because trust documents typically are not public documents like articles of incorporation. Also, trusts typically do not file officer statements that generally are required of corporations. The law regarding the liability of trustees and regarding trust interactions with other persons and entities, however, is not as well developed as the law in these areas with respect to corporations. The lawyer should review the expected activities and needs of the client to see if the trust form is suitable for the foundation.

Some states have adopted limited liability company statutes that allow a limited liability company (LLC) to be organized as a nonprofit entity.[17] The body of law on using these entities as charities is not well developed at all. As this law develops, however, there may be some circumstances in which an LLC might be considered for a foundation or aspects of a foundation's operations. Some nonprofits are using LLCs as holding companies for real estate to contain liabilities. The LLC should not be considered without the involvement of an experienced lawyer, who can determine if this novel structure is a feasible form for the foundation and who can identify the potential problems of a foundation organized as an unorthodox entity.

Choice of Jurisdiction

The final aspect to be considered in the formation of the foundation is the state laws under which the foundation will be formed. The state laws will affect the internal governance requirements, the state taxation of the entity, and the state regulatory supervision of the foundation. As with a choice of legal entity, while the lawyer should explain the issues to the client, the lawyer should generally guide the choice of jurisdiction.

Each state has its own rules regarding the internal operations of corporations created under that state's law or trusts administered under the state's laws. Of particular interest to foundations would be provisions affecting transactions between the foundation and its managers,[18] and meeting procedure requirements, particularly the procedures for taking actions without a formal meeting.[19] It may also be important to consider the required minimum number of managers.[20] Another issue to be considered is the powers granted to the foundation entity under state law.[21] Finally, the compensation, indemnification, and limitation of liability of foundation managers afforded by the state's laws should be considered. The lawyer for the foundation should review these rules with the client and discuss the activities that the client is considering to be sure no conflicts will exist.

If a foundation is incorporated in a state that has a corporate income tax, the foundation likely will need to obtain a determination of tax-exempt status from the state tax. This likely will involve additional filings, both at formation and annually. In addition, real and personal property taxes and other types of taxes also should be considered in selecting the jurisdiction in which the foundation will be formed. It is important to note, however, that even if a foundation is not incorporated under the laws of a state, if it has sufficient operations in a state, it may still be subject to tax in that state and need to file for tax-exempt status. If the foundation will not have operations in a state with burdensome tax requirements, however, it likely does not make sense to inadvertently impose such requirements on the foundation by incorporating under the state's laws. The lawyer for the foundation should work to minimize tax filing burdens on a foundation by minimizing the foundation's contacts with difficult states as much as can be done in light of the foundation's activities.

The level of supervision of charitable organizations by the states, usually by their attorney general's offices, varies from state to state. If a foundation will not have significant operations in a state whose attorney general actively regulates and supervises charities, then the foundation likely should not be incorporated in that state.

It is not reasonable to expect a lawyer to know the nuances of all 50 states' trust and corporations laws. The lawyer should be familiar with the laws of the state in which he or she practices, and perhaps, one or two other states. Knowledge of alternative states' laws is particularly important if the lawyer's home state has laws with potentially problematic limitations.[22] The lawyer also should be familiar with the tax requirements of the state of his or her practice and one or two alternatives if tax compliance is a burden in the lawyer's home state. Finally, the lawyer should have knowledge regarding the activities of the state regulators, such as the state attorney general and any other government body that supervises charitable activities. The client needs to disclose the expected geographic scope of the foundation's activities so that the lawyer can effectively use his or her knowledge of situs options for the foundation's benefit.

APPLICATION FOR TAX-EXEMPT STATUS AND OTHER REGULATORY APPROVALS

Once the type of entity has been selected and it has been formed in the desired jurisdiction, the foundation will need to seek tax-exempt status from the Internal Revenue Service and, possibly, the state in which the foundation is formed or operated. The foundation may need to obtain other regulatory approvals, such as for solicitation activities. The lawyer should be able to advise the foundation of all of the approvals it must obtain, and should be able to obtain approvals that have significant filing requirements.

The lawyer should obtain from the client all of the information required by the regulators. The lawyer can then organize that information in the form that each regulator requires. The term *charitable* as used in the United States Income Tax Code is broad and encompasses many activities.[23] Properly described, the IRS will approve the application for tax-exempt status for a wide variety of charitable endeavors. If the description of activities touches on or implies involvement in narrow, prohibited activities for charities, however, the application process can become bogged down or even fail. A lawyer must guide the client in identifying a charitable purpose and in describing that purpose in an appropriate manner. Furthermore, the lawyer should ensure that the application is complete and that all basic fundamental requirements are satisfied, such as governing instruments that include required dedications to charitable purposes, limitations on political activities, and the proper private foundation prohibitions where necessary. It is important, however, that the client make the decision and provide the underlying information regarding the foundation's operations. The lawyer should not be left to make up the program of the foundation, or it will reflect the lawyer's values rather than the client's values.

The lawyer should be strategic about completing an application for tax-exempt status. The application process should consider all potential aspects of the operations of the foundation to obtain the exemption on the most favorable basis for the foundation possible and to avoid having to seek further rulings from the IRS confirming that future operations do not jeopardize the tax-exempt status of the foundation. The application for tax-exempt status affords a private foundation an opportunity to obtain approval from the IRS of any program of grants to individuals for travel and study. If those activities are carried out by a private foundation without prior IRS approval, the payments will be taxable expenditures.[24] That approval can be obtained in the process of applying for tax-exempt status. If the approval is not obtained at the time, the foundation will need to seek a separate ruling, which can be a more extensive process than obtaining the approval of tax-exempt status.[25]

The IRS may have questions about a foundation's activities or operations. The lawyer must be able to respond to the IRS in a manner that effectively expedites the application process. In general, if the lawyer is knowledgeable and courteous, and promptly provides information requested by the IRS, he or she will succeed at obtaining a determination of tax-exempt status in a timely manner. At times, an IRS reviewer will incorrectly apply a rule or regulation. In most circumstances, however, if the lawyer for the foundation directs the reviewer to the proper authority and leads the reviewer through a reasoned analysis, the issue will be resolved. Belligerence and arrogance will never advance a foundation's cause with regulators. A foundation lawyer who is obnoxious to regulators will not be an effective advocate for the foundation.

If the foundation is incorporated in or operates in a state that imposes an income tax on the entity used to form the foundation, the foundation may need to apply for tax-exempt status with the state taxing authorities. The state tax authorities may impose additional governing instrument requirements or adjustments to language other than those required to satisfy the Code requirements. The lawyer should be aware of these requirements and nuances. The lawyer should use information, schedules, and narrative from the federal application for tax-exempt status to the fullest extent possible in any state applications. In some states, an exemption from real or personal property taxes or sales taxes may be required.

A typical foundation does not have an extensive fundraising program. If the foundation will be soliciting support from the public, it may need to comply with the state and local solicitation registration requirements in the areas in which it will be seeking funding. If the fundraising program is widespread, this can be a significant burden because the foundation can be faced with filing requirements in hundreds of jurisdictions. The lawyer should be able to advise the foundation of these requirements. Depending on the complexity of the registration requirements, the foundation may or may not need the lawyer to draft these applications.

UNIQUE TAX RULES FOR FOUNDATIONS

The Internal Revenue Code exempts foundations from tax in order to promote charity. The Internal Revenue Code contains several limitations and restrictions on foundations to ensure that they remain dedicated to their charitable purposes and are not diverted for private benefit. The foundation lawyer must be familiar with these limitations and be able to guide the foundation in complying with the limits of the Internal Revenue Code.

Private Foundation Rules

If a foundation is a private foundation as defined in the Code,[26] the foundation will be subject to several restrictions applicable to private foundations. In general, a private foundation must distribute 5 percent of the value of its assets annually. Private foundations are prohibited from engaging in a variety of transactions with the creator of the foundation. Private foundations are prohibited from holding large blocks of closely held businesses. Excessively risky investments are prohibited in private foundations. Finally, a variety of expenditures from private foundations will result in an excise tax on the foundation, including the giving of grants or scholarships for travel or study without prior IRS approval.

As noted previously, the lawyer for the foundation initially needs to determine whether the limitations on a private foundation would be unduly burdensome for the proposed activities of the foundation. If the private foundation limits will conflict with the operation of the foundation, an alternate structure should be used. If the foundation will be operated as a private foundation, the lawyer needs to make the foundation managers aware of the basic requirements of the structural limitations on private foundations and sensitize them to the situations that would be affected by these rules. A foundation manager does not need to know all of the details of the private foundation rules, but the foundation manager must know when the private foundation rules may be implicated and when to call the foundation lawyer.

A private foundation is required to distribute 5 percent of the value of its assets annually toward charitable purposes. The lawyer for the foundation (and its accountants) needs to be aware of the timing and methodology rules for calculating compliance with the distribution rule. The lawyer also should be familiar with options such as working with a community foundation that is available when a private foundation is having difficulty meeting its required minimum distribution. Other aspects that may need to be considered include the ability to exclude assets from the calculation base if they are used for the foundation's exempt purpose and identifying all expenditures that count toward the minimum distribution requirement.

Private foundations are prohibited from engaging in a wide variety of transactions with substantial contributors to the foundation and their families and related businesses (collectively, "disqualified persons").[27] A foundation likely will want to consult with its counsel any time it considers a transaction that may involve or affect any of the disqualified persons. These rules apply to indirect acts of self-dealing, and it is not always apparent when an indirect transaction is taking place. Furthermore, the prohibition includes a ban on the use of foundation assets for the benefit of a disqualified person. This prohibition may apply to a wide variety of transactions. Not every transaction that in some way involves the foundation and a disqualified person, however, is a prohibited transaction. The foundation lawyer should be able to help the foundation distinguish between transactions that are clearly permissible under these rules and transactions that clearly are not permitted, and to evaluate the transactions where the results may be unclear.

Private foundations are prohibited from holding investments that jeopardize their ability to carry out their exempt purpose.[28] An investment that is excessively risky relative to its expected return is a jeopardy investment. The foundation lawyer should be aware of the context in which this rule is applied to help the foundation and its investment advisors structure the foundation's portfolio to satisfy the prohibition on jeopardy investments.

A private foundation may not be used to hold large blocks of corporations in which disqualified persons own large amounts of stock. The foundation lawyer needs to be aware of the holding limits and the options available to the foundation to dispose of excess business holdings when a foundation receives a gift or bequest of stock constituting an excess business holding.

Certain private foundation grants require special procedures or prior IRS approval. Grants to foreign charities, to other private foundations, or to nonexempt entities all require special procedures and documentation. A grant program for payments to individuals for travel or study requires prior IRS approval. The lawyer for the foundation should be knowledgeable regarding these procedures and requirements. In addition, however, the foundation lawyer should be able to identify alternatives such as working with an existing public charity or a community foundation to achieve the foundation's goals.

Excess Benefit Transactions

A foundation that is formed as a public charity, primarily the support organization, is subject to the excess benefit transaction limitations. These rules impose an excise tax on insiders who receive an excess economic benefit from a transaction with a foundation and on the foundation managers who approved the excess benefit transaction. An excess benefit transaction occurs when the goods or services received by an insider exceed the value of the goods or services provided by the insider to the foundation. The insiders who are subject to the excess benefit transaction rules are disqualified persons with respect to the foundation. The definition of *disqualified person* for the excess benefit transaction rules includes any person who is in a position to exercise substantial influence over the foundation.

The foundation lawyer should be able to help the foundation identify transactions that would be covered by the excess benefit transaction rules. This primarily is a question of identifying disqualified persons. Because the excess benefit transaction statute is relatively new, there may be many circumstances under which it is unclear whether a person is a disqualified person if he or she does not fall into one of the per se categories such as a director or officer. If the foundation is entering into a transaction with a disqualified person, it will need to ensure that no excess benefit is being provided. If the foundation managers prove that the transaction followed certain procedures, including obtaining adequate documentation and obtaining the approval of a majority of independent directors, in many instances it is presumed that a transaction does not provide an excess economic benefit. A foundation can take several important procedural steps to minimize the risk that it will engage in an excess benefit transaction and the risk of liability for a tax on the foundation managers. The lawyer for the foundation should be called on to guide the foundation through these procedures. Particularly with respect to the presumption, the lawyer should provide detailed directions regarding the steps to be followed and the information needed. The foundation should follow these steps in their entirety.

Unrelated Business Income

Although charitable organizations are normally exempt from tax, if a charity regularly engages in a business activity that is not related to its exempt purpose, the charity will be subject to tax on that income.[29] This tax is the Unrelated Business Income Tax (UBIT). There are numerous exemptions from UBIT that cover most forms of investment income and certain fundraisers normally associated with charities, such as the sale of donated tangible personal property or bingo. Even a normally exempt activity, however, will be taxable if it is financed with debt. A foundation lawyer needs to be familiar with the UBIT rules in order to help the foundation avoid unnecessary payment of tax.

A foundation should have its lawyer review all of the income-producing assets that the foundation will acquire. Typically, this will be a simple review, and most portfolios that a foundation would consider will not generate UBIT. The foundation lawyer, however, should be able to catch common sources of inadvertent UBIT, such as limited partnerships that operate businesses or have debt, or margin activity in an account. If the foundation will be making private equity investments of any kind, the lawyer should review the potential for UBIT in the disclosure documents as well as other features of the investment for the foundation.

The foundation should consult with its lawyer in setting up fundraising programs. Improper wording of recognition of donations; transactions involving the use of the foundation's name, mailing lists, or other property; or certain sales programs can all result in UBIT if structured improperly. Generally, however, there is a way to engage in most fundraising activities without generating UBIT. The foundation lawyer should be able to help the foundation structure its fundraising activities so that the funds raised will not be subject to UBIT. For example, a sales activity will not generate UBIT if it is carried out entirely by volunteers.

Whenever a foundation borrows funds, its lawyer should review the UBIT implications of the borrowing. A foundation that acquires property that will not be used in its exempt purpose with debt will be taxable on the income from the property, including the gain on the sale of the property. This rule not only covers debt that is secured by the property, but also debt that would not have been incurred but for the acquisition of the property. Accordingly, whenever a foundation takes on debt, the foundation lawyer should review the debt to be certain it will not be attributed by the IRS to income-producing assets generating UBIT.

Lobbying Limits

The foundation may wish to participate in the legislative process for many reasons, but the Code places strict limits on the types and level of political participation in which the foundation is permitted to engage. If the foundation violates these restrictions, it can face substantial penalties in the form of excise taxes on prohibited political expenditures, or even have its tax-exempt status revoked. In order to avoid those sanctions, the lawyer for the foundation must understand the rules that prohibit certain types of political activities. The foundation should consult with its lawyer before engaging in political activity of any kind because a violation of the rules can be disastrous for the foundation. Even minor participation in a political campaign can jeopardize the foundation's tax-exempt status.

The Code contains several rules designed to ensure that charitable organizations do not use tax benefits to subsidize attempts to influence legislation. Specifically, an organization will not qualify for tax-exempt status under IRC Section 501(c)(3) if a "substantial part" of the activities of the organization involve carrying on propaganda or otherwise attempting to influence legislation. Unlike publicly supported charities, private foundations cannot elect to use the Code's lobbying safe harbor provision and must abide by the vague "substantial part" standard. The Code prohibits charitable organizations from influencing legislation directly through communication with government officials, indirectly attempting to influence legislation through grassroots lobbying, or influencing public elections.[30] A charity is also prohibited from participating in political campaigns by either supporting or opposing any candidate for public office.[31] Counsel should be aware of these restrictions and advise the foundation to avoid improper activities.

Counsel for a foundation also should be able to advise the foundation on permissible political activities that fall outside the Code's definition of "lobbying" or prohibited involvement in campaigns. A foundation is free to interact with legislative bodies when it is merely making available the results of a nonpartisan study.[32] The organization also may provide technical advice or assistance to a governmental body in response to the government's written request. The broadest exception allows a foundation to communicate directly with a legislative body regarding issues that affect the operations of the organization itself.[33] A charitable organization is therefore allowed to seek legislation protecting its own existence, and to aid its own purposes. Counsel must be able to advise the foundation on the character of its proposed activities, to ensure that they are permissible forms of legislative involvement.

GENERAL OPERATIONS

The operations of a foundation require the same guidance as a business, except that each issue has additional unique requirements related to the tax-exempt status of the foundation. The areas in which foundations need guidance include employment law, litigation, contracts, intellectual property, and real estate. The foundation lawyer must be able to competently represent the foundation in each of these areas. In all likelihood, this role would be fulfilled by multiple lawyers because each area is a specialty. Each of these specialists must, however, have a general familiarity with the unique requirements of nonprofits and must work with a lawyer with detailed knowledge of the nonprofit rules.

The foundation may not know whether its lawyer is familiar with the special rules applicable to charities. The best way to address the concern is to raise the issues with the lawyer. The foundation should inquire specifically whether an activity would do any of the following: (1) affect its tax-exempt status, (2) cause private benefit or be a prohibited transaction, or (3) generate unrelated business income.

The lawyer either will be able to analyze the issues, or, it is hoped, will obtain the assistance of counsel who can evaluate the issues.

Employment Law

One of the major areas of compliance for any business, as well as foundations, is employment law. In general, employees of foundations are entitled to the same rights as employees of for-profit businesses. Accordingly, the foundation must be advised regarding appropriate compensation, withholding, family and medical leave, harassment, and termination policies. The tax-exempt status of the foundation adds several dimensions to this analysis. The foundation lawyer needs to guide the foundation regarding basic principles of employment law and the special requirements for tax-exempt employers.

With respect to private foundation managers, compensation must be reasonable so as to avoid a self-dealing transaction.[34] For non-foundation managers, excessive compensation would constitute private benefit, jeopardizing the tax-exempt status of the foundation.[35] While the foundation lawyer cannot tell the foundation how much compensation is reasonable, the lawyer should be able to advise the foundation regarding procedures it must follow in approving compensation. The lawyer also should identify the types of information that the foundation should obtain in evaluating compensation.

The retirement and fringe benefits that can be offered by a foundation are similar to those that can be offered by for-profit businesses, but important differences exist. The lawyer for the foundation should be familiar with the unique requirements for tax-exempt organizations. Use of business compensation programs in a tax-exempt entity can result in disqualified plans or unexpected tax results.[36]

Litigation

Like any business, a foundation may become involved in litigation. Like advising a business, lawyers for the foundation must advise the foundation regarding the strengths and weaknesses to balancing the costs and risks of pursuing the case versus potential settlement. In most instances, litigation strategy should be a dispassionate economic decision. In a few circumstances, however, the case may relate to the exempt purpose of the foundation, and it may be more than an economic decision regarding the strategy of the case. Unless the foundation is a legal defense fund or other organization with a primary mission to pursue litigation, however, a foundation should carefully consider whether it ever wants to further its exempt purposes through litigation. Litigation is, at best, a costly way to further an exempt purpose.

An important issue in litigation involving a foundation is whether any of its officers or directors have been named in the suit. It is an extremely onerous burden for a volunteer director to retain counsel to defend him- or herself in a lawsuit brought against the foundation. Before any litigation is commenced, the foundation may want to consult with its lawyer to assess general liability and director and officer insurance as well as particular riders that may be needed for specific activities of the foundation.[37] For example, foundations with employees will want to consider harassment policies. Where there are multiple employees, the foundation could be liable for the conduct of one employee toward another employee. A foundation that has programs involving the supervision of children also will want special insurance riders to cover those activities.

In addition to protecting officers and directors in litigation, a lawyer for a foundation must be sensitive to the potential conflicts of interest between the officers and directors on the one hand, and the foundation on the other hand. Such a conflict may arise in particular when a taxing or regulatory authority has questioned a transaction between the foundation and one of its officers or directors. At the outset, all parties would seek to prove that the transaction was proper. If the transaction was not proper, however, a conflict arises because the foundation would seek to undo the transaction and recover from the officer or director who received the benefit of the transaction. The foundation also may seek to recover damages from the officers or directors who breached their fiduciary duty by approving the transaction.

One area of litigation that does not generally affect most businesses but may affect the foundation is contested probate litigation. A foundation that receives benefits under a will or a trust may find its interest challenged by family members of the donor. An interest under a will or trust is an asset of the foundation. Accordingly, in carrying out their fiduciary duties, the directors of the foundation must prudently pursue the interest. This does not mean that the foundation should pursue all interests in estates at all costs, but a foundation also should not readily settle a case, giving up property to which it has a solid claim. To be sure of securing its gift under a will or trust, the foundation should apprise its lawyer whenever the foundation is the beneficiary of such a gift. Notice will allow the lawyer to evaluate whether there are any like problems with the gift. For most cases the foundation can be passive during the administration of an estate or trust. In the few circumstances where a foundation must protect its interest in an estate or trust, it is generally best for the foundation to have its lawyer be involved from the outset of the administration. Early participation gives the lawyer the greatest flexibility to protect a gift and, in some instances, the maximum leverage in settlement discussions. If the lawyer is brought into a problematic administration of a will or trust late in the process, deadlines to exercise important legal rights may have lapsed.

Contracts

The foundation may enter into a variety of contracts. Some of these contracts may be negotiated agreements specific to the foundation and the other party to the contract. Other contracts will be form agreements supplied by the vendor that are not subject to negotiation or modification. Depending on the circumstances, the foundation lawyer may need the skill and experience to negotiate an agreement on behalf of the foundation. Under these circumstances, the lawyer needs to be able to constructively work through issues and effectively come to a beneficial agreement between the other party and the foundation. While some agreements may not be subject to negotiation, review by the foundation lawyer may be helpful so that the foundation is fully apprised of all of its rights and obligations under the proposed agreement. This will allow the foundation to make an informed decision whether the benefits under the contract outweigh any of the potential risks or costs.

The considerations mentioned for a foundation lawyer giving guidance with respect to a contract so far are the same considerations that would apply for any lawyer representing a business. In addition to these considerations, however, the foundation lawyer must be aware of certain special considerations relating to the foundation's tax-exempt status. If the contract provides for payments to the foundation, the lawyer must analyze whether the payments could be considered unrelated business taxable income for the foundation. If business activities can be attributed to the foundation under the agreement, any payments will likely be unrelated business taxable income.

The foundation lawyer also should consider with respect to any contract the prohibition on private benefit and private inurement that apply to the foundation, as well as the excise tax on excess benefit transactions or the self-dealing prohibitions when applicable.[38] Sometimes the fairness of the transaction is assumed if it is with a third party, but it is possible for a foundation to enter into an agreement with a person who is not an insider that provides an uncompensated economic benefit, jeopardizing the tax-exempt status of the foundation.

One particular type of contract to which a foundation may be a party that requires special attention is the pledge. Under basic tenets of contract law, a pledge to make a future gift without any consideration is not enforceable.[39] Some states have made written charitable pledges enforceable based on public policy.[40] In other states, courts have enforced pledges using the basic contract law theory of detrimental reliance.[41] Detrimental reliance occurs when a party takes a detrimental action in reliance on a promise to make a gift.[42] Still other courts have enforced pledges on the theory that the consideration for the pledge is the contributions by other donors to the charity.[43] The foundation lawyer should be aware of how to make the pledge enforceable under the applicable state law, and perhaps, just as important, should be able to advise the foundation under what circumstances it is desirable to have the pledge be enforceable. For accounting and self-dealing rules, it may be advantageous for a pledge not to be enforceable. The financial accounting standards require that enforceable pledges be treated as an asset of the foundation, but ascertaining the value of a pledge can be difficult. If a pledge is made to contribute a specific dollar amount or a specific piece of property, a future renegotiation of that pledge may result in a self-dealing transaction.

Another type of foundation agreement generally not used in business is the grant agreement with other organizations and with individuals. These agreements need to have adequate and reasonable safeguards to ensure that the grant funds are used for intended purposes. In the case of a private foundation, depending on the type of organization or person receiving the grant or the purposes of the grant, the Internal Revenue Code and regulations impose requirements that certain provisions be included in the grant agreement.[44] Failure to include the required provisions can result in an excise tax on the foundation. The lawyer for the foundation needs to provide the foundation with grant agreements that meet basic tax and legal requirements. The lawyer also must have practical knowledge of the operations of potential recipients to design effective grant procedures. Finally, a lawyer for the foundation should be sensitive to the accounting requirements applicable to grant agreements, particularly when structuring a multiyear or renewable grant.

Intellectual Property

Foundations that support scholarship and writing, sponsor art works, or otherwise fund endeavors that create copyrightable material or material otherwise protectable under intellectual property laws need to be advised how to establish and protect their rights in this property. Furthermore, foundations that distribute or share materials need to be sensitive to and understand the rights of others who may have developed the materials being used by the foundation. At the basic level of protecting its own rights and not infringing on the rights of others, the role of an intellectual property lawyer for a foundation is similar to that of an intellectual property lawyer for a business. Foundations, however, have special considerations in the intellectual property area.

Business clients usually want to restrict use of their copyrighted or protected material. A foundation that has developed copyrightable materials, however, will often want to share those materials with the general public on a low-cost or no-cost basis. Accordingly, the foundation may be willing to have others copy its materials under certain circumstances without receiving compensation. The foundation may, however, want limits such as requiring attribution of the source or may not want the materials duplicated in contexts that are disparaging or offensive to the foundation. In other instances the foundation may want compensation for its materials, particularly to recover the cost of producing copies that are being distributed.

The foundation lawyer needs to be able to develop plans to distribute materials as the foundation desires without losing control of the copyright. The tax-exempt status may impact the appropriate distribution agreement structure. The sale of copyrighted materials needs to be structured so that it will not result in unrelated business taxable income for the foundation.

In assembling its educational materials, the foundation may desire to use material copyrighted by others. Under limited circumstances, a foundation can use the copyrighted materials of others without seeking their permission or providing any compensation to them under the doctrine of "fair use."[45] The lawyer for the foundation must be able to advise the foundation when its uses are subject to the fair use doctrine and under what circumstances the foundation will need to obtain permission to use copyrighted materials.

Intellectual property issues sometimes come to the surface for a foundation when it is negotiating agreements regarding its Web site. A well-drafted agreement for hosting a Web site will clearly delineate ownership of the content of the Web site and who is responsible for any infringing material posted on the Web site. The lawyer should be familiar with the various financial arrangements for Web sites. Many firms offer "free" Web hosting based on the idea that the foundation's content can be used to gain sponsors or advertisers. The application of the unrelated business income tax to Web activities is not settled.[46] The foundation lawyer needs to keep abreast of this evolving area of law.

Real Estate

Either for its administrative needs or as part of its exempt-purpose activities, the foundation may enter into real estate transactions. The foundation will have basic concerns present in any real estate transactions, such as negotiating price and terms in face of uncertain future needs and markets. Depending on the circumstances, a real estate deal may contain several contingencies and notice requirements that the foundation lawyer will need to help the foundation navigate.

Real estate transactions are a common source of related-party transactions that may pose problems under the excess benefit or self-dealing rules. It is not uncommon for a founder, officer, or director of a foundation to want to make office space available to the foundation. It may be most convenient to house the foundation operations near or in the same offices as the family business. The foundation lawyer must know when these arrangements are permissible and how to structure them. The reverse transaction also must be reviewed carefully where the foundation has excess office space and a related party wishes to lease some of that space.

The foundation may use real estate in its exempt-purpose activities, such as providing low-income housing or operating a facility. If the real estate will generate revenue, the foundation lawyer will need to be able to advise the foundation whether any of that revenue will be unrelated business taxable income. Admission to the foundation's museum would not be unrelated business taxable income, but depending on the circumstances, revenue from a restaurant in the same building may or may not be unrelated business income.

Real estate investments are often leveraged with debt. For foundations this debt can result in debt-financed unrelated business income. The foundation lawyer must be able to structure realistic transactions to avoid unexpected, unrelated business taxable income.

Holding real estate exposes the foundation to the risk of environmental liability. Although the foundation lawyer must be aware of this risk, he or she also must be aware of the impact of tax-exempt status on typical strategies for limiting liability. Real estate is often held in a separate entity to contain liability. Such an entity may not qualify for tax-exempt status or local property tax exemptions, however. The foundation lawyer must be able to help the foundation balance these considerations in structuring real estate holdings. To be most effective, the lawyer should be retained early in the process of acquiring real estate, before any agreements are signed. This timing is important to give the lawyer maximum flexibility in helping the foundation structure its ownership of real estate.

CORPORATE GOVERNANCE

Foundation managers will need guidance from the foundation lawyer on carrying out their legal responsibilities. These responsibilities will flow from three areas: (1) general corporate law or trust law, depending on the foundation entity, (2) the specific state law provisions for charitable corporations or charitable trusts, and (3) tax rules that affect governance. Another area in which a foundation will need guidance is the restructuring of its governance. Foundation managers often want guidance from the foundation lawyer regarding their personal liability risk.

Basic Duties

There are important distinctions between duties of a director of a corporation and of a trustee, at a top level of analysis, but the obligations for both capacities are substantially the same. Persons serving in both capacities have a standard of care they must perform for the benefit of the foundation. The foundation lawyer needs to advise foundation managers as to the duty owed, to whom the duty is owed, and what conduct is required to satisfy the duty. When available, the lawyer should provide relevant examples of proper and improper exercises of the duty by other governing bodies in similar situations. There are three broad areas of analysis with respect to the governance of a foundation: general operations, investment management, and fiduciary liability.

The generally applicable standard for most operational decisions of a foundation is the business judgment rule.[47] The business judgment rule requires that the foundation manager acted in good faith on the basis of reasonable information.[48] It is a standard that looks at the process by which the decision was made more than the result of the decision. The manager of a foundation has wide latitude to make operational decisions on the organization's behalf, as long as the manager complies with the legal standard of the business judgment rule. The rule presumes that the foundation manager made decisions in the organization's best interests because the director or officer of a foundation has access to information about many factors influencing the organization's business decisions. Therefore, although the manager's decision may ultimately be detrimental to the organization, a court will hesitate to substitute its own judgment in place of the judgment of the foundation manager. The court will only question the foundation manager's decisions if evidence shows that the manager acted in bad faith, had a conflict of interest, or was not well enough informed about the subject of the business judgment to make an appropriate decision.[49] The business judgment rule involves scrutiny of the foundation manager's decision-making process, rather than the substantive result of the decision. Accordingly, the foundation lawyer should lay out to the foundation manager the process that should be followed to make operational decisions. In particular, the lawyer should identify the type of information that the foundation manager should review.

Investment Decisions

One area in which the foundation manager will face a specialized duty is management of the foundation investments. Most states impose statutory duties regarding the standard of care of a director's managing assets, the factors that should be considered, and the circumstances under which investment management decisions can be delegated.[50] The lawyer for the foundation should guide the foundation manager through the process required by the state's investments standard. Although the lawyer should not be making the investment decisions for the foundation, he or she needs to be familiar with basic investment concepts such as asset allocation, total return investing, modern portfolio theory, and the relationship between time horizon and risk. All of these investment concepts are incorporated in most states' standards for institutional investment management. The lawyer should identify for the board all of the factors that the law requires the board to consider. The board should consider the mission and goals of the foundation and identify the relative importance and needs based on those factors. The foundation investment advisors would then recommend the appropriate investments and asset allocations based on the factors and goals identified by the board. Working in concert with the investment advisors, the lawyer should help the foundation draft an investment policy statement that documents the procedures and the deliberations of the board in determining its investment policy, showing that the appropriate information was gathered and appropriate factors were considered.

Foundation managers must regularly monitor the performance of the foundation investments to determine that the asset allocation desired by the foundation is being achieved and to compare the performance of the portfolio with the benchmark indices identified in the investment policy statement. If the policy is not being followed, the investment manager should be directed to align the portfolio to the policy. If the foundation managers do not wish to align the portfolio to the policy, then they should reconsider the policy and make appropriate adjustments. The lawyer for the foundation should keep the foundation managers apprised of the type of review that they should be conducting. Lawyers should also keep the foundation managers mindful of the need for periodic oversight.

The Uniform Management of Institutional Funds Act gives foundation managers an opportunity to delegate responsibility for managing investments to committees or professional fund managers.[51] If foundation managers follow proper procedures in making the delegation, which include procedures to ensure that the choice of investment manager is prudent, the foundation managers will be protected from liability for losses in the portfolio. The foundation lawyer should apprise the managers of the opportunity to delegate responsibility and liability, and guide them in the procedures for proper delegation. Furthermore, the lawyer should guide the foundation managers in the review and oversight that is required of them when they have delegated management of assets to a committee or investment manager.

Foundations are often in the position of entering into contracts with board members, officers, or their families. Foundation managers are generally required to follow special procedures when approving insider contracts. A foundation lawyer should be called on to advise the foundation managers of the procedures, documentation, and information required for approval of an insider transaction. Insider transactions also have significant implications for the tax-exempt status of the foundation and potential excise taxes. The tax rules often also impose procedural requirements. The foundation lawyer needs to coordinate the decision-making process to ensure that it satisfies all of the overlapping state and tax procedure requirements.

When working with counsel for a foundation in making decisions, it is important to be sure that the foundation lawyer is called on to advise the foundation regarding the right procedure to follow in making the decision, but is not called on to tell the foundation what is the right decision. That is, the foundation lawyer can advise the foundation of what steps should be followed and what records should be kept to document that the board has made a prudent decision. The foundation lawyer should not be called on to tell the board, however, which of two alternatives is prudent. A qualification to this distinction is in the area of precedent. In researching the standard of care for the directors and identifying the factors they should consider and the persons to whom they owe a duty, the lawyer will review cases and rulings on prior decisions of directors of charitable organizations. In some instances, the lawyer will find cases with facts that are similar or analogous to the situation faced by the foundation. In these instances the lawyer should help the foundation board determine whether the foundation's situation is sufficiently similar to the case that its ruling can be relied on to establish whether a decision is prudent or whether important characteristics distinguish the facts in the case from the situation faced by the foundation such that a different outcome may result.

Tax Rules Affecting Governance

In addition to state law considerations, federal tax law may affect certain decisions. In particular, where a foundation is considering a transaction with an insider with respect to the foundation, only certain transactions may be allowed, or specific procedures may be advisable.[52] In these decisions, it is essential that the foundation develop information to support its decision. In most instances, the lawyer from the foundation may be able to advise the foundation about the type of information needed, but counsel likely will not be a good source of that information. For example, the foundation lawyer may be able to advise the foundation managers to review salaries of comparable foundations in setting the salary of the foundation president, but most lawyers would not be good sources of information regarding comparable salaries. For a foundation subject to the excess benefit rules,[53] the foundation managers will be able to shift the burden of proof regarding the reasonableness of a transaction from themselves to the IRS if the foundation managers follow the proper procedures in reviewing the decision and obtain the proper information. To be sure that the foundation protects itself in reviewing insider transactions, the foundation should consult with its lawyer at the outset, not after an agreement has been reached.

Restructuring

A foundation can exist in perpetuity. During this extended period, it may be necessary to reorganize the foundation structure. The terms of a foundation trust agreement may need to be modified, or the corporate structure may need to be changed. The lawyer for the foundation needs to be aware of the circumstances in which a reorganization or modification of structure would make sense. The lawyer must also be familiar with the rules governing the reorganization of the foundation's legal structure. Finally, the foundation lawyer must be aware of the additional roles that the IRS or the attorney general of the state in which the foundation is organized may play.

One reason to change a foundation structure is that the governing provisions pose a limitation on the operations that adversely affects the foundation. A trust instrument may contain investment limitations, or the articles of incorporation may limit the purposes for which foundation funds can be spent. The lawyer should consider whether there is at least a good-faith argument that a proposed action is within the existing purposes of the foundation. If only the attorney general would have standing to question the use of funds, assuming that it is a legitimate use of funds, there may be no reason to go through the expense of modifying the governing instruments. The lawyer should also consider whether any state law provision would override the limitation in the governing instrument.

If no other options seem viable other than changing the governing instrument, the foundation lawyer would first review the governing instruments to determine whether they provide any mechanism for changing the provisions. If not, then the lawyer for the foundation would look to state law provisions. Particularly in the case of trusts, state law may offer several grounds and procedures for modifying the governing instrument. The lawyers should select the simplest applicable procedure for making the desired modification.

From time to time, foundations may wish to reorganize by either merging or splitting into multiple foundations. Family dynamics often lead to the division of a foundation. A divorce or sibling disagreements may be resolved by dividing a foundation into separate entities so that each disagreeing party has an entity over which they have complete control. If the foundation is a private foundation, a division needs to be structured so that it does not trigger the private foundation termination tax[54] or cause one of the entities to have expenditure responsibility over the operations of the other entity.[55] The foundation lawyer should be able to recommend and execute a division of a foundation when it is desirable.

Just as business corporations sometimes merge for strategic reasons, foundations may also be merged. Two small foundations with similar purposes may be more effective as a single entity. A merger also is an effective mechanism for changing the situs of a foundation that is a corporation. A new nonprofit is formed in the state to which the foundation wishes to move its situs, and then the new corporation and the old corporation are merged with the new corporation as the surviving corporation. A foundation also may want to spin off a portion of its assets or operations to segregate liabilities or to obtain a favorable tax status for those operations, such as qualifying as an operating foundation. A reorganization can allow the foundation to obtain these benefits.

Reorganizations can be highly effective in solving certain foundation problems or creating opportunities. They can, however, be complicated and costly. The foundation lawyer needs to assist the foundation in determining when one of these transactions is justified and when a simpler solution will address the issue.

Liability of Nonprofit Directors

The foundation should protect itself from legal liability by purchasing insurance coverage. Although insurance will not entirely insulate the foundation from liability, it is the most effective way to protect the organization from many kinds of lawsuits. A foundation should purchase two types of insurance policies: general liability, and directors and officers (D&O) insurance. A general liability policy protects the foundation against many claims for negligence and other torts, covering claims for bodily injury or property damage. It protects the foundation when a plaintiff names the organization in a lawsuit, including respondeat superior claims where the organization is held responsible for the actions of its agents.

In contrast, a D&O policy does not protect the overall organization; it only covers the directors and officers in litigation relating to the foundation when they are individually named in the lawsuit. Directors and officers insurance is especially important for foundations because many directors of nonprofit organizations may not otherwise have the resources to shelter themselves from liability. The lawyer for the foundation should look for a D&O policy that pays defense costs throughout the course of a lawsuit, rather than leaving the director to pay out-of-pocket expenses and wait for later reimbursement, which could take months or even years.

Some states have enacted legislation to protect the directors and officers of nonprofit organizations against liability. The California state legislature has enacted two statutes, but they offer limited protection. California Corporations Code section 5047.5 states that a plaintiff has no cause of action against a director or officer of a nonprofit organization who acted in good faith, within the scope of normal duties, and in the best interests of the corporation. But the statute applies only to nonprofit organizations that already maintain a general liability insurance policy. That policy's limits must correspond with the annual budget of the organization—over $1 million for a nonprofit organization whose annual budget is over $50,000—and the statute protects only the directors and officers when the general liability policy covers the type of damages at issue.[56] The Cal. Corp. Code section 5047.5 will not apply when the director or officer engaged in self-dealing transactions, transactions involving a conflict of interest, or actions brought by the attorney general. The statute also will not apply to any intentional, reckless, or wanton acts, gross negligence, or actions based on fraud, oppression, or malice. The director or officer must be an uncompensated volunteer.

Another California statute limiting nonprofit organizations' D&O liability is Cal. Corp. Code section 5239. The statute protects the foundation's directors or officers against claims that are covered by the organization's general liability policy or D&O insurance, or the individual's own insurance policy. But even if the damages are not covered by insurance, the director or officer will not be liable if the board of the organization and the individual director made "all reasonable efforts in good faith" to obtain insurance. The statute contains restrictions similar to Cal. Corp. Code section 5047.5, and only protects the nonprofit organization's directors and officers from liability if they are uncompensated volunteers.

The Delaware legislature has enacted similar provisions to limit liability for nonprofit volunteers.[57] Delaware law protects nonprofit volunteers from negligence liability in connection with the organization's activities.[58] The statute contains several exceptions, allowing liability for willful, wanton, or grossly negligent conduct, and for acts involving the operation of motor vehicles in the course of an organization's activities. The Delaware legislation allows proof of the volunteer's conduct to establish the liability of the nonprofit organization through the doctrine of respondeat superior. Although the individual director or officer may be immune from liability under 10 Del. Code section 8133, therefore, a plaintiff may find it easier to hold the organization liable.

State legislatures have limited the liability of nonprofit organization volunteers, but those laws may not provide enough protection. As the California and Delaware examples illustrate, state legislation will protect an organization only under certain circumstances. Under both states' laws, the director or officer of the nonprofit organization must be a volunteer. State statutes may not clearly apply at the outset of litigation, leaving the director to pay for expensive legal defense until the judge can discern that the director is not liable under the statute.

Because state laws do not completely shield a foundation's directors and officers against liability, the organization should primarily rely on its insurance policies for protection. Therefore, the organization will still need to acquire both general liability and D&O insurance coverage. The foundation should obtain a general liability insurance policy on D&O insurance of at least $1 million. The foundation lawyer should advise the foundation of the scope of any of the state statutes protecting directors and officers from liability. The lawyer should help the foundation structure its insurance for the maximum protection of the foundation and its officers.

CONFLICTS OF INTEREST

The lawyer for a foundation needs to be careful to avoid conflicts of interests between his or her representation of the creator of the foundation and the foundation itself. A foundation lawyer has often worked with the creator of the foundation for an extended period before forming the foundation. This lawyer may represent several of the creator's business interests. Naturally, the creator will want the lawyer to continue representation in the area of the foundation. Business lawyers are aware that conflicts of interest can arise between owners and their businesses, particularly if the business is not 100 percent owned by one person. When a business is wholly owned by an individual, ultimately all of the duties and obligations flow to the same owner, and conflicts of interest don't arise. With respect to conflicts, the foundation is like the business with outside owners. The foundation should be wholly dedicated to public and charitable purposes and should serve no private interests, including those of the creator of the foundation.

A conflict of interest is obvious when the foundation and its creators or a family member are entering into an agreement with each other. Generally in this circumstance, the foundation and the founder should have separate counsel. The other circumstance where separate counsel may be necessary is when the foundation and its creator are jointly entering into a contract, such as both entities investing in the same fund or both entities entering into a lease with one landlord for office space. Depending on the circumstances, the foundation may or may not need separate counsel in these arrangements. If the lawyer will represent both the foundation and its creator, he or she may want to have a written agreement regarding the joint representation that, among other things, addresses what will happen if a conflict between the foundation and its creator develops in the future.

The lawyer for the foundation should be primarily responsible for addressing conflicts of interests in his or her representation of the foundation, but the foundation managers should raise these issues with the lawyer whenever there seems to be a potential conflict to ensure that the lawyer is considering and will address the conflict issue.

Obviously, representation with a conflict of interest will reflect poorly on the lawyer. The foundation managers, however, are also subject to criticism if they fail to ensure that the foundation has adequate independent representation when needed.

LEGAL OPINIONS AND PRIVATE LETTER RULINGS

In reviewing certain transactions or activities of the foundation, the foundation may consider obtaining a legal opinion from the lawyer or a private letter ruling from the IRS. An opinion is a formal legal analysis in which the law firm will be liable if the legal conclusions are not correct. A private letter ruling is a formal response from the IRS to a question posed by a taxpayer. The lawyer for the foundation should be able to advise the foundation of the circumstances when a legal opinion or private letter ruling is required. Because both opinions and ruling requests entail a great deal of work for the lawyer, the lawyer may have a bias in favor of them.

In certain transactions, foundation managers can protect themselves from liability if they have obtained a legal opinion regarding the transaction. Because of the liability assumed by the firm, however, legal opinions typically are costly. Legal opinions should only resolve legal questions. The opinion must rely on the factual information provided by the client. These facts will be set out in the opinion. If the facts set out in the opinion do not match the actual situation facing the foundation, the opinion will not be valid. It should also be noted that law firms will tend to qualify and limit the scope of their opinions as much as possible to minimize the actual exposure in giving the opinion. Generally, a foundation should seek an opinion of counsel only in the rarest of circumstances when it is essential. This might be the case when dealing with a significant transaction that could be affected by the self-dealing or excess benefit rules, and the foundation is seeking to protect outside directors. The foundation may also need to obtain opinions in transactions where it is buying or selling significant assets to unrelated third parties or is borrowing significant sums of money. In these transactions the other party or a lender may request an opinion confirming the status and authority of the foundation. Finally, if the foundation is engaged in a transaction that takes advantage of a particular law that requires tax-exempt status, such as low-income housing credits or tax-exempt bond financing, an opinion may be required. In general, however, foundations should avoid requesting opinions of counsel because they will tend to be expensive and may offer little or no benefit. If the foundation would like a record of legal advice it has been given, it may ask for a letter confirming the advice or a memorandum of law on the subject. Such correspondence will document the advice without carrying the premium of an opinion.

The IRS regularly publishes private letter rulings addressing the various private foundation restrictions and limitations. Private letter rules are responses from the IRS to particular taxpayers who have asked the IRS to rule on the tax implications of a particular set of facts. In some instances, these rulings address novel situations for which the rules do not provide a clear answer. Several rulings each year, however, will address situations that could have been resolved by a foundation lawyer with careful analysis of the available authorities. The foundation lawyer should be able to distinguish between the circumstances where the foundation can comfortably proceed without requesting a ruling from the IRS and those occasional situations where the authorities do not resolve the situation, and the facts reasonably might be interpreted as causing a violation of one of the private foundation prohibitions. Unnecessary ruling requests are a waste of foundation resources.

FINDING FOUNDATION COUNSEL

Although the role of the lawyer for a foundation is analogous to that of a general business lawyer, general business lawyers are rarely equipped to provide guidance to a foundation. The corporate or trust laws governing the operation of the foundation may be similar to general business corporation law, but the lawyer must be familiar with the unique provisions governing nonprofit entities. The tax rules for nonprofits are not discrete and focused only on particular transactions or particular times. Tax laws permeate and affect all aspects of the foundation's operations. If the foundation has sophisticated operations, it is unlikely that a single lawyer will be able to service all of those needs. A lawyer who is familiar with the corporate governance requirements for a foundation is often also familiar with the tax laws governing the foundation's operations. The challenge comes when a foundation needs an employment law or litigation specialist who is familiar with the unique rules governing that body of law, but who is also sufficiently familiar with the unique tax and corporate law aspects of a foundation to address those needs in the foundation context.

Good business lawyers understand the businesses of their clients. The same is true for foundation lawyers. Foundation lawyers should understand the business of nonprofit organizations. This understanding often will come from personal involvement in nonprofit organizations, serving as a volunteer or a member of a board of directors. Similarly, a lawyer who has solicited donations will be better equipped to advise a foundation in a negotiation with a donor. A lawyer who has helped a nonprofit apply for grants is better equipped to help a foundation draft its grant review policies. In addition to general knowledge of nonprofit business operations, the lawyer for the foundation should become familiar with the particular foundation's operations. This would come from site visits to some of the foundation's projects or attending meetings of the foundation grant review or scholarship committee. This background will allow the foundation lawyer to be a general strategic advisor to the foundation. In addition, it will help ensure that the legal advice will be practical and can be followed and implemented by the foundation.

A small foundation with basic operations may be able to find a single lawyer who is able to address most, if not all, of the foundation's legal needs. A larger foundation with more complex transactions likely will need expertise beyond that which can be maintained by any one person. Such a foundation will likely have a primary lawyer expert in the tax-exempt organization area, but will need the assistance of specialists in real estate, employment, litigation, or intellectual property law. The larger foundation will need to be represented by a law firm that has attorneys who can handle all of its different needs and that represents enough tax-exempt organizations that the attorneys in the other disciplines have represented nonprofits within their discipline and are sensitive to their special needs and considerations.

The search for foundation counsel should be conducted in the same manner as any search for professional services. The foundation should consult with other foundations to get recommendations of potential lawyers and firms. In addition, the local bar association may have a committee devoted to tax-exempt organizations, and members of that committee may be potential candidates as lawyers for the foundation. Staff or directors of the foundation may also meet potential lawyers at educational seminars conducted by associations of nonprofits or associations of foundations.

Initially, the foundation will want to solicit basic biographical and professional information from the potential lawyers. This information should include, where appropriate, some information about other lawyers in the firm who may be working on the foundation's matters. At this stage, the foundation also may want to request a list of some existing foundation clients that can be called as references. In reviewing the written material, the foundation should look for experience with nonprofits, quality educations, and participation professionally and personally with nonprofits.

After reviewing the information from various lawyers, the foundation board or executive director, either in person or over the telephone, will want to interview a few of the candidates. The amount of time that the foundation expects from the potential lawyer and whether the foundation should expect the potential lawyer to come to personal meetings should be based on a realistic assessment of the volume of work that the foundation expects to generate. The selection based on the interview should be confirmed with calls to the references.

Many foundations do not follow a structured procedure in identifying the foundation lawyer. Often, the family estate planning attorney who may have created the foundation becomes its lawyer. If this attorney services numerous clients who create foundations, he or she may be knowledgeable in foundation operations and capable of continuing to meet the foundation's needs. If, on the other hand, the lawyer only occasionally works with foundations, another lawyer may be helpful. Board members may be friends with or neighbors of lawyers. Before retaining one of these acquaintances as the foundation lawyer, the foundation should review the lawyer's credentials and references, and possibly consider other candidates. If any of the foundation managers are resistant to this type of process, they should be reminded that their fiduciary duty applies to the process of selecting a lawyer. Just as a prudent process must be followed in selecting the foundation's investment advisors, the choice of attorney also must be made on a prudent basis.

CONCLUSION

The complicated tax and legal limitations imposed on foundations make the lawyer an important part of any foundation management team. For that team to function well, the lawyer should be aware of all the significant activities of the foundation and should bring recommendations to steer clear of legal problems at an early stage. The lawyer should be creative and practical so that the foundation has maximum flexibility to achieve its charitable objectives. The foundation needs to keep the lawyer informed of its operations and carefully follow recommendations of the lawyer that the foundation accepts. Ultimately, the role of the lawyer is the same as that of all the other foundation managers—to help carry out and promote the charitable objectives of the foundation. These objectives will be most effectively carried out if the lawyer has the background, experience, and temperament to provide guidance to the foundation, and if the foundation managers understand the role of the lawyer so that the managers can ask the proper questions of the lawyer and provide the lawyer with the information he or she needs to complete the required analysis.

NOTES

1. Throughout this chapter, *foundation* shall generically refer to a private philanthropic entity for a client that may be a private foundation or a support organization. See notes 7 to 16.
2. Throughout the chapter, the term *manager* refers to directors, officers, or trustees of a nonprofit organization as is applicable.
3. See IRC section 509(a).
4. See notes 7 to 12 and accompanying text regarding limitations of private foundations.
5. Treas. Reg. section 1.170A–9(e)(ii).
6. A donor-directed fund is a less common alternative to the donor-advised fund that may be considered. These funds are required to distribute income annually and can exist only for the life of the creator of the fund and the life of his or her spouse. IRC section 170(b)(1)(E)(iii).
7. Internal Revenue Code of 1986 as amended (IRC). See notes 26 to 28 and accompanying text.
8. IRC section 170(d).
9. IRC section 170(b).
10. *Id*. section 4944(a)(1).
11. *Id*. section 4940.
12. *Id*. section 4945(d)(3), (4).
13. Others include medical research foundations under IRC section 170(b)(1)(A)(iii), educational institutions with regular curriculum under IRC section 170(b)(1)(A)(ii), public-supported charities under IRC section 170(b)(1)(A)(vi), and charities that derive revenue from their exempt-purpose activities. IRC section 509(a)(2).
14. *Id*. section 509(a)(3).
15. *Id*.
16. *Id*.
17. See, e.g., Del. Code section 18–106(a).
18. California Corporations Code section 5227 prohibits more than 49 percent of the directors of a charity or their family members from being board members. If any family member is compensated, a board of only family members will not be legal under this statute. Such a provision does not appear in most other states.
19. Compare California Corporations Code section 5211(b), which requires unanimous consent of directors for an action without meeting, with Nev. Rev. Stat. 82–271(2), which allows action without a meeting by a majority of the directors.
20. Compare Cal. Corp. Code section 5213(a), which provides that the president cannot be secretary or treasurer, with Nev. Rev. Stat. 82–211, which allows one person to hold all offices.
21. E.g., Cal. Corp. Code section 5140(k) authorizes a nonprofit to act as trustee of charitable trusts.

22. E.g., California's limitation on foundation directors with a financial interest in foundation operations. See note 18.
23. Treas. Reg. section 1.501(c)(3)–1(d).
24. See last paragraph of section on Private Foundation Rules.
25. *Id.*
26. IRC section 509 (a).
27. IRC section 4941.
28. IRC section 4943.
29. IRC sections 512, 513, 514.
30. IRC section 4945(e).
31. IRC section 4955(d).
32. IRC section 4945(e).
33. *Id.*
34. IRC section 4941(a)(2).
35. IRC section 501(c)(3).
36. Business employers can make an unfunded promise to make a future payment to an employee without tax consequence to the employee. For a tax-exempt entity, under Section 457, such a promise can result in immediate taxation of the employee.
37. See notes 56 to 58 and accompanying text.
38. IRC section 4941; 4958.
39. Restatement (Second) contracts section 71.
40. See, e.g., *Jewish Federation of Cent. New Jersey* v. *Barondess*, 234 N.J. Super 526 (1989).
41. Witkin, Summary of California Law (9th Ed., 1987) Contracts, section 257.
42. The textbook example is the nephew who signs a contract to purchase a car in reliance on his uncle's promise to pay for the car. In this case, the court would enforce the uncle's promise.
43. See, e.g., *Hirsch* v. *Hirsch*, 32 Ohio App. 2d. 200 (1972).
44. IRC section 4945.
45. *Nimmer on Copyright* (MB) section 13.05.
46. See Catherine E. Livingston, "Tax Exempt Organizations and the Internet: Tax and Other Legal Issues," *Exempt. Org. Tax Rev.* 419 (March 2001).
47. In the case of trusts, where trustees are acting in an area of discretion not in contravention of a particular provision of the trust or higher duty imposed by law, courts have extended to trustees broad latitude similar to the business judgment rule applicable to directors of charitable corporations.
48. American Law Institute, Principles of Corporate Governance section 4.01.
49. See *Id.* at section 4.01(c) (1994).
50. See Cal. Prob. Code section 18500 *et. seq.*
51. *Id.*
52. See IRC section 4941.
53. IRC section 4958.
54. IRC section 507(c).

55. IRC section 4945.
56. Cal. Corp. Code section 5047.5.
57. Title 10 of the Delaware Code section 8133.
58. *Id.*

CHAPTER 8

The IRS Eyes the Foundation World

By Douglas Mancino, Esq.

PERSPECTIVES

Tax law has always exerted a strong influence on the development of foundation-based philanthropy in this country. It is not coincidental that the first megafoundations were created soon after the institution of income taxes (and the first and only deduction, charity) at the turn of the twentieth century. In the interim—with the most significant action being the Tax Reform Act of 1969—Congress and the IRS have been as closely watched by foundations and their advisors as they have been watched. Monitoring the often subtle shifts in policy is not an easy job.

Douglas Mancino, a partner at McDermott, Will & Emery's Los Angeles office, has represented all types of nonprofit organizations in tax, business, and financial matters for more than 25 years. He advises organizations and individuals on the formation of nonprofit organizations such as public charities, private foundations, and trade associations, and oversees corporate transactions such as mergers and acquisitions, joint ventures, shared services, and conversions from nonprofit to for-profit status.

Private foundations represent more than one-fifth of all tax-exempt charitable organizations that file information returns with the Internal Revenue Service (IRS). Private foundations are also one of the most highly regulated types of charitable organizations from a tax point of view. In 1969, after studying the activities of private foundations and identifying several real and perceived abuses of them, Congress added provisions to the Internal Revenue Code (the Code) that affect the grantmaking and investment activities of private foundations and that govern transactions between a private foundation and its directors, officers, or other disqualified persons.

GRANTMAKING ACTIVITIES OF PRIVATE FOUNDATIONS

One of the principal activities of private nonoperating foundations that entitles them to obtain and maintain their section 501(c)(3) tax-exempt status is their grantmaking activities. The IRS has regularly ruled that making grants to individuals and other organizations exclusively for charitable, educational, scientific, or other exempt purposes qualifies a private foundation for tax-exempt status as an organization described in section 501(c)(3) of the Code. Unlike public charities, which enjoy considerable latitude with respect to their grantmaking activities, private foundations are subject to statutory provisions that prescribe the minimum amounts that must be distributed periodically, limit the types of grants that a private foundation may make, and impose a variety of restrictions on how and to whom such grants may be made.

Minimum Distribution Requirements

One of the abuses that troubled Congress in 1969 was that many private foundations were paying out insufficient amounts of their income or corpus for grants. Section 4942 now prescribes minimum distribution requirements that must be met by nonoperating foundations and imposes an excise tax on the undistributed income of an operating foundation under certain circumstances. Private operating foundations are exempt from the minimum distribution requirements.

Section 4942(a) imposes a tax on the "undistributed income" (income not distributed within one year following the year in which it is earned) of private foundations for any taxable year. The tax is equal to 15 percent of the amount of the income that remains undistributed as of the first day of the second year following the year in which the income is earned. An additional tax of 100 percent of the amount that remains undistributed after the initial tax has been imposed can also be incurred if correcting distributions are not made in a timely fashion. Failures to make required distributions because of incorrect valuations of assets are not taxed if certain requirements are met.

Distributable Amount

Private foundations are required to make minimum distributions of at least 5 percent of the excess of the aggregate fair market value of all assets of the foundation other than those used or held for use directly in carrying out the foundation's exempt purposes, reduced by the acquisition indebtedness with respect to the assets. This minimum distribution amount is reduced by the sum of the taxes imposed on the private foundation for the taxable year.

A private foundation's undistributed income thus consists of the distributable amount reduced by the amount of qualifying distributions. Importantly, calculation of the distributable amount applies only to the foundation's assets and not to assets held by separate charitable remainder and similar trusts of which the foundation is the ultimately beneficiary.

Qualifying Distributions

The primary purpose of the minimum distribution requirement is to ensure that some minimum level of grants, loans, or other expenditures for charitable purposes (including administrative expenses) is made annually by private foundations. The distribution requirements are designed to give private foundations a fair amount of flexibility in the methods they select to satisfy these requirements and to permit private foundations to increase their endowments (if they choose) by adopting a reasonable investment strategy that yields returns in excess of the minimum required to be distributed.

In general, any grant made to public charity to accomplish one or more charitable, educational, scientific, or other exempt purpose is treated as a qualifying distribution. The only exception to this general rule is for grants made to public charities that are controlled by the private foundation or disqualified persons with respect to the private foundation.

Grants made by a private foundation to another private foundation are treated as qualifying distributions only if the recipient private foundation distributes the grant proceeds within a prescribed period, and the grantor private foundation obtains adequate records or other sufficient evidence from the recipient private foundation showing that the required distributions were made by the recipient organization.

Grants to individuals for charitable, educational, scientific, or other exempt purposes are treated as qualifying distributions. Thus, for example, grants to individuals for scholarships, for research, or to reward past accomplishments are charged against the distributable amount; however, certain types of grants to individuals are subject to expenditure responsibility requirements.

As with grants to individuals, grants to nonexempt entities for charitable purposes may be charged against a private foundation's distributable amount, but they too must be made in compliance with the expenditure responsibility rules.

Set-Asides

From time to time, private foundations can expect to receive grant requests that can or should be funded over a period of years rather than in one lump sum. To accommodate these kinds of situations and to allow these commitments to be treated as qualifying distributions on a current basis, a private foundation must formally request approval as a set-aside by the IRS, as long as the set-aside is payable within 60 months after it has been set aside. In addition, the private foundation must establish to the satisfaction of the IRS that the specific project for which the amount is set aside is one that can be accomplished better by the set-aside than by the immediate payment of funds. The types of specific projects for which a set-aside is appropriate include relatively long-term grants or expenditures that must be made in order to ensure the continuity of particular projects or program-related investments or grants made as part of a matching program.

Charitable Assets

Expenditures made by a private foundation to acquire assets that it will use directly in carrying out its exempt purposes are treated as qualifying distributions. An example of this type of expenditure is the acquisition of a research facility and related equipment by a medical research organization or the purchase of paintings or other works of art for public display.

Administrative Expenses

In general, reasonable and necessary administrative expenses are treated as qualifying distributions. The administrative expenses must be incurred in connection with grantmaking; expenses incurred with respect to investment activities are not counted for this purpose, but rather are allowed as deductions in calculating the amount of net investment income subject to taxation.

Taxable Expenditures

In order to ensure that private foundations do not misuse their funds, section 4945(a)(1) imposes a 10 percent tax on each taxable expenditure. In addition, section 4945(a)(2) imposes a tax on any director, officer, or other foundation manager who agrees to making an expenditure knowing that it is taxable. This tax is equal to 2.5 percent of the amount of the taxable expenditure (up to $5,000) and is imposed on directors, officers, or foundation managers unless their agreement is not willful and is due to reasonable cause. Additional taxes of 100 percent and 50 percent (up to $10,000) are imposed, respectively, on both the private foundation and the participating directors, officers, or other foundation managers if a tax is imposed on the taxable expenditure and the expenditure is not corrected. Section 4945(d) identifies several categories of taxable expenditures.

Lobbying Expenditures

The term *taxable expenditure* includes any amounts paid or incurred by a private foundation to carry on propaganda or otherwise attempt to influence legislation. The regulations under section 4945 incorporate the definitions of "attempts to influence legislation" contained in section 4911. Also, the regulations make clear that the special rules for electing public charities' communications with their members do not apply to private foundations. Consequently, whether a private foundation's communications with its members (assuming it has any) are lobbying communications is determined solely with reference to whether it constitutes a direct or grassroots lobbying communication and does not take into consideration the special exception available to public charities for certain communications with their members.

Private foundations are not treated as having paid or incurred amounts for lobbying merely because they make grants to other organizations on the condition that the recipients obtain a matching support or appropriation from a governmental body. In addition, private foundations are not treated as having made taxable expenditures of amounts paid or incurred in carrying on discussions with officials of governmental bodies as long as certain conditions are met: (1) the subject of these discussions must be either an existing or a new program jointly funded by the foundation and the government; (2) the discussions must be undertaken to exchange data and information on the subject matter of the program; and (3) the discussions may not be undertaken by foundation managers in order to make any direct attempt to persuade governmental officials or employees to take particular positions on specific legislative issues other than the program.

Electioneering and Voter Registration Activities

As a general matter, amounts paid or incurred by a private foundation to influence the outcome of any specific election or to carry on, directly or indirectly, a voter registration drive are treated as taxable expenditures. A private foundation is considered to be influencing the outcome of a specific public election if it participates or intervenes, directly or indirectly, in any political campaign on behalf of or in opposition to any candidate for public office. Candidates for public office include individuals who offer themselves, or who are proposed by others as contestants, for elective national, state, or local public office. Attempts to influence the outcome of a specific public election include publishing or distributing written or printed statements or making oral statements on behalf of or in opposition to a candidate, paying salaries or expenses of campaign workers, and conducting or paying the expenses of conducting a voter registration drive limited to the geographic area covered by the campaign. If an organization meets certain requirements, amounts paid or incurred by the foundation are not considered taxable expenditures even if they involve voting registration drives.

Grants to Public Charities

Private foundations typically make most of their grants to public charities to accomplish their exempt purposes. Grants to public charities are not taxable expenditures. In general, the primary responsibility of the private foundation in connection with its proposed grants to public charities is to establish that the organization is in fact a qualified public charity.

Generally, this proof requires the private foundation to obtain a copy of the proposed grantee's determination letter issued to it by the IRS and an affirmative representation from the proposed grantee that the determination letter has not been revoked. In addition, if the private foundation proposes to make a substantial grant to an organization and has reason to believe that the proposed grantee's public charity status may be adversely affected by the grant, further steps must be taken to obtain financial and other information that will help establish, to the satisfaction of the private foundation, that the public charity status of the proposed grantee will not be jeopardized by the grant.

From time to time, private foundations are approached by individuals or organizations seeking to use an established public charity as a conduit through which to make a proposed grant. If the private foundation does not earmark the use of the grant for any named secondary grantee and an agreement, oral or written, does not exist whereby the private foundation may cause the recipient organization to select a secondary grantee, the private foundation's grant is generally treated as made to the public charity itself rather than to the secondary grantee.

Grants made to a governmental entity are generally treated as grants to a public charity and do not require the exercise of expenditure responsibility. If a private foundation makes a grant to a political subdivision and the grant is earmarked for use by another organization, the grantor private foundation need not exercise expenditure responsibility for the grant if the government agency has obtained advance approval from the IRS of its grantmaking program and the government agency exercises expenditure responsibility for its grants.

Grants to Other Private Foundations

Private foundation grants to other private foundations are not taxable expenditures, provided they exercise expenditure responsibility for the grants. Expenditure responsibility requirements obligate the foundation to exert all reasonable effort and to establish adequate procedures to see that the grant is spent solely for the purpose for which it was made, to obtain full and complete reports from the grantee on how the funds are spent, and to make full and detailed reports on the expenditures to the IRS on Form 990-PF annually. The IRS has identified a series of steps to establish that the private foundation has exercised expenditure responsibility for grants.

Grants to Noncharitable Organizations

Private foundations occasionally receive grant requests from organizations that do not qualify as charitable organizations. An example might be a request from a business corporation seeking to fund research concerning a health-related problem affecting residents of a particular community. Another example might be a grant request from a trade association described in section 501(c)(6) seeking to fund a specific research or educational project.

It is perfectly appropriate for private foundations to make grants to non–section 501(c)(3) organizations if they wish to do so, provided that the grant itself is intended to further a charitable, educational, scientific, or other exempt purpose, and that the private foundation exercises expenditure responsibility with respect to the grant. If these requirements are not met, however, the grant will be a taxable expenditure. In addition to the general expenditure responsibility requirements, if the proposed grant is to be made to a non–section 501(c)(3) organization, the grant agreement must obligate that grantee organization to maintain the grant funds (or other assets transferred) continuously in a separate fund dedicated to charitable, educational, scientific, or other exempt purposes. The grant agreement must also obligate the grantee to return any unexpended amounts promptly to the grantor foundation.

Grants to Individuals

Private foundations may make grants to individuals as long as the grants are designed to accomplish one or more charitable, educational, scientific, or other exempt purposes; however, additional steps must be taken to avoid taxable expenditure treatment if the grant or similar expenditure, such as a loan, is going to be made to an individual for travel, study, or similar purposes. In these cases, the grants must be made pursuant to written grant procedures that are submitted in advance by the private foundation to the IRS for its approval. The courts have routinely rejected "substantial compliance" and similar arguments made to explain or rationalize the failure of the foundation to obtain the necessary advance approvals. The individual grant procedures must provide for a selection process that is objective and nondiscriminatory and that is reasonably calculated to result in performance by the individual grantees of the activities that the grants are intended to finance. Also, the procedures must require the individual grantees to provide regular reports to the grantor foundation with respect to carrying out the purposes of the grant. Special requirements apply to employer-sponsored grant programs to ensure that grants to employees or members of their families are for charitable and not compensatory purposes.

INVESTMENTS OF PRIVATE FOUNDATIONS

Net Investment Income Excise Tax

In 1969, Congress enacted an excise tax on the net investment income of private foundations for the ostensible purpose of financing the administration of the extended provisions applicable to private foundations. The tax is currently 2 percent of the net investment income of a private foundation for the taxable year. This tax is paid annually, and estimated taxes must be paid in quarterly installments.

Private foundations are eligible to reduce the tax from 2 percent to 1 percent if the foundation's qualifying distributions for the current year exceed the sum of the average payout ratio for the base period, multiplied by the net value of noncharitable assets for the current year, plus 1 percent of the net investment income for the current year.

Jeopardy Investments

General Rules

Section 4944(a)(1) imposes a tax on any private foundation that invests its funds in a manner that jeopardizes carrying out any of its exempt purposes. The tax is equal to 5 percent of the amounts invested for each year or part thereof in the taxable period. In addition, if the private foundation is subject to the tax, any director, officer, or other foundation manager who participates in making that investment may also be subject to a 5 percent tax (up to $5,000) if that person knew that the investment would jeopardize carrying out the foundation's exempt purposes and if the participation by that person was willful and not due to reasonable cause.

If the investment is not removed from jeopardy after the imposition of the initial tax, second-tier year taxes of 25 percent and 5 percent (up to $10,000) can be imposed, respectively, on the foundation and any directors, officers, or foundation managers who refuse to agree to remove any part of the investment from jeopardy.

In general, only a small range of investments is likely to result in a serious risk that the foundation or its directors, officers, or managers would be subject to the section 4944 taxes. These investments are generally made where there has been a failure to exercise ordinary business care and prudence, under the facts and circumstances at the time the investment is made, in providing for the long- and short-term financial needs of the foundation to carry out its exempt purposes.

In determining whether the requisite standard of care and prudence has been met, such factors as the expected return, the risks of rising and falling price levels, and the need for diversification within the investment portfolio are taken into account. Also, whether the investment of a particular amount jeopardizes the carrying out of the foundation's exempt purpose is determined on an investment-by-investment basis, each case taking into account the foundation's portfolio as a whole.

No category or type of investments is treated as a per se violation of section 4944; however, the regulations identify the following types or methods of investment that are scrutinized closely to determine whether the directors and officers of a private foundation have met the requisite standards of care and prudence:

- Trading in securities on margin
- Trading in commodity futures

- Investments in working interests in oil and gas wells
- The purchase of puts, calls, and straddles
- The purchase of warrants and selling short

It is important to recognize that when the regulations under section 4944 were drafted, there was no recognized market for trading in options, and many of the sophisticated investment vehicles (e.g., notional principal contracts and other forms of derivatives) did not exist. Many of these investment vehicles and products are now a part of prudent investment strategies of many organizations. Nonetheless, before a private foundation embarks on an aggressive investment strategy, it should use care to obtain legal advice to confirm that its particular strategy, taken in context, satisfies the applicable standards; however, the IRS will not issue a ruling that the use of a proposed investment procedure by a private foundation precludes the imposition of tax under section 4944.

Some examples of jeopardizing investments are (1) loans made by private foundation to its attorney advisor; (2) the payment of premiums and interest with respect to a whole life insurance policy subject to a loan to the donor-insured that was donated to a private foundation; (3) the acquisition of a hotel; and (4) the exchange of common stock in a corporation by private foundation (which constituted its sole asset) for preferred stock in another corporation. In another case, a private foundation was determined to have engaged in jeopardizing investments when the foundation managers invested substantially all of the foundation's funds in a company that was publicly traded on a stock exchange and was the employer of several of the foundation's managers. The IRS rejected the foundation managers' argument that their special involvement with the company would enable them to manage the portfolio of the foundation better, and concluded that the risks undertaken in placing the entire portfolio in the stock of one company were so great as to cause the investment to be a jeopardy investment.

On the other hand, the purchase of a bingo hall in order to raise funds for a private foundation's charitable purpose was held not to be a jeopardizing investment, nor was the purchase of gold mining stock, because the purchase of such stock was consistent with the foundation's policy of investing as a hedge against inflation. Similarly, the investment of a small percentage of a private foundation's portfolio in a venture capital pool was held not to be a jeopardy investment.

Compliance with section 4944 does not relieve the foundation or its managers from responsibility to comply with other federal or state laws. Thus, private foundations and their managers must use care to comply with federal and state securities registration, insider trading, short-sale, disclosure, or fraud statutes, as well as state laws that prescribe permitted or impermissible forms of investments. Conversely, compliance with state laws does not exempt or relieve private foundations or their managers from the obligations under section 4944. Thus, for example, even if the fiduciary duty standards imposed by state law are satisfied, that fact alone does not exempt or relieve the foundation or its managers of exposure under section 4944.

Special Exceptions

Investments that are gratuitously transferred to a private foundation are excluded from its coverage; however, if consideration is paid by the foundation directly or indirectly, the foundation is treated as having made an investment to the extent of the consideration.

Also, investments acquired solely in connection with corporation reorganizations, such as mergers, recapitalizations, and liquidations, are not subject to section 4944. The "solely" requirement would presumably preclude the application of the exception to purely consensual exchanges of investments (e.g., exchanges of securities between investors in the same corporation) that are not corporate reorganizations described in section 368(a).

Finally, the IRS has ruled that investments acquired by a private foundation at a time when it was classified as a public charity will be excluded from the application of section 4944.

Program-Related Investments

Many private foundations have decided that their charitable purposes may be carried out more effectively by making investments in selected high-risk businesses for the primary purpose of indirectly accomplishing a charitable purpose by providing assistance to the business. An example of this type of investment is the purchase of stock in, or the extension of credit to, a minority-owned small business corporation that is located in a deteriorated urban area. Program-related investments were pioneered by the Ford Foundation during the 1960s.

Congress recognized that these types of investments, by their very nature, involve extremely high risks and might otherwise be regarded as jeopardy investments. Consequently, section 4944(c) provides expressly that program-related investments will not be considered as investments that jeopardize carrying out a private foundation's exempt purposes. To be classified as a program-related investment, the investment must possess three characteristics:

1. The primary purpose of the investment must be to accomplish one or more charitable purposes. An investment meets this description if it significantly furthers the accomplishment of the private foundation's exempt activity and if the investment would not have been made but for the relationship between the investment and the accomplishment of the foundation's exempt activities.

2. No significant purpose of the investment may be to produce income from the appreciation of property. Satisfaction of this requirement is determined in part on whether investors solely engaged in investing for profit would be likely to make an investment in the business or project on the same terms as the private foundation. That an investment produces significant income or capital appreciation is not, in the absence of other factors, conclusive evidence of a significant purpose involving the production of income from the appreciation of property.

3. No purpose of the investment may be to influence legislation or to support a candidate for public office.

The concept of program-related investments has typically been used by private foundations to support minority-owned businesses, to help finance urban redevelopment, and for similar purposes. In appropriate cases, however, a private foundation may find it desirable to use program-related investments to help accomplish other charitable purposes. An example would be research for a cure for AIDS conducted by a medical researcher who needs additional funding for the project and cannot obtain it or can obtain it only from commercial sources on terms that are overly restrictive.

Excess Business Holdings

In general, the excess business holdings of a private foundation are the holdings it would have to dispose of to a person other than a disqualified person in order for its remaining holdings to be permitted holdings as defined later. Section 4943(a)(1) imposes a 5 percent initial excise tax on the total value of a private foundation's excess business holdings for each taxable year of the foundation during the taxable period, as defined in section 4943(d)(2). If the foundation fails to dispose of its excess business holdings after the initial tax is imposed, section 4943(b) imposes an additional 200 percent excise tax on the undisposed excess business holdings.

Significantly, the section 4943 excise taxes are only imposed on the private foundation, and no tax is imposed on the foundation managers whose actions or inaction may have given rise to the taxes. Nonetheless, these individuals may have personal exposure under state laws if their actions or inaction were willful or otherwise breached their fiduciary duty to the organization. As previously noted, the organizational requirements of private foundations in section 508(e) require compliance with section 4943 and may create a separate basis for a state surcharge or similar action against the foundation managers.

Ninety-Day Grace Period

If a private foundation acquires excess business holdings other than as a result of a purchase, the foundation has 90 days from the time it knew or had reason to know of the event that created the excess business holdings within which to dispose of them without being subject to tax. The 90-day grace period also applies to excess business holdings that result from the purchase or acquisition of interests by disqualified persons. Determining if a private foundation knew or had reason to know of the acquisition of holdings by disqualified persons is based on several factors, including (1) the foundation having in place reasonable procedures for discovering such holdings, (2) the diversity of foundation holdings, and (3) the existence of large numbers of disqualified persons who have little or no contact with the foundation or its managers.

Holdings Acquired by Gift or Bequest

Private foundations that acquire excess business holdings by gift or bequest generally have five years within which to dispose of them. The period can be extended to 10 years in cases involving an unusually large gift or bequest or holdings with complex business structures if the foundation establishes to the satisfaction of the IRS that certain conditions exist and that it has taken certain prescribed steps.

Permitted Holdings in Corporations

Private foundations are permitted to own up to 20 percent of the voting stock of a corporation. If disqualified persons also own voting stock in the same corporation, the permitted holdings of the foundation are reduced by the amount of voting stock held by the disqualified persons. Private foundations are permitted to own any amount of one or more classes of nonvoting stock of a corporation if all disqualified persons actually or constructively own no more than 20 percent of the voting stock in the corporation. Any equity interests that do not have voting powers attributable to them are nonvoting.

Debt obligations and nonstock instruments. Debt obligations, including debts that are convertible into voting or nonvoting stock, as well as warrants, options, and other rights to acquire stock are not considered equity interests for purposes of section 4943. The criteria developed by the IRS and the courts are used to determine whether hybrid securities are treated as debt or equity for section 4943 purposes.

Permitted Holdings in Partnerships, Trusts, and Other Unincorporated Entities

Private foundations are permitted to own up to 20 percent of the profits interest in a partnership (general or limited) or a joint venture classified as a partnership. Similar rules presumably apply to membership or other interests in limited liability companies classified as partnerships. As with stock holdings, permitted holdings in partnerships are reduced by profits interest held by disqualified persons.

Capital interests in partnerships are equated with nonvoting stock, and thus if disqualified persons together own less than 20 percent of the profits interest in a partnership, a private foundation may own a capital interest greater than 20 percent.

Special rules apply to ownership interests in other entities, such as trusts and unincorporated associations, that are intended to equate the interests of a private foundation in the entities with stock for purposes of determining the permitted holdings a private foundation may have in the entities.

Private foundations are precluded from operating a sole proprietorship. This prohibition has the effect of preventing private foundations from conducting most unrelated trades or businesses.

A private foundation is permitted to own up to 2 percent of the voting stock and 2 percent of the value of all outstanding classes of stock in a corporation. The holdings of private foundations described in section 4946(a)(1)(H) are aggregated for purposes of calculating whether this de minimis rule is available. Once the 2 percent de minimis amount has been exceeded, the calculation of a foundation's excess business holdings disregards the 2 percent de minimis rule. Importantly, this rule applies only to holdings of stock in corporations and not to holdings in other forms of entities, such as partnerships or trusts.

The permitted holdings of a private foundation in a business enterprise can be increased from 20 percent to 35 percent under limited circumstances. First, the private foundation and all disqualified persons may not hold more than 35 percent of the voting stock in a corporation or equivalent interest in another form of enterprise. Second, the foundation must establish to the satisfaction of the IRS (i.e., by obtaining a ruling) that effective control of the business is in the hands of persons other than disqualified persons or the foundation itself. Effective control is defined as "the possession, directly or indirectly, of the power to direct or cause the direction of the management and policies of a business enterprise, whether through the ownership of voting stock, the use of voting trusts, or contractual arrangements, or otherwise." It is not enough to show merely that neither the foundation nor the disqualified persons have effective control.

TRANSACTIONS BETWEEN A PRIVATE FOUNDATION AND ITS DIRECTORS, OFFICERS, OR OTHER DISQUALIFIED PERSONS

In General

Transactions between a private foundation and members of its board of directors, officers, substantial contributors, and various individuals or organizations related to these persons must be monitored and reviewed carefully. Before the enactment of the Tax Reform Act of 1969, section 503 of the 1954 Code imposed an arm's-length standard of conduct on dealings between a private foundation and its founders and major contributors to prevent private foundations from being used by these persons for their personal benefit. Potential sanctions for violation of these standards included the loss of the foundation's exempt status for at least one year and the disallowance of deductions to donors for contributions made during the period.

Congress's perception of the ineffectiveness and inequity of these standards and sanctions prompted it to include provisions in the Tax Reform Act of 1969 that generally prohibit outright, rather than regulate, most direct or indirect transactions (defined as acts of self-dealing) between a private foundation and certain classes of individuals, and that shift the tax cost of the sanctions from the foundation to the disqualified person involved in the act of self-dealing. The decision to prohibit self-dealing transactions rather than subject them to an arm's-length standard was "based on the belief that the highest fiduciary standards require that self-dealing not be engaged in, rather than that arm's-length standards be observed."[1] The breadth of the self-dealing rules is considerable, and it is irrelevant whether a person had an intention to violate them.

Sanctions on Acts of Self-Dealing

One of the sanctions on acts of self-dealing is contained in section 4941(a)(1), which imposes an excise tax on a disqualified person of 5 percent of the amount involved in each act of self-dealing between the disqualified person and a private foundation. In addition to the initial 5 percent excise tax, section 4941(b)(1) imposes a second-tier excise tax on the person of 200 percent of the amount involved if the act of self-dealing is not corrected in a timely manner. These rules are broad in application and often harsh in effect. Moreover, the regulations make it clear that "it is immaterial whether the transaction results in a benefit or a detriment to the private foundation."[2] Thus, for example, even though a private foundation obtains significant financial or other benefits by reason of the transaction, if the transaction is regarded as an act of self-dealing, it thereby subjects the disqualified person to the penalty excise tax.

In addition to the penalty excise tax imposed on a disqualified person for self-dealing, directors, officers, and other foundation managers who knowingly participate in an act of self-dealing (e.g., by voting to approve such an act) are subject to a tax of 2.5 percent of the amount involved (up to $10,000) with respect to the act of self-dealing, unless their participation is not willful and is due to a reasonable cause. Further, a director, officer, or other foundation manager who refuses to agree to partial or full correction of an act of self-dealing is subject to a tax equal to 50 percent of the amount involved (up to $10,000).

Correction of Acts of Self-Dealing

In order to correct an act of self-dealing, the transaction must be undone to the fullest extent possible. This may mean the retransfer of property or the return of amounts received. In any case, the foundation must be placed in a financial position no worse than that in which it would be if the disqualified person had operated under the highest fiduciary standards.

Direct Acts of Self-Dealing

Section 4941(d) defines the term *self-dealing* broadly to cover numerous forms of routine and nonrecurring transactions between a private foundation and a disqualified person. Although certain transactions are excepted from that definition, a transaction not excepted is an act of self-dealing regardless of whether the foundation's position is enhanced or harmed.

Sales and Exchanges of Property

Sales and exchanges of property between a private foundation and a disqualified person are acts of self-dealing unless they fall within exceptions. This rule applies to real and personal property as well as intangible property. If real or personal property is subject to a mortgage or lien that the foundation assumes, the transaction is treated as a sale or exchange. If the real property is transferred subject to a mortgage or lien that is not assumed (where the recourse of the lender or lienholder is limited to the property itself in the event of a default), that transfer is also treated as a sale or exchange, but only if the mortgage or lien was placed on the property by the disqualified person within a 10-year period ending on the date of the transfer. If a lien is insignificant in relation to the fair market value of the property transferred (e.g., a property tax lien where the liability has accrued but payment is not yet due), it may be disregarded.

Leases of Property

Leases of property between a private foundation and a disqualified person are acts of self-dealing. This provision clearly applies to leases of real and personal property. It is not clear, however, whether it would apply to transactions involving intangible property through licensing and similar arrangements that technically are not leases, although other self-dealing definitions may apply to these transactions.

A disqualified person is permitted to lease property to a private foundation without charge for the use of the property as long as the property is used exclusively for charitable purposes. The lessor is permitted to pass through maintenance costs incurred for the use of the property as long as the maintenance is provided by third parties and not the disqualified person; however, the pass-through of costs related to the property itself but not to its use (e.g., property taxes or the cost of services provided directly or indirectly by the disqualified person) is treated as a charge for the use of the property, and thus is an act of self-dealing under section 4941(d)(2)(C).

Loans and Other Extensions of Credit

In general, lending money, as well as any other extension of credit between a private foundation and a disqualified person, is an act of self-dealing. This treatment extends to direct transactions, including a secured or an unsecured loan made by a private foundation to a disqualified person or by a disqualified person to a private foundation; however, it also applies to loans made by a private foundation or a disqualified person to an unrelated third party that ultimately come to rest with either a private foundation or a disqualified person. For example, if a third party obtains from a private foundation a purchase money loan that is secured by the property and subsequently transfers or sells the property to a disqualified person, an act of self-dealing occurs when the disqualified person assumes or takes the property subject to the loan. Similarly, if a disqualified person issues a debt instrument to a third party that is later transferred to a private foundation, an act of self-dealing occurs upon the transfer.

Certain interest-free loans made by a disqualified person to a private foundation are excepted from treatment as acts of self-dealing, as are certain general banking and trust functions where the lender or trustee is a disqualified person. In addition, contributions of promissory notes, pledges, and similar written or unwritten promises to make future contributions or gifts are expressly excluded from treatment as loans or extensions of credit. The phrase "extensions of credit" undoubtedly includes loan guaranties, pledges of collateral, letters of credit, and similar forms of credit support.

Furnishing Goods, Services, or Facilities

The furnishing of goods, services, or facilities between a private foundation and a disqualified person generally constitutes an act of self-dealing. This prohibition applies to a broad range of items, including office space, automobiles, secretarial help, furniture, housing, libraries, publications, and artwork. When a private foundation provides services or other items to a disqualified person or foundation manager, careful planning requires the foundation and disqualified person to determine whether the exception for goods, services, or facilities furnished on the same basis to the general public, the exception for compensation for personal services, or some other exception applies.

Disqualified persons are permitted to provide services, facilities, or goods to private foundations without charge, and may pass through costs incurred while using property (e.g., for transportation, insurance, and maintenance) as long as payments for such costs are made directly to the provider and not to the disqualified person.

Payment of Compensation

Payment of compensation, as well as payment or reimbursement for expenses for any purpose, is an act of self-dealing. The breadth of this definition requires careful consideration if the reasonable compensation for personal services exception is used.

Transfer or Use of Foundation Income or Assets

An act of self-dealing occurs if a private foundation's assets are transferred to, or used by or for the benefit of, a disqualified person. This expansive category applies to the payment of any tax imposed on a disqualified person under Chapter 42 as well as to loan or lease guarantees, purchases or sales of stock or securities to manipulate the price for the benefit of a disqualified person, making grants to satisfy a pledge or other legal obligation of a disqualified person, and to many other types of transactions. If the only benefit received by a disqualified person is incidental or tenuous, however, the fact that the benefit exists will not cause the transaction to be treated as an act of self-dealing. For example, giving public recognition to a substantial contributor is not an act of self-dealing in itself, nor is making grants to public charities located in areas served by a corporation that is a substantial contributor or on whose board a substantial contributor or foundation manager serves.

Indirect Acts of Self-Dealing

Section 4941 applies to indirect as well as direct acts of self-dealing. Neither the statute nor the regulations identify specific acts of self-dealing; rather, they prescribe several transactions that expressly do not constitute indirect acts of self-dealing.

Exceptions to Self-Dealing Treatment

Narrowly drafted exceptions provide limited relief from the harsh application of the self-dealing rules in the case of certain transactions that are deemed to be necessary to accomplish a private foundation's exempt purposes or are of such a character as not to create potential abuse.

Furnishing Goods, Services, or Facilities to a Disqualified Person

In circumstances where a private foundation makes goods, services, or facilities available to the general public, the private foundation is permitted to provide such items to a disqualified person on the same basis as it makes them available to the general public. As of May 16, 1973, these items must be furnished as part of a related trade or business.

The threshold issue is determining whether the items are in fact being made available to the general public. Qualification for this exception requires meaningful public use of the goods, services, or facilities, such as general sales of books or magazines or access to the facilities. This means, for example, that a disqualified person (e.g., a board member) with respect to a nursing home could be admitted to the home as long as the home generally maintains an open admissions policy.

The second issue is determining whether the goods, services, or facilities are made available to a disqualified person on at least as favorable a basis as they are made available to the general public. This requirement is applicable to all terms, including availability, pricing, payment terms, and similar items. Disqualified persons are permitted to pay more for the items than the general public, but situations where they pay the same or less should be scrutinized. For example, discounts off charges for a facility for board members or officers would not be permitted because, by definition, those discounts are not generally available. Similarly, waivers of admission fees or access to limited, upgraded accommodations made available to disqualified persons should be evaluated carefully.

Compensation for Personal Services

Private foundations are permitted to compensate disqualified persons for personal services, as well as reimburse disqualified persons and make reasonable advances for expenses related to the provision of such services. Payments to individuals as well as entities (e.g., law firms or accounting firms) may qualify under this exception.

The payments must be for personal services; payments for property, services other than personal services (e.g., manufacturing), or other items are not excluded. Thus, for example, payments made for property other than that used to provide personal services are not exempt. In *Madden* v. *Commissioner*, the petitioner argued that the exception for personal services applies to any service where capital is not a major factor in the production of income. The Tax Court, on the other hand, rejected a broad interpretation of the term *personal services* and concluded that the provision of maintenance, janitorial, and security services did not meet the definition of personal services.

The regulations generally limit cash advances to reasonable amounts not in excess of $500 absent special circumstances, such as extended travel or special assignments. Also, the compensation for personal services exception is not applicable to payments made to government officials because the payments are expressly addressed in a separate statutory exception.

Interest-Free Loans

A disqualified person is permitted to make interest-free loans of money to a private foundation as long as the proceeds of the loans are used for charitable, educational, scientific, or other purposes specified in section 501(c)(3). This exception has application to other financial arrangements that include credit enhancements, such as loan guarantees and indemnification agreements provided by disqualified persons to a private foundation without charge or cost to the foundation. Care must be taken to ensure that such cost-free credit enhancements are enforceable under the laws of the state in which they are made.

Corporate Transactions

If a transaction between a disqualified person and a private foundation (e.g., a sale or exchange of property) occurs pursuant to a liquidation, merger, redemption, recapitalization, or other corporate adjustment, organization, or reorganization, the transaction is not treated as an act of self-dealing if certain conditions are satisfied.

TRANSACTIONS BETWEEN PRIVATE FOUNDATIONS AND CERTAIN GOVERNMENT OFFICIALS

An agreement to make a payment of money or other property to certain government officials constitutes an act of self-dealing unless the agreement or payment falls within one or more limited exceptions. It is important to note, however, that in order for the act of self-dealing to occur, the government official's participation must be knowing.

This treatment of agreements between private foundations and government officials was originally intended to prevent private foundations from unduly influencing government officials by financing leaves of absence and similar travel or study grants; however, the prohibition's scope is much broader: it applies to many completely appropriate transactions and ultimately prevents private foundations from offering programs that provide more than nominal financial support to government officials. It should also be noted that government officials who become or are treated as disqualified persons for other reasons, such as because of their board service, are subject to the self-dealing prohibitions that apply generally to disqualified persons.

CONCLUSION

Following the enactment of the comprehensive rules affecting private foundations in 1969, legal practitioners and others predicted the demise of the private foundation. The complexity of the provisions, the operational and other changes demanded by them, the perceived harshness of some of the provisions, such as the self-dealing prohibition, and generally the enormous amount of effort required to bring existing private foundations into compliance made many in the foundation world believe that the private foundation as a useful vehicle for grantmaking was at an end. Nothing could have been further from the truth. By the early 1990s, the IRS, after completing a taxpayer compliance measurement program for private foundations, concluded that private foundations were in a high level of compliance. In addition, Congress made permanent the easing of restrictions on contributions of appreciated, publicly traded stock to private foundations. Furthermore, the costs of compliance with rules such as the minimum distribution requirements and the expenditure responsibility rules became lower as foundations became more comfortable with those rules and requirements. Thus, rather than declining in number, the number of private foundations grew from approximately 27,000 in 1975 to almost 48,000 in 1995. Correspondingly, the value of assets held by private foundations grew from $108.5 billion in 1975 to more than $263 billion in 1995.

During that same period, however, sophisticated and attractive alternatives to private foundations have emerged, such as donor-advised funds. Thus, several conclusions can be reached concerning the impact of the IRS placing its focus on private foundations: (1) a significant class of tax-exempt charitable organizations that was perceived to be involved in various forms of abusive transactions has been brought into compliance with a complex and comprehensive array of rules and regulations; (2) private foundations have become useful philanthropic tools for more than the dynastic families, such as Ford and Rockefeller; and (3) rather than becoming a dying breed of philanthropy, private foundations remain attractive philanthropic vehicles for the foreseeable future.

NOTES

1. Reg. section 53.4943-3(b)(3)(ii).
2. Reg. section 53.494(d)–2(a)(1).

CHAPTER 9

Beyond the Numbers: A View from the Accountant

Interview with Diane Cornwell, Tami Wilson, and Steve Cobb

PERSPECTIVES

The most visible document to all observers of a foundation's activity, especially the IRS, is Form 990. The next most revealing document would be the audited financials. Both of these documents lie in the purview of accountants. Increasingly, foundations have been asked to have such information readily accessible to the public. With the development of online search engines such as GuideStar, anyone can view these documents with the click of a mouse. Is this changing the way philanthropy manages or governs itself? Does this change the nature of the relationship with our accountants? And are there issues the accountant deals with that the foundation world chooses to downplay?

This chapter is an interview with Diane Cornwall and Tami Wilson. At the time of this discussion, Diane and Tami were with Andersen. Diane Cornwall was a tax partner with their Louisville, KY office and led the firmwide practice for tax-exempt organizations, which included foundations. Cornwall supported Andersen partners nationwide in dealing with nonprofit and foundation clients. Tami was a partner in Assurance and Business Advisory. She served as the lead Assurance partner on private foundations in Los Angeles. Joining the editors for the interview is Steve Cobb, vice president and chief financial officer for the California Community Foundation and former chief financial officer for the Milken Family Foundations.

Frank Ellsworth: What are the main differences between an auditor/client relationship, for a tax-exempt foundation versus a non-tax-exempt entity?

Tami Wilson: There is a big difference in the relationships between the tax-exempt and the for-profit entity. The private foundations, although handling large amounts of assets, tend to have more simplified procedures and operations because they run with a smaller staff and outsource primarily all of the management of the investments. Whereas with a large for-profit entity you are dealing with a wider array of services and the relationship is broader. The tax-exempt relationship is really much more focused because it is a focused-purpose entity. There is a lot more sharing of information among private foundations. In Los Angeles, it's a very tight community. A lot of the private foundation personnel know each other, are in organizations together, and there is a lot of information sharing among the people running the foundation. In the for-profit companies you do not see a lot of sharing of ideas among entities as they are competitors. As far as the audit relationship is concerned, because of the lean staffs in the private foundations, we find there may be more tactical accounting questions.

Diane Cornwell: And I want to say from the tax side, in many cases there is not a lot of deep in-house tax expertise. In some of the larger foundations there may be, but it's not uncommon for the organization to rely much more heavily on an outsourcing concept, to answer questions and to help with the tax returns.

FE: A question that comes to mind—the nonprofit organizations now are required—their Form 990s appear on GuideStar. I think you all know. And there's been some discussion about private foundations having to disclose some kind of information. Do you have any reaction, opinion, as to whether you think this is good? Should it happen? Are their issues related to this . . .

DC: Private foundations already have public disclosure requirements and, in fact, they have had to disclose information longer than other charities. Private foundations for many, many years have been required to publish a notice in a newspaper saying they are making the information returns available for public inspection and people can review them.

Of course, new requirements to provide actual copies when requested via mail and organizations collecting and publishing information on the Web (e.g., GuideStar) are significantly increasing the availability and use of such information.

This is resulting in an increased focus on Form 990 PF or the Form 990 more as a public relations document. Part of what we're starting to see is that the days when preparation of these information returns is done with little internal review at the last minute are gone. Before, the board members and most of the top executives would never see the returns before they were filed. Now there's starting to be a much greater awareness that these returns are going to be telling the foundation's story. The information is going to be showing up more and more, so it is really important how the information is presented. No one wants to be surprised at the executive or the board level.

Steve Cobb: I think that's very true and, in fact, goes back five or six years. I had referred to "Well, it's an information return. It doesn't really matter what's in there." But now it matters a lot. It's on the Web; you can do all kinds of research. People—I think there's been a proliferation of inquiries because it's on the Web because it generates questions. I think, Frank, that was one of your points. It can generate—even though you're disclosing information—it can generate a question that isn't quite answered, whether it's about compensation or about investment or for both private foundations and community foundations about grantees.

FE: *Is there a clear way of reporting the cost of management as opposed to cost of program? And if that sounds like a loaded question, it is, because I often—when I'm looking at the 990s of private foundations someone will say, "Well, Frank, help us understand what's the cost for this foundation and what's the cost for that," and I have trouble easily doing that. Is that just sort of a special problem I've encountered or would others have that problem?*

TW: Part of this issue goes back to the financial statements. There is some interpretation as to how you split your costs into categories and how many categories you use. Some foundations do much more summarized presentations of their expenses and some do much more detailed presentations. The more detailed expense presentations allow for more accurate comparisons; however, you cannot compare all foundations because they are managed differently. Assets may be managed by outside advisors or in-house. It also depends on the type of programs they have. Some foundations have one person that basically handles all the grant-making, some discharge that task to the board, and others have multiple offices with people in the local community dealing with the different grant requests. So foundations are often not comparable. The types of grants are also different among foundations. Some foundations want to provide ongoing support, while others only do grants for very specific purposes. For some foundations one large multiyear grant will be 90 percent of their grantmaking and then you do not need a large staff because you are not doing the volume of grants. All of these differences have significant impacts on the costs.

Joe Lumarda: In your experience—I mean, hearing you talk about the grant of a foundation—is there an evolution in the industry where the relationship between the firm—the accounting firm—and the foundations gets more involved—it's deeper in a sense? Do you understand more about the programmatic side because it's something that helps the relationship in general? I mean, in the past maybe it was just "Give us the numbers" and we looked at that and "Yeah, you make grants but that's not something I need to know." Do you see that growing even more?

TW: You do need to have an understanding of the private foundation and how it operates in order to be able to do a good job auditing them. In the grantmaking process there is a lot of risks. If somebody really wants to get around the system, that is how they are going to do it. So you need to understand the controls over the grant process. Also, grants can affect the tax-exempt status.

We want to understand what grants the foundation is making, and whether the grants they are making are in line with their purpose. Beyond the tax-exempt status issue, it is a trustee or board issue. If grants are not being made in line with a purpose, then you want to make sure that the trustees and the board are aware of that and it is a conscious decision.

DC: Another area that's important to understand is the scope of things that are looked at for the performance of an audit, detailed tax compliance review, or preparation/review of a tax return. For example, the things that a tax professional might ask for purposes of assisting in putting together a tax return would likely differ from the steps taken if one was doing a detailed tax compliance review. Sometimes there may be an assumption on the part of management or specifically at a board or the public level that when a tax return is prepared/reviewed, a preparer has verified the documentation behind the information being presented. When a tax return is prepared, in many cases the preparer accepts information as provided by the organization but is not required to otherwise be verified directly. Now, as auditors, there is a different level of verification required, but the approach is determined within set materiality and risk factors of the organization. So there can still ultimately be issues identified by the Internal Revenue Service on audit in some of these organizations even when there has been external assistance.

TW: I agree because we definitely look at controls over the system and then we do a sample. So we're not testing every transaction.

FE: *I think it's helpful, Diane, that you're reminding us and the readers, the difference between audit and tax. Why don't we focus a little bit and look at the top, say, two or three issues that are audit issues and then let's do the same with tax. Why don't we start with what are the top audit issues based on foundation?*

TW: I think the top audit issues that we look at are the controls over investments and grants.

FE: For investments, do you look to the detail of an investment policy statement and whether the individuals, in essence, are in accordance with that?

TW: We will generally, yes, look at the investment policy statement and verify that the investments and the investment managers are in accordance with that policy. Most foundations have controls in place to do that because they are also concerned with the management of their investments. In those cases, we will look at those controls on a scope or sample basis. We will also look to see whether the foundation is reconciling between what an investment manager reports, and the custodian reports, and what the private foundation is reporting, because that is an important process of identifying errors and making sure that they are corrected and that the overall investment process is working well and that you have good communication between the foundation, the investment managers, and the custodian. In the grant process we review for compliance with tax guidelines, compliance with foundation policy, and proper authorization. We also ensure the foundation is accruing for the grants payable and disclosing any contingent grants.

FE: On the question of cost basis, I see different ways of calculating cost basis with foundations. I'm curious, is there a required one, a preferred one? Why is it that there's a range on that issue? It's also very confusing to trustees.

TW: It's confusing for everyone. We really look at the investments at fair value. We don't get overly concerned about the original cost of the investments. Management is really looking at the overall improvement of the portfolio from year to year rather than against original cost. There is not really a standard method. Foundations use one of three methods: last in first out, first in first out, or average cost, usually dependent on how the custodian tracks original cost. The fact is that original cost is not going to impact how much you have to spend. That is based on the current fair value of the assets.

FE: Would I get into trouble if I said wouldn't it be great if fair value was the approach used rather than cost basis?

TW: Well, fair value is the approach used on the financial statements.

FE: Because what I find is often having to interpret with trustees . . .that it's the cost basis that comes to their attention and they don't quite understand it. So when I play this role, I have to try to explain fair value.

TW: Most of the trustees I know are not concerned about the cost basis, they're really looking at the value of the portfolio on a current basis, and management also gets flash reports all the time on what the current value of the portfolio is and that report is based on fair value. That's really what I see. I really haven't seen a whole lot of people focused on original cost.

FE: Do you think the size of the foundation plays some role there? Am I correct in assuming that you're dealing with mostly larger foundations?

TW: Could be. I work with foundations with assets of $100 million dollars or greater.

FE: Because what I hear is from the smaller foundations and I would be interested, Diane, at your reaction as you listen to this. Do you think there is a difference on an issue like this between a larger foundation and a smaller foundation?

DC: Yes, because when you have a larger foundation you're more likely to have more sophisticated financial management, and they will likely have interim records which report the information on a fair value basis. I think the internal reporting within a smaller organization is going to be largely a function of what has been set up in the past and what internal data is easily available. They may or may not ever put the information on a fair value basis, and depending on the state, may or may not be required to have a financial statement audit. So depending on the size and sophistication of the foundation, it is not uncommon to have those that are not audited. Therefore the books and records may be kept on a historical basis as they do not produce GAAP financial statements.

JL: How would you describe the ideal trustee to have for a foundation in light of some of these audit and tax issues? I'm assuming that you all would say it's important for every foundation board to have someone who understands the tax and audit process and the appropriate reports. Could you talk a little bit more about what that ideal trustee might look like?

TW: From the audit and tax perspective, you would want somebody with that background. It helps to have somebody who understands financial statements and also understands audits and knows what questions to ask. Having someone who is either a tax attorney or has a tax background is helpful to understand some of the tax implications. It is probably two different members as it is rare to find people that have that combined experience. I also believe you need somebody who really understands that as a trustee they have a responsibility and they need to be asking questions. I never mind when trustees ask questions. That is what they should be doing.

SC: I think that's a key question. You know, it's a difficult question to answer, and I think the difficulty lies in one of the questions that's on our sheet and people come in with maybe great business backgrounds, a great understanding of the for-profit world and the way the for-profit financials look, and then they come in and they go, "Whoa, what's this?" And we even acknowledged the current attempts to introduce some parallels and terminology that both worlds can understand and work with. And half the time you're educating while informing. How do you educate a board member that may be well-informed on nonprofit boards but they look at foundation financials and say, "Well, you tell me what's going on because I can't make heads or tails of that."

JL: And I know for example, the California Community Foundation at our fiscal year-end, we have $35 million in a securities lending program. I can tell you that our investment committee understood at the meeting where it was discussed, but now we have a set of financial statements *with a one-paragraph disclosure about this $35 million. I'm just not sure that the financial statements are keeping up with their job of trying to explain the financial status of the organization. I think that's an emerging issue, as you pointed out.*

TW: I think it is a continual education process. Trustees that have a lot of experience from other boards may not need that, but with those that are newer to private foundations, it does take two or three tries to understand the process. When we meet with the board we actually walk them through the financial statements. It is a good exercise to go through what the different statements mean and what is behind the various line items on the statements and what is in the financial statement footnotes. For example, I would explain what a line item means and why there is a big change from year to year, and a lot of times, it will bring up questions. This process gives the trustees enough information to ask questions because they feel they understand it. The trustees are very, very bright people in their fields, who know a lot about business and a lot about investments, but when it comes to the captions in the financial statements and the terminology, they get thrown off a little. So once you start describing what's in the various accounts and what the major changes are, if there's new footnotes, key footnotes, and any recommendations we have, that's really going to help. We usually also do the same communications to the audit committee that are required for public companies. This would include things such as the scope of our audit, disagreements with management, changes in significant accounting principles, and a variety of other things.

FE: *I wonder if this does argue for orientation of new trustees with regard to a general picture. Let me just step back for a minute. The majority of private foundations are family foundations. That's a very different dynamic often with the board than with a larger foundation, which, I think, is saying it's even more important to try to help trustees understand what the process is by providing a common vocabulary—what the red lights are that you as a trustee should be looking for. But I think* *orientation in this area—at least in my experience—is lacking. There's an assumption that you'll get it sooner or later.*

TW: That is an excellent recommendation. When you have new trustees join the board, whether they have experience on other foundations or not, they should be oriented to your foundation because every foundation is different and it is important to communicate that. The training should include key terminology, the financial statements, the investment management, the grantmaking, and the tax issues.

FE: *Before we shift to major tax issues, can you think of other audit issues that are lurking out there that we should pay more attention to?*

TW: One thing that comes to mind is valuation of alternative investments. There are some foundations that are investing in this area and some that have moved away from them. So it depends on whether your foundation is involved in these. The management of these alternative investments is key, and there is some thinking in the foundation community right now that the really good alternative investments you cannot get into, so that leaves the other ones that you really do not want to be in. There was maybe a big push for these before, but people may have backed off a little bit.

FE: *Do you find a time that boards or particular trustees are pushing you for opinions on investments? I mean you mentioned alternative investments and we all know there are some that say never do it and some that say you should. I mean do you often ever find—the accountant finds himself, herself, in that position as being asked for an opinion on that kind of stuff?*

TW: People do ask for our informal opinion on various subjects including that and they often ask to find out what some of the other foundations are doing. So part of it is because they know we deal with a lot of other private foundations and they are interested in what the other foundations are doing. Management of the foundations has a great support network and talks a lot to the other people in the industry. There are some really good organizations that they belong to. For the trustees, I do not think there is as much interaction among trustees of the various private foundations as there is between the management of the foundations so that they do not get the same sharing of thoughts and ideas that management does.

FE: *Shall we shift here to tax issues? Major tax issues that you see in foundations, what are they?*

DC: I think the first thing that you have to put on the list is maintaining tax exemption. This is because tax exemption is the most fundamental aspect of who they are and yet it often can be taken for granted. Because the Internal Revenue Service has not historically been really active in challenging tax exemption, I think organizations and boards may assume that once you get exemption, that is behind you. We think it's important to continue to stay focused on this very significant organization asset and ensure that the organization has a continuing file supporting "Why we are exempt." Specifically, what have we told the IRS we're exempt to do? Are we reporting any significant activity changes to the IRS? Are we making sure we are not running afoul of any of the rules that might endanger exemption, for example, political activity?

FE: *Well, if a trustee were to say to you, "What are the components? What do I as a trustee, or a board, need to know in order to make certain that the foundation remains tax exempt?" Is there a list? I know you just mentioned some. I thought that was interesting because I was making a note of a couple of them that wouldn't have come to my mind. Where can they—a foundation that's come to you, have you got that in writing, those major components?*

DC: Basically when you think about the fundamental requirements of being tax exempt, they include, first, the organization must be organized appropriately. The organization requirement is usually taken care of when the foundation is established. This includes certain magic language in corporate articles and bylaws or trust documents. It is then required to notify the IRS of any changes in those documents. Most organizations are pretty good at complying with this requirement since there is a question in the information returns (Form 990-PF/990) that asks whether there have been changes to those documents and, if so, requests a copy. The second requirement is that the organization be operated exclusively for charitable purposes. The courts and the IRS have concluded exclusively means mostly. This means the foundation has gone to the IRS at some point and presented a case for why they are tax exempt and what their activities are going to look like. For those organizations whose operations evolve over the years, it's important to revisit this periodically. As they put in new programs, or change existing programs, they should consider and document what, if any, impact the changes have on the continuing operations as they relate to tax-exempt status. What, if any, additional information should be sent to the IRS as part of the tax filing? There also is a question in the information return inquiring about significant changes in operation that sometimes is overlooked. Board members may want to consider confirming that the ongoing exemption question is being considered and updated each year.

TW: There are a few ways here that foundations can get in trouble without really realizing it, and one of these is when a program changes. You have to look at these changes in relation to their impact on your tax-exempt status. For example, some foundations may decide to give grants to for-profit entities, and that requires a certain amount of additional oversight when you do that. There are many things you can do that affect your tax-exempt status, and sometimes it is just a matter of setting up the new program in the right way to avoid any problems later.

FE: *I think your comments are particular timely. I've had a couple dozen calls from foundations that want to move into helping the families in the aftermath of the recent events, and that raises the question then, "How can a foundation give grants, if you will, to go to specific individuals?" I think you're sort of right on saying that if you haven't been in* *that area before with the foundation, you really need to think how you do it. Do I understand you correctly?*

TW: Yes, definitely.

DC: The IRS just published on their Web site the new disaster relief document about how to set up new organizations and get exemptions for them. It highlights the issue of whether or not an organization can get exemption if it is going to assist individuals and if it too narrowly defines the class of recipients. Often someone determines, "This is a good cause, I should be able to do that." But clearly you have to identify the class of people that are going to benefit. How broad is it—can it be construed to be "the general public"? Is it a single disaster fund, or is it going to stay around once this disaster has been dealt with? Those are all fundamental questions.

JL: *You alluded to political involvement and what sometimes can jeopardize a tax-exempt status. How clearly defined are the guidelines with regard to what a foundation can do in the area of political involvement?*

DC: They're pretty clear. A section 501(c)(3) organization is prohibited from political activity. There is a difference, however, between political activity and legislative lobbying. A private foundation is not supposed to do lobbying either, whereas a public charity that's not a private foundation can engage in insubstantial lobbying. Political activity is generally defined as supporting anybody running for office, and sometimes this can happen inadvertently. For example, if travel and entertainment reimbursements are not carefully scrutinized or the policy is not made clear, the organization might fund tickets to a political dinner where a portion of the payment is going to support a candidate's campaign. An individual gets a request, they attend, and they get reimbursed through their expense account. That's a violation technically on the foundation's exempt status. Practically, when you find an issue of this type, you fix them. For example, an organization may consider the payment compensation to the individual and report it as such, or require the employee to pay it back. If the IRS identifies the issue on audit, it typically results in a negotiated settlement, assuming it is not a pervasive issue, yet it is very troubling. Since it is an exemption issue, you certainly would not want any kind of pattern of it.

Another area of potential exposure could be use of assets by/in a political campaign. For example, the organization has good facilities and allows a candidate to come in to tour the facility and make a statement. Depending on all the facts, this could cause concerns and should be carefully considered.

JL: *What about an area I believe is even fuzzier: public policy (political) education program. So this foundation wants to support what might look like an educational program, but that program is identified with a very specific political purpose. Do foundations need to be concerned about that kind of political involvement?*

DC: The short answer is yes. Anything that could be construed to be political needs to be carefully reviewed and documented to make sure that the activities would truly be deemed educational. And, the other thing that should be kept in mind is the IRS gets the benefit of hindsight. So, if the only thing that gets supported by the hypothetical foundation always happens to benefit one particular political party, it could be a more difficult case to make that it was not politically motivated or part of a political agenda. This would be contrasted to the foundation that could show where they supported educational initiatives impacting both sides.

FE: *Other tax issues. We sort of didn't want to pass by quickly the fundamental one of tax exemption and maintaining it, but I gather that you have some others as well.*

DC: The second broad category to review is compliance. By compliance, I mean more than just "How do I fill out my tax return?" As a private foundation there are various technical rules regarding what the foundation can and cannot do, for example, with disqualified persons (i.e., substantial contributors, founders, family members, companies that are primarily funders, etc.). Congress wanted to discourage any transaction between those parties and related private foundations, so they set up what they call the self-dealing rules as one compliance area where certain transactions are not allowed, even if they are completed at fair market value. If the self-dealer participates, he or she, as well as the foundation, can be subject to penalties. It is important that board members understand that there are specific rules and guidelines that a private foundation must consider. This is an area where people sometimes inadvertently create issues. Once there is an issue, when the tax return is completed, there are specific questions about whether or not there are any of those types of violations and, if so, if and when they have been corrected. Many of these penalties can accrue each year that there has not been correction.

FE: *Are there any issues that are relating to compensation?*

DC: Compensation is another area of concern generally for many organizations. For example, a foundation can have self-dealing if it is paying "unreasonable compensation." From a practical perspective, I have not seen the IRS assert "unreasonable compensation" in many cases. It is becoming interesting, however, as we start to see more and more incentive-type compensation being developed by different organizations. In fact, in one of the recent *Chronicles of Philanthropy*, there's a discussion about the prevalence of incentive compensation and how it relates to fundraising. If it's a family foundation, fundraising compensation is not likely going to be an issue. But there are some questions from family foundations regarding whether or not compensation is reasonable for participating family members. The analysis generally starts with what the person actually does for the foundation. If the organization outsources all the operations and only makes a few grants, the compensation must be reviewed within the context of what the organization is, what it does, and what the individual contributes to the organization in exchange for the compensation. The compensation, of course, includes not only the salary but any benefits as well.

SC: And under compliance, you mentioned jeopardy investments. I'm wondering in this world of more common familiarity with hedge funds, derivatives, futures, and alternative investments such as Chilean telecommunications through short or long strategies and so forth, is there even any such thing as a jeopardy investment?

DC: One of the keys here becomes looking at the portfolio as a whole. A "prudent man" rule would be used to determine whether the organization might be invested in any one thing that could be viewed as high risk. If the higher-risk investment is a small piece or part of a balanced portfolio approach within an overall stated investment policy, there would likely not be an issue of jeopardy investment.

TW: I would agree with you, and I think the larger, more conservative foundations actually stay away from a lot of that stuff because it is difficult to understand and difficult to manage. It is high-risk stuff so, you sit there saying, "Well, I don't really understand this. It's really high risk. Is that really what I should be getting involved in?" I mean, if you have small portions of it, I think there is less concern. I would have to say most of the foundations I am involved with have some derivatives that are more along the lines of trying to hedge foreign currency exposure on instruments they have in foreign currency. So that is probably about as sophisticated as I've seen them get, with a few getting into alternative investments at no more than 5 percent of the portfolio. Not a whole lot of other types of instruments because they are very difficult for the trustees and management to understand unless they are people who are really educated in this area, and even for a lot of these people it may be difficult to really understand all the repercussions and risks involved.

DC: Another tax area to consider is unrelated business income. This is especially true when you have alternative-type investments (e.g., partnerships or limited liability companies). Whenever I see a portfolio that includes some of those kinds of investments, I immediately have tax questions regarding whether or not there could be unrelated business income ramifications. Many view those kinds of investments as equivalent to stock because they are passive types of investments (i.e., they do not exercise management oversight). But for tax purposes, these are entities with a different set of rules used to determine unrelated business income. Finally, excess business holdings must also be reviewed. If a foundation owns too much of a particular investment (in conjunction with other disqualified persons), there can be an excess business holding violation resulting in penalties.

JL: *The comment by Steve regarding Chilean telecommunication investments made me think of another side of the foundation coin with our shrinking world. Have you seen a growth in people being interested in making grants offshore, and what is your role in bringing them up to speed on all the compliance and regulatory issues in that regard?*

DC: Yes. Not only are U.S. charities wanting to look overseas, but what we also find is there are more foreign organizations that are looking at how to raise or invest money in the U.S. For U.S. organizations making grants overseas, they should look at their grantmaking procedures to ensure they meet the necessary requirements (e.g., maintaining expenditure responsibility in many cases).

FE: *Following up on this, was there anything that you heard through the tax world when President Bush said, "Well, there's some charitable fronts also, and people who make grants should be concerned about making grants to international organizations that may fund other than charitable activities"?*

DC: I am not personally aware of any organization that I have been involved with where the money that has gone overseas has gone to an organization that has made the suspect list thus far. But I think it will cause everybody to relook at their procedures: who they give money to, what kind of documentation is in their files to support the legitimacy of the organizations, and how their money is being spent.

FE: On a different topic issue, there's been much discussion about the spending policy of private foundations. What are some of the issues there, and as you look into your crystal ball, do you think there'll be any changes?

DC: Do you mean in relation to grants or other expenditures?

FE: No. The spending policy required to give the minimum 5 percent.

DC: I have the impression that more of the criticism lately has gone towards the public charities who do not have a spending minimum. There was an article in *USA Today* that identified endowments of selected large institutions and universities. It talked about how much money has been raised and questioned whether or not they should still be fundraising.

FE: I certainly do hear it, Diane, coming from the nonprofit side of house. I do hear it there. But I'm thinking here more specifically on the 5 percent. There's been a lot of discussion, is this minimum or maximum? Is it enough? Now whether this is just political discussion or whether there's some substance to be—behind it, I think there are some foundations—type of foundation folks that are wondering whether this is something that they may have to deal with—that is, an increase in the distribution.

DC: It's possible. Though, when you look at the 5 percent level in relation to what advisors recommend regarding how much money an organization should take out of an endowment if it wants to retain its corpus in perpetuity, it is only about 6 percent on average. I have been involved in a lot of meetings with a lot of different investment advisors as both a board member and as a tax advisor. It seems that the 6 percent average is the most any will recommend (and this assumes the favorable investments returns realized in the past). It seems it would be imprudent to require an organization to adopt a higher annual payment requirement when many of the foundations rely on a perpetual endowment concept.

FE: *Yeah, I would even just sort of fine-tune it and say the trend with the nonprofits is moving from 6, to 5, to 4 percent, and particularly given the investment events of the last 18 months or two years and with a decline on yield and dividends and all of that, I suspect that it's going to go even more firmly toward the 4 percent with the nonprofit. As we come to the end here, and I think we should—each of us be thinking of anything we had wanted to say or a question that we had wanted to ask.*

  And I guess my concern echoes what you're saying, that if I am a reader of this chapter, would I be able to walk away from reading this chapter knowing what you all think are major areas that trustees need to be concerned about as they look at their roles as trustees of foundations from the accountant's perspective?

SC: The one question that comes to mind is this—after listening to Marcus Owens, who used to be in charge of the exempt organization section of the IRS and other regulatory agencies, saying that we (IRS) are understaffed and we can't do as many audits, we can't look at the applications as deeply as we'd like, so are there any either managers or trustees who kind of take that into account when they are making decisions about what is disclosed or what they put into some of these financials or in their returns?

TW: I do not think that management looks at its disclosures and thinks, "Oh, I probably don't need to disclose as much because they're not really looking at this stuff" as much as if an error does happen or someone does do it a different way or isn't aware of the rules, there is nothing there to catch it and there's no one there to say, "Oh hey, you know what, you're really not supposed to do it that way." That would be more my impression. Diane, you can probably expand on that.

DC: I would agree with that. The real question may be "Where do we put resources?" For example, if a financial statement audit is not required under state law and you have limited funding sources (e.g., a family), a board may determine a financial statement audit is unnecessary. A similar determination may be made regarding outside assistance with tax compliance; however, because of the additional scrutiny returns are now getting, we are seeing an increase in the number of organizations that want assistance either in preparing or reviewing tax filings.

JL: *Well, thank you so much for your time to address these current and emerging accounting issues with foundations.*

Artists Beware

When all is said and done, and when our civilization as we know it crumbles, who will be remembered? The politicians, the tycoons, the socialites? None of them. Our civilization, as with earlier cultures, will be known primarily by its artists, authors, musicians, and its architects.

Art and artists are the cornerstones of our culture, for good and for bad. One of the most fascinating artists working in the 1950s and continuing through the early 1990s was Sam Francis, a maverick colorist who had studios in Paris, Bonn, New York, Los Angeles, Palo Alto, and Tokyo during his lifetime.

Francis was born on June 25, 1923, in San Mateo, California. His father was a professor of mathematics and his mother was a concert pianist. The artistic focus of his parents was the guiding passion in his long life. He loved fine books, music, good wine, philosophy, art and, most of all, beautiful, exotic women.

Sam Francis was well educated; he had earned bachelor and master of arts degrees from the University of California at Berkeley. In the late 1960s, he received an honorary PhD from Berkeley. He was a world-famous artist who was celebrated wherever he went. His art was shown in all of the great museums and galleries in London, Paris, Berlin, Madrid, Tokyo, New York, Chicago, and Los Angeles. His works are part of the permanent collection of more than 85 museums worldwide.

Francis's art was published in numerous books, pamphlets, magazines, catalogs, and monographs. In the early 1980s he founded the

Litho Shop with master printers George Page and Jacob Samuel to print his etchings and lithographs, and Lapis Press with Jan Butterfield and Jack Stauffacher to publish books on the visual arts, poetry, psychology, literature, philosophy, and limited editions of artist books. Both the Litho Shop and Lapis Press are still producing works of art.

Sam collected homes, horses, wine, art of other artists, and wives. Since 1950, he had the strength and fortitude to marry five talented and exquisite women, all of whom were involved in the arts, and produce four children. Two of his wives were Japanese, two were American, and his widow is of English descent.

Sam lived an honored, exciting, and interesting life, and he enjoyed every minute of his existence. He was highly organized in his work and usually disorganized in his personal life. He accumulated wealth and many possessions, but he failed to adequately provide for his heirs on his demise. In 1990, he was diagnosed with prostate cancer and sought alternative medical treatments in Mexico. His cancer progressed rapidly, and on November 4, 1994, he died from complications arising from the cancer.

During the final four years of his life, Sam struggled to paint and made numerous attempts to develop a proper set of legal documents to protect his art and provide for his widow and children, but he never completed that crucial task. As a result, his documents testamentary were inadequate to protect anyone except the IRS.

Following the death of Sam Francis in late 1994, his will and trust were admitted to probate in the Superior Court of Los Angeles County, and an executor was approved by the Court to administer the estate. When the heirs of Sam Francis read the contents of the will and trust, the widow and four of his children filed separate actions to contest it, asking that the document be voided by reason of fraud and duress. When the contesting parties appeared in court, there were more than 10 lawyers representing all of the diverse views and each of the contestants. One of Sam's children filed a separate action against the widow for the wrongful death of her father, blaming the widow for nonfeasance.

More than three years of nasty litigation followed, during which time the Court removed the executor from office and appointed a new administrator. Millions of dollars in legal fees were spent, and finally the new administrator negotiated a global settlement of all claims against the estate. The Settlement Agreement gave the widow her community property rights in the estate, together with a widow's allowance, and all the children were treated equally financially. Each heir was entitled to choose five paintings from Sam Francis's works. The balance of the estate, mainly the bulk of Sam Francis's art, was given to the Sam Francis Foundation for charitable uses.

The failure of Sam Francis or his counsel to provide for adequate tax planning and the fair distribution of his vast number of works of art cost the estate millions of dollars in estate taxes and legal fees, which otherwise could have been given to his tax-exempt foundation.

In general, professional artists are totally consumed with their work and tend to avoid making decisions to protect the future of their art, and so neglect their loved ones. The completed work of an artist at his or her death is valued for estate tax purposes at the appraised value of the work. A prolific artist like Sam Francis would have accumulated in his studio at the time of death many thousands of works, which would be appraised at an astronomical number. If the artist has not taken the time during his or her busy schedule to hire competent tax experts to prepare documents testamentary, the bulk of the estate will go to Uncle Sam. Unfortunately, the United States tax laws do not permit death taxes to be paid in art, as does the French government—thus the Picasso Museum, the Miro Museum, the Monet Museum, and many others. Too many famous American artists die without proper estate planning, and as a result, litigation usually ensues. The estates of Mark Rothko, Robert Motherwell, Andy Warhol, and Sam Francis are but a few examples.

Artists are urged to seek expert tax advice early in their careers before they accumulate a large inventory. It is important that consideration be given to the form of a tax-exempt foundation, which would exist during the entire career of the artist. The foundation would be the recipient of yearly gifts from the artist, as well as bequests from the artist's estate after death.

The organization of the foundation is central to its well-being and survival. Trustees named should be well known to the artist, business wise, and have good reputations. Close friends, spouses, and other relatives are often chosen, and generally well represent the artist. Historically, the artist's attorney and accountant are the most frequently named trustees, but they do not always represent the best interests of their clients. Choose carefully!

FREDERICK M. NICHOLAS

President
The Sam Francis Foundation
Los Angeles, California
September 1, 2002

Index

Index

Index

Index

Index

World War I, 57
World War II, 57
Worldwide Initiatives for Grantmaker
    Support (WINGS), 48, 51
Wyganski, Kuba (interview), 63–72

Y
Yamamoto, Tadashi, 79